Diana die
6 weeks befor

on Aug 31

Its a wonderful read
and about 10 pages
of our trips together
starting on page 136

She was a very special
lady + very important
in my life

Betty Lou

A Cheerful Heart

*Life is Not a Bowl of Cherries,
so Stay Out of the Pits*

DIANA HOLT

iUniverse, Inc.
New York   Bloomington

A Cheerful Heart
Life is Not a Bowl of Cherries, so Stay Out of the Pits

iUniverse books may be ordered through booksellers or by contacting:

iUniverse
1663 Liberty Drive
Bloomington, IN 47403
www.iuniverse.com
1-800-Authors (1-800-288-4677)

ISBN: 978-1-4502-5950-7 (pbk)
ISBN: 978-1-4502-5951-4 (cloth)
ISBN: 978-1-4502-5952-1 (ebk)

Library of Congress Control Number: 2010913591

Printed in the United States of America

iUniverse rev. date: 9/21/2010

Preface

Being an active member of Al-Anon for nearly thirty-four years, and sponsoring an Alateen group for ten has been an eye-opening experience. Attending my Church for over twenty-five years has reinforced my beliefs and given me strength.

For as long as I can remember, I have wanted to share some of my life experiences in order to give 'Hope' to someone out there in this world.

Writing the poem 'My Train of Life' and having it published in the Canadian Library of Poetry as well as the North American Library of Poetry made me realize that I could write and be helpful to people.

The little books I wrote in the 'Grandma's Silver Series' have brought me so much delight. How heart warming it is to know that my little books have already brought pleasure to children in many countries: Africa, Peru, England, United States, and Scotland that I am aware of. Not to mention across Canada. My love for children is so deep. This warms my heart.

There were aspects of my life that probably could have been handled differently and may have saved me lots of heartache. Today I feel the assignments God gave me were very instrumental in the discovery of skills I did not even know I possessed.

Growing up on a farm and coming to a huge city at age fourteen was overwhelming. I was naïve and everything was very unnerving. It took a long time to get comfortable in this new environment. And, what a ride it has been. I wonder if my parents would have made the big move if they had known what was in store for us? I will never know the answer to this question.

My dream in opening my mind and heart to people is to help everyone I can by sharing my search for a life worth living. Exposing my soul will be worth it, if I can help just one human being live a better life.

Many times a slogan, a Bible verse, a phrase or a quote has helped to make my day better. I have included many in my book and have hundreds more that I would love to share.

The joy that comes with sharing with people is indescribable. My dream is that this book will be helpful in times of distress, and enjoyable in good times. Putting this into words has certainly helped me.

With 'A Cheerful Heart', Diana Holt

Acknowledgements

It was a lot of hard work creating a cheerful heart, and I could not have done it without help from God, Friends and Family.

No matter what we are going through right now, I know it will change. I realize that we have a choice in how we live our lives. We can become miserable, irritable, cranky, and defeated. Or, we can learn as we go along and work on creating 'A Cheerful Heart'.

There have been many challenges along the way. My challenges may not be like yours, but the tools for healing and cheerfulness will be similar no matter what the situation.

Many of my dear ones have died, but the most painful was the loss of my twenty-one year old son. I learned heaps during his illness. We had a lot of time to share and I would not give that time away for anything. Although it is still hurtful to think about the suffering he had to endure, I selfishly appreciate what I have learned. I could do nothing at all about the rest.

In the beginning, my thoughts were: Who wants to hear what I have to say?

Does anyone care about all of this stuff? Will anyone even read it? Why would anyone want to read about my life? Will my children be upset? How will my family react?

There are many people in my life who have encouraged me to write. They know me well and feel that my sharing will help. My sister-in-law, Marion, has always encouraged my writing. My dear friend Berta never gave up telling me to get it done. Selene, Nettie, Barbara, Krystyna, Nellie, Rolly, and many others kept encouraging me to keep typing. They said they were waiting for the results. Nearly every time we talked, Eileen told me I could do this. My family just accepts the fact that I love to write.

Thank you to Selene Berg, Barbara McNabb, Betty Lou Williamson, Nettie Olsen, Krystyna Korzeniowski and Lorretta Cherkas for proofreading my work. Thank you to Ron Bradshaw, for always being so ready to help me with the new technology.

I really do appreciate everything that all of you have done and said, and the time that you have spent in supporting my pursuit.

With much love, Diana Holt

Contents

To my sons
Don, Randy, and Tim

To my grandchildren
Mandie, Charles, Randy, Victoria, Anthony, Nick, and Keshia

To my great grandchildren
Alexandra, Austin and any more that may come.

And, to my friends who have encouraged me every step of the way.

I would like to dedicate this book to my sons, Don, Randy and Tim. They have been with me through many phases and challenges. Thank you boys. I Love You!! My deepest sadness comes from not having Randy with us to share this story. Randy died at the age of twenty-one from a rare virus. He always inspired me to do what I love.

My grandchildren and great grandchildren have added more joy to my life than they can even imagine. They have taught me to love, laugh often and hard, and to delight in the simple things. A huge 'Thank You' goes to my children for giving me the opportunity to rejoice in all that being a grandma brings.

All the children I come in contact with one way or the other have been a blessing and have brought delight to my life. In my opinion, children are the zest for life. Thank you.

A 'Huge Thank You to God' for being with me throughout everything I am sharing and more. For never giving up on teaching me. Thank you for keeping me healthy and focused. My work would never have been completed without God's help. I am happy He never gives up on me.

My friends believed in me in times when I did not, encouraging me to write with words like "Keep going" "People will get help from it" "Just keep typing" "Don't stop now". With support from everyone, how could I not complete my goal? 'Thank you'!!

I am sure each time I would start to write, my family and friends would think, "Oh boy, here she goes again", but they never said it out loud.

With love and thanks.

Chapter 1

FEAR

Fear is the darkroom where negatives are developed!!
(Found in the Kidney Foundation Newsletter)

When life gets to the stage where there is no faith, 'Fear' is the dominant feeling. This was how I spent part of my life till I re-learned some of my coping skills.

I gave 'Fear' the opportunity to take over my life.

Up to my fourteenth year, Dad, Mom, my brother and I lived on a 160-acre farm in Alberta. My brother, David, was five years younger than I was. We did not have electricity, and we carried water to the house from a well. To us 'logging on' meant putting another log in the stove or heater, and 'monitor' was keeping an eye on the flame. The school David and I went to was a two-room school with grades from one to ten. Since our neighbours lived a mile and a half away across the field, the animals were our friends.

After grade ten, I had to live in a dormitory to attend school about eleven miles from home. In September I moved into the dormitory. It was at this time that my parents decided we should all go to Vancouver, so that we could be together. Dad felt there were more opportunities for us there.

In December 1949 we had an auction selling our farm equipment, cattle, horses, chickens, ducks, geese and turkeys. All our household items were either given away or sold. The most heartbreaking of all was leaving our beloved pets that went to our neighbours. Our dogs, Maxie, a border collie cross, and Brownie, a shorthaired brown mongrel, were our best friends and soul mates. Leaving them behind was devastating for all of us.

With many mixed emotions, we piled into our car with our personal belongings and headed for Vancouver, British Columbia.

Dad was not familiar with this type of driving, and Mom was probably as frightened as we were. No one said much. Dad just kept driving. I am not sure how he was feeling. He was very quiet and that was not his nature. We were all in kind of a trance about what was happening. Being responsible for the safety of us probably made Dad more frightened than any of us.

It was a fairly tranquil ride, till we got to the mountains and cliffs. We were in awe of many things that we had never seen. Where we came from, in a car on a main highway, you could see miles ahead of you. We were watching all the curves in the road. The cliffs wow!! The biggest thing we ever witnessed where we lived were the ditches on each side of the road leading to our school. This was frightening and exciting all at the same time.

My brother, David and I spent a lot of time on the floorboards of the back seat. We could not see the cliffs and winding road if we stayed down. In 1949, the mountain roads were not like they are today. We would stay down and play, then get up and watch for a while, and so on.

The route Dad chose was through Edmonton, then south into the United States. I do not remember going through the border in Montana, but I know that we had to do that to get here. I was probably on the floor of the car. We went through the northern part of Montana to Washington and on to the British Columbia Washington Border Crossing. Douglas Crossing was sensational for us, because we knew that we were nearing our new life in Vancouver. I am not clear about what happened there. I just knew that we were on our way.

Although we knew it wasn't too far, it seemed forever to get to our destination. We went over Patullo Bridge and had to pay. We had never gone over a bridge with a toll before. On through New Westminster along Kingsway to Vancouver, finally arriving at aunty Katie and uncle Pete's.

There was much celebration when we got there, as it was only a few days before Christmas. Decorations were brilliant everywhere. This was all new to us. The most brilliance we had on the farm was from a few candles lit for a little while. These are my memories of Christmas from the Alberta farm.

MEMORIES OF UKRAINIAN CHRISTMAS
'On The Farm'

My fondest memories of Christmas are of '**Christmas on the Farm**', when I lived in Alberta with my parents, Catherine and Nick, and my brother David. Our Uncle Jim also lived with us. Uncle Jim and Dad sort of raised each other. Grandma died when Dad was seven and Uncle was one, and Grandpa died when Dad was 15 and Uncle was 9.

Here they were on the farm, two boys alone. Well Dad was not a quitter and he loved his brother, so together they began this life of farming and living together. A few years later, Dad married our Mother. In those days marriages on the prairies took place in strange ways, especially in our culture. Dad's cousin took him to visit a farm where mom lived with her parents and two brothers.

I don't know exactly what happened, but a wedding was planned. A year later I was born, and so my Uncle sort of became my brother. My days as a youngster were much more unique than they would have been without him. Uncle made Christmas on the Farm much more exciting. He was just a youngster too. We were great friends, and I don't ever remember him treating me unfairly.

Now for our Christmas: On Christmas Eve, hay was brought in and placed under and on the table. A tablecloth went over the hay. This represented the stable. A bundle of wheat, called a sheave, was brought in and kept in the house until after the New Year Celebration. This was for a manger effect.

There were twelve varieties of food for the Christmas Eve Feast. The twelve different foods represented the twelve disciples. We began with wheat cooked with poppy seeds and honey, soups, fish, mushrooms, broad beans, pickled herring, peroghes, cabbage rolls, jellied fish, dried fruit such as: prunes, apricots, apples, peaches and raisins. Sometimes we had canned fruit and vegetables that Mom preserved in jars. After midnight we could have meat. All the food was cooked in oil, not animal fat. Animal fat was not allowed till after midnight.

A round loaf of bread called a 'Kolach' was made with a hole for a candle in the middle. The candle was lit at suppertime and burned all night. This was our 'Centrepiece', and it represented 'The Star of Bethlehem'.

The most thrilling part of Christmas for me was decorating the 'Christmas Tree', which we always did this on Christmas Eve. The tree came from our farm, that was chopped down by Dad and Uncle, since this was considered a 'man's job'. Decorations were simple, but oh my goodness, we sure did enjoy this part. A few glass baubles were placed very carefully here and there on the tree. We only had very few. A lot of families did not have any, so this was extra special. We were very fortunate indeed. Mostly the ornaments on the tree were made of crepe paper and popcorn strung with a needle on thread. The most 'extraordinary' part was the candleholders. These were made similar to clothespins, and had a round hole on the top to hold a tiny candle. The candles were fastened to the tree branches and were lit before or during supper. Wow, as youngsters, we were in awe of amazement during the whole evening. Can you imagine the danger there was in this? We lived seven miles from the nearest town. No one ever heard of a fire department. Our nearest neighbour was one and half miles across the field and three miles by road. No one had a car, and if they did it often could not be started in the winter.

It was even harder travelling by horse. If the winter was severe, even getting the horses ready was a chore. Water was brought in from the well. We never thought about the danger. I wonder if our parents did? If the winter was not too severely cold, we may have company.

We opened our presents on Christmas Eve, and most of our gifts were hand made and we only had one or two things each at most. We also had stockings hung up. If we had not behaved, we got a rotten potato in the stocking, but usually the stocking consisted of a few nuts, some dried fruit, maybe an orange and sometimes a candy. I remember one year I found a rotten potato in my stocking and I was very upset. I don't remember why I got it, but I do remember I never got another. Sometimes, if the weather was not too stormy and we did not have company, Dad would hitch the horses to the sled and we would go to a neighbour's for an hour or so. We had jingle bells on the harnesses, a bench in the sled and we covered with down quilts (hand made). This was a '**fabulous**' part of winter there. We knew the stars and gave them names. The 'little dipper' and the 'big dipper' were our friends.

Christmas Day was quiet. Sometimes we went to church. Many times we just stayed home and read and played games. If we were lucky, maybe some neighbours would come over.

The second day of Christmas (Boxing Day), some hay was put in a dish with silver money and water was added. Everyone washed in this basin, for 'Good Health' and 'Wealth' for the coming year. If we could get to church, this water was blessed.

The third Day of Christmas, the hay was collected from the house, and set on fire where the most traffic took place, which was the gateway where the cattle and the people went through. This was done for 'Good Health' for the coming year. We could jump over or walk over this spot after the fire. Oh how we cherished this moment!!

New Year's Eve we went to visit friends. Mostly these were our neighbours, or they came over to our place. The adults played cards and told stories. We played 'Button, Button, who has the Button', or 'I Spy with my Little Eye'. My favourite game of all was 'Dress Up' in our parents' clothing, and if we had old curtains, it was even better. We then could pretend we were 'Having a Wedding'. 'Hide and Seek' and 'Hit the Can' were two games we could play if the weather was not too cold. When we got bored, we sometimes played a game that went like this. Someone smacked you on the butt (how hard depended on a lot of things). If you guessed who did it, he or she was it, and so on. We also played cards, and eavesdropped to hear the adult stories. This was easy to do, since there was no insulation and the houses were not that big.

A very memorable time for my brother and myself is New Year's Day. My brother was born five years after me, and uncle was now becoming a young man. On New Year's Day, the custom of the time was to go to neighbours, relatives or friends. We did this in order to wish 'Good Luck' for the New Year. Often we chose to go to our Great Uncle's. However, if the weather was wretched we just chose somewhere closer to home. When we arrived, we threw rye and wheat in the doorway as soon as they opened the door. We threw the grain in a sowing manner and chanted these words:

Sheeshy, vrodychy, zhetto eee pshenecheey,
Na shchashche, Na zdorohvie,
Na say novae reek,
Shobe vam she vroodelo leepshe neesh vtoreek!!
(These are English letters written in Ukrainian pronounciation).

This chanting means: "We are sowing this grain, rye and wheat, so that you may have 'Good Luck', 'Good Health' and 'Better Crops' than you did last year. This was a very important part of the New Year Celebration. It was a lot of fun for us kids, and I was very fortunate because in those years boys played a very important part in the lives of our ancestors, but because our parents were trying hard to be modern, I was allowed to take part in this ritual. This was mostly done by the boys. The first ones to arrive got the most money for the chant. You must remember that we had to wait for the chanters to come to our place before we could go out. We always waited for at least one visit before we left home. As we grew older, this custom seemed to diminish.

What fun it was to go to Uncle's!!! Besides the chant and the money, there were fourteen children in this family and we were always treated 'royally', often staying for supper as well. The combination of various ages of people around us was stimulating and we learned a lot of things there. Everyone was very friendly and we felt 'special'. Company in the winter was a rarity and very much enjoyed. They always had sixteen people at mealtime. Looking back I realize that we probably blended in and we always helped. What a marvellous time for my brother and myself! Our parents also had a 'Great Time'. This family was very talented, playing instruments of all kinds. They cooked great things and every visit was a new adventure. Dad taught himself to play the violin and so he joined in and Mom enjoyed the women and children of all ages and interests. The older kids always made a fuss over my brother and me and we lapped this up like little puppies. Since we only had each other, this was a treat for us. We tried to be the first ones at Uncle's or wherever we went to do the chant. Getting places took time, as everyone lived a fair distance away. This taught patience as well.

Going out during the holidays was not always possible, because very frequently we could not get out of the yard, with snow storms, etc. This is why the visits to our Great Uncle's farm stands out in my mind.

Electricity was something we only heard about. Our source of light was a 'coal-oil lamp'. As we got older, we had the more modern 'lantern'. We never thought much about all of these things as this was the way life was. We burned wood in the stove and the heater and coal at night, when we could afford to have it. You must keep in mind that our winters were in the 20 to 60 degrees below zero Fahrenheit. Thank God for down comforters. Most of us had these. We all had chickens, ducks and geese, so the women made comforters and pillows during the cold winter months. Early in the mornings, the whole family stood around the heater. Often there was frost around our nose and mouth, and plenty of ice on the windows. Dad was kind to us and let us use a five-gallon pail to do our 'toilet duties' first thing in the morning. The rest of the day we used the 'out house' (a hole in the ground with a wee building built over the hole). There was a bench seat inside with two holes. We were 'sitting pretty' since Dad put in a smaller hole for us kids. We got very excited if we got fresh fruit of any kind. We liked the fruit, but we **loved the paper** it was wrapped in. It was much softer than the catalogue pages!! We never heard of toilet paper!! I never appreciated these things then, but now I realize how fortunate we were. Our parents tried to make life easier for us as much as they could, with what they had, and because Uncle Jim lived with us, our life was more fun.

One particular winter, Uncle was old enough to go to Edmonton and work for a while. I really remember this Christmas!! Uncle was away all winter and we all missed him like crazy. We were so very stirred up because he was coming home for Christmas.

That Christmas Eve will be in my memory for as long as I live. He brought me a 'beautiful doll'. This doll is treasured in my heart forever. She was the only real doll I ever had as a child. We used to cut paper ones out of the catalogues and dress them with the clothing we cut out. Catalogues were used for many things in those days. They were very important to us. I had my doll till some neighbourhood children accidentally broke her. She is not gone. She remains in my memory and in my heart. Uncle did not ever think she would mean this much to me. This was a very Special Christmas indeed!!

As our Mother grew and learned, she found the recipe for 'Date Squares' also known as 'Matrimonial Cake'. Dates were very scarce and a rare treat. Only at Christmas time did Mom bake Date Squares. She would bake this cake and put it in the cellar which was a room dug under ground, with a hole cut in the kitchen floor with a door that lifted up. We played marbles in the hole that held the lifter for the cellar door. Dad built shelves in the cellar, and we stored vegetables like carrots, turnips and potatoes there, and Mom kept her home canned fruits, jams, jellies, and vegetables in jars down in the cellar. This is where she put the Date Squares. There were 'salamanders' down there too. For Christmas we also got a case of 'Orange Crush' pop and a few other goodies. Everything went in the cellar. All of this I remember as very exciting and special, but the Date Squares are still my favourite. My brother and I would sneak down the cellar whenever Mom and Dad would go out to milk the cows or feed the animals. It was only last year that Mom told me that she knew all along that we would sneak down there and eat the cake. She said she knew she'd have to make another one just before Christmas. She too, did not know how important this was in my life, and enjoyed hearing about it in her old age.

This was our 'Christmas on the Farm' when we were youngsters in Alberta. These are 'Warm and Happy Memories'.

This was written approximately 1991.
My brother died on October 28, 2001
Milt's sister Ivy died October 2002
Mom on January 7, 2003 and
Dad on May 25, 2005
Milt died on January 17, 2006
Milt's sister Myrt died August 2006
Gabrielle, my best friend, died January 2007

I am so pleased that they were able to read this story and that my brother enjoyed it. It was found in his wallet the day of his death. He never did tell me he liked it, but I know he would not have carried it around if he didn't. Dad did not understand much that I wrote, but Mom enjoyed hearing about the cake.

At Aunties, everyone had a room to sleep in except me. I was already frightened by all the hoopla, but nowhere for me to sleep?

Our aunt was a very flexible lady and she could come up with ideas no one else did. She decided that my cousin, who was about 21 at the time, and I could share his room. He worked graveyard shift and was always up by 10:00 p.m. to get ready for work. So here was the plan: I would go to bed at 10:00 p.m. and sleep till 7:00. Jim would come in and wake me by saying, "Wakey, wakey, rise and shine. You've had your sleep, now let me have mine." We would have a chat. I would get up. He would go to bed. That bed was never cold. Today, people may frown upon that idea, but for several months it worked. I had a bed to sleep in and so did Jim.

Now there was another dilemma. We had been in Vancouver for four months and the only place I had been is school. Aunty asked me, "Are you not interested in going to see the shops along the drive?" I replied, "Oh yes, but I am waiting for the rain to stop". "Oh my goodness", she said, "It doesn't stop raining here till May".

That was how I lived, a fourteen-year old Prairie Chicken. Not sure what to do. Eventually I ventured out into the world around me, fearful of everything. "We live in an Art Gallery of divine creativity, and yet are content to gaze only at the carpet." From the book 'God came near'.

After four months, we moved into a big house with another of Dad's sisters. At Aunty Clara's, I shared a room with another cousin. She had so many beautiful clothes. I felt so underdressed when I saw what she had. Mom made most of my clothes till we moved to Vancouver, when she bought me a brown skirt with pleats in the front and a white sweater. I remember the skirt well. These were the first store bought items I had besides underwear.

I admired my cousin's drawer full of angora sweaters for several weeks, then one morning she said, "If you want to wear one of my sweaters, I don't mind". Wow!!! Was I pleased? I knew exactly which one I would wear. It was a pretty green colour and I had admired it all this time. I put the sweater on and went on with the rest of my morning, to discover that I was itchy everywhere. The problem was that I was allergic to the wool. It was not such a big deal after that.

We enrolled in school right after Christmas. I attended Vancouver Technical School. If you think this was simple – think again? I was scared out of my shoes to start there after living in the country all my life, but start I did.

I was so naïve at age fourteen when we came to Vancouver. This story I read reminds me of that time.

A rancher got into his pickup and drove to a neighbouring ranch and knocked at the door. A young boy about nine opened the door. "Is your Dad home?" the rancher asked.

"No sir, he isn't", the boy replied, "He went into town".

"Well", said the rancher, "Is your Mother here?"

"No sir, she went to town with Dad".

"How about your brother Howard, is he here?"

"No sir, he went with Mom and Dad."

The rancher stood there for a minute, mumbling to himself.

"Is there anything I can do for you? I know where the tools are if you want to borrow one. Or maybe I can take a message for Dad?"

"I really wanted to talk to your Dad. It is about your brother Howard getting my daughter, Suzie, pregnant." The boy thought for a minute, "You would have to talk to Dad about that. I know he charges $500.00 for the bull, and $50.00 for the hog, but I really don't know how much he gets for Howard".

A lot of fear, but also excitement dominated my life by this time. My cousin was a smoker and wanted me to try it, so I did. I could not understand what was so great about it. I took a puff or two. It was bitter and hot. There was nothing enjoyable about that cigarette. Thank goodness I felt that way about this adventure. She continued to smoke for many years.

I really wanted to become a nurse. My parents could not afford to send me to school past Grade 12. I had decided that I would find a job and put myself through school.

Attending Vancouver Technical School was a challenge of its own. The building was huge, with different teachers for each subject. I was used to one teacher for seven grades, and another for grades eight to ten. Now here were all these rooms. When we were registering, I met Eileen who also came from a small community. We then went our separate ways, meeting again in the basement of the school, totally lost. Thank goodness we met. We felt safer because there were two of us. This is not to say we weren't frightened about the trouble we would be in and how we were going to find our way around this monstrosity. We were truly lost. It is now many decades since this happened. Eileen is still a dear friend.

Eventually we were settled in home and school. Eileen and I were good friends and spent much time together in each other's homes. One evening she called me and said there was someone at her house that wanted to meet me. I spoke with Dave on the phone finding him very pleasant to talk to. He had the deepest voice. I was fascinated by his voice. We spoke to each other daily and met three weeks later. Right away, we were very comfortable with each other. He told me that he would help me with the cost of nurses training. I was really looking forward to doing this, also very pleased that someone I hardly knew was willing to help me.

Really wanting to earn some money and school was out for the summer, I went to a little restaurant in our neighbourhood. I stood at the counter sheepishly. When approached, I asked if they needed any kind of help there. I told them a story I had cooked up, saying that I worked in a little place on the prairies and it had since been sold. I was told that they did not require any assistance at that time.

I guess the look on my face showed the disappointment. A man who was at the counter came up to me and asked, "Are you looking for work?" I sheepishly replied, "I really want to work for the summer". He said, "Just wait here for a moment". He went to the back of the premises and came back with a sealed envelope. He told me, "Go downtown to Richards and Hastings. There is a place there called The Pall Mall Restaurant. Go there and ask for

Paul. Give him this envelope and he will give you a job". I did what he told me to do and I did get a job as a waitress.

This was so thrilling. A lady named Mary watched over me and asked, "You have never done this before, have you?" I told the truth. "I really need to work, because I want to be a nurse, and I need new clothes for school". She then proceeded to teach me what I needed to know. Within two weeks I was working in the dining room where groups of people came. Soon I was earning more tips than wages.

God was already at work in my life, but I did not know that then.

I worked at the Pall Mall for three years during summer holidays and other school breaks, plus long weekends. The tips I made were plentiful and I put them in a tin can I transformed into a piggy bank. When September came, I planned to use the money to purchase new clothes for school. I looked into my can. There was very little money there. My brother had taken my tip money and spent it.

I was angry. My parents handled it like it was a normal thing for a boy to do. This disturbing situation is still very fresh in my mind. I was upset, angry and fearful of what else of mine he would take. Never again did I leave money or anything of value visible or handy. I was so disappointed. I did not have as much money for clothing for school as I thought I would have.

While working at the restaurant, I met a group of gospel singers. They were pleasant and treated me well, leaving a good tip. One of them asked if we could write. We became pen pals. He sent me a photo of himself and I did the same. Mom somehow saw the picture and told me to stop writing to this man. I did not understand. She told me that Dad would disown me if he knew I was writing to a black man.

In the meantime Dave and I continued to see each other, being together whenever it was possible. He worked on the tugs and was away a lot. I was only sixteen when he gave me an engagement ring. I knew my parents would not approve, so I would wear it in the daytime. After school, I put it in the back of a little picture that hung in our hallway. It had a little lady painted on the front of the concave glass. I can still see that picture when I think about it.

After a few months, things happened that upset me. I bought a shirt, a birthday card, wrote a letter, and put the ring in the shirt pocket. I packaged the whole thing and mailed it to Dave. The next day Mom sent a parcel to our uncle and aunt on the prairies and included the picture, where I had been storing the ring. Whew!!

When Dave received the package, card and letter, he was surprised. I felt I had good reason to be angry with him. He called and apologized and I told him to leave me alone for a while.

When his nephew was getting married, Dave called and asked me to go with him to the wedding. I accepted. What a wedding it was and what a grand time we had. I felt so special in my new red dress that fit me well. The colour was perfect too. He was pleased that we were there together and asked me if we could start over again.

Mom and Dad did not want me to be so involved with anyone at such a tender age. I often told them I was going to a friend's when in fact I was going to meet Dave. This did not make me feel very good, but it sure did help the home situation. They loved my friend Theresa and never minded me going there, so this was working for now. Theresa and I were best friends and spent lots of time together.

At one point I went to visit family on the prairies and asked Theresa to keep my boyfriend occupied so he wouldn't be lonely. She still talks about this and feels very honoured to have been so highly trusted. I know I would do this even now.

After nearly three years Dave and I were married. My dress was beautiful white satin covered with lace. I made my long veil and embroidered white petals on it. The tiara was very royal looking with white pearls and white leaves. Everything was perfect for our new beginning.

The week prior to the wedding, all my aunts were over. There was a lot of buzzing around. We were cooking for the wedding and visiting, making flowers to decorate the cars, and baking. The wedding was wonderful with about 250 people and all the trimmings. It was a traditional Ukrainian wedding including the presentation during the reception, similar to the receiving line at other weddings. The difference being that we, the wedding party were behind a large table covered with a white tablecloth. On the table was a large plate. People came to the table and put money in it if they wanted to, or gave us a wrapped gift, or both. We shook hands and kissed the guests as they wished us well. This is one day I will never forget.

Excited about my new life, I had many dreams and wanted them to all come true. Rolly, one of Dave's friends, and an usher at the wedding, lent us his car. We went to Portland, Oregon for our honeymoon, returning along the West Coast. After arriving on our own turf once more, we decided to go and visit Dave's parents on the Sunshine Coast. I really wanted to go home. I was homesick, but I did not tell him that. While waiting for the ferry, we heard a song being played for us. My cousin, who had been a bridesmaid at the wedding, put in the request. I felt better and enjoyed the trip. Circumstances had changed. I would not go into nurse's training now.

With both of us working, we were able to purchase our own little house. It was a one-bedroom home, a kitchen, with sawdust burning stove, living room, bathroom and a basement with a sawdust-burning furnace, and it was ours. There was a little two-room run down shack beside it.

This was an exciting time. The sawdust burning stove and furnace were interesting. In today's times, people would laugh at this kind of heat and cooking arrangement. Heating was a demanding job. We would go downstairs and give the hopper a thump to move the sawdust down into the furnace. Sometimes this would cause lots of smoke and different situations, but it did keep us warm. Cooking with sawdust was another story, but baking was a challenge. If I was going to bake bread, I had to be sure the sawdust was in such a place in the hopper that it would slowly drop and burn evenly. If you had too much sawdust, it would either be really hot or would quench the fire for a while and then burn heartily. I would have to be there and watch it carefully. Eventually I did learn how to use it properly and it worked well. What a memory.

Concerned about how we would make our mortgage payments, purchase a fridge and pay all our bills, I had a plan. We cleaned the shack up, painted it and put in a little oil heater. One young man we knew came to live there, as well as two others. They slept in the little hovel, which was warm and clean now. Their meals were with us and I did their laundry, thus being able to buy a fridge, and do whatever we needed to do.

Things were going great, but about a year into our life together, my husband began complaining about a sore knee. After several visits to the doctor, it was decided that there was some inflammation there. A few weeks later, he arrived home after work with a knee that was swollen, red and hot. Back to the physician he went. He was put into the hospital for further tests.

He called me at work to come and see him during my lunch break. He told me he had something to tell me. When I got to the hospital he explained that the prognosis was bad. Dave had Cancer in the knee. The news came as a complete shock. There had been much discussion by the medical people and the decision was to amputate the leg above the knee leaving a five-inch stump, thus being able to fit him for an artificial limb.

His plan was that I should leave him and start a new life. My feeling was that I married him for better or worse, till death do us part, and I wasn't buying into this idea. Of course he was happy with my decision, but wanted me to have the option.

This was a frightening and horrible experience. It is many years now and I can still see the canopy over his leg, to keep the sheets from touching it. I had a hard time with this dilemma. It made my stomach turn when I was finally able to actually look at the stump. After the surgery we were told that if he remained cancer free for five years, he would probably be fine.

My husband was recovering from the amputation, and after about three weeks in hospital he was discharged. It was quite an adjustment. However, it was great to have him home. We were so happy that this ordeal was over and we could start living again.

Eventually family and friends contributed enough money so we were able to purchase an artificial limb. He was happy to be able to start over. Slowly and with much practice, he did use the limb.

One morning, several weeks after Dave was home from the hospital, my Mom called while I was asleep. I jumped out of bed to answer the phone. The artificial limb was leaning against the bed. I hit the bedside table, cutting my chin and bruising my face. A few stitches, a swollen face and a black eye, I was okay. After several days went by, I discovered I did not fall because I got up quickly and surprised by the limb. It was because I was pregnant.

It was so wonderful to have him home. Now I was pregnant!! How were we going to live when I could not work any more? I had not learned to live 'One Day at a Time' at this point.

A few months before the baby was born, I had to give up my job with a prominent insurance company and we moved in with my parents. We rented our little house to my best friend Theresa and her husband, with the idea that we would move back when one of us was able to work again. Theresa, and her husband were expecting a baby as well.

Moving in with my parents was not easy. It took some adjusting, for us and for them. Mom was used to doing things her way. I had some ideas that were different from hers. Dad was trying to adjust to the big change. It didn't take long to get into a routine. Mom and Dad went to work. My brother was still in school. I stayed home doing the housework and the cooking for all of us while taking care of my husband. We were all waiting for the new baby, and for Dave to be walking and driving again.

We managed to purchase a vehicle with the help of both sets of parents. They loaned us enough to purchase this car. It was a beautiful black Pontiac car with an automatic transmission. Since it was my husband's left leg that was amputated, he could drive the car.

My father-in-law told me that if I had a boy, he would give me $100.00 and $10.00 if I had a girl. I just wanted a healthy baby.

On the way to the hospital, my husband was pleased and excited. This is when he told me, "If this cancer should return, I want you to marry again. Give our child a father, and you deserve a life". I was not hearing any of it. In my eyes all would be well. He probably felt something I did not even want to think about, because I wanted us to get back to a normal life. We were with Mom and Dad for a few months when our son was born.

The birth was a difficult one and eventually I was put to sleep. I am not sure what happened after that, except I was happy to see my wonderful baby boy after I woke up. While I was in the hospital, I developed a terrible itch.

It nearly drove me crazy. My body was one big red mess and itchy. In those years the hospital sheets were changed daily and they were starched. I asked them not to change my sheets. My husband brought me gloves, pyjamas and socks. This all helped, but I was happy to be out of there.

Our baby was born on August 6, 1956. We called our son, Donald, and I did get the $100.00, which was great because we sure did need it.

Shortly after Donald's birth, Dave's cancer returned.

This was a time of deep anxiety. I had a new baby, a sick husband and the inevitable certainty of death. The medical people did not believe in telling the patient that it was terminal, so I could not discuss it with my spouse. How I wanted to explain to him the reason that he felt like someone was putting a pillow over his face. I wanted him to know how much he meant to me. How badly I wanted him to live. My heart was aching, but I had to put on a bold front.

Our doctor told me that the cancer had spread throughout my husband's internal organs. He would soon need morphine for the pain. If I learned how to give the morphine shots, Dave could stay at home. The doctor made arrangements for me to come to this office where they taught me to give the shots by using an orange. There was not much to putting the needle into an orange. Putting it into my husband's body was a different story. He was patient with me and I eventually got real good at doing this. I was now a nurse with no official training.

I could not talk about our future. Today, I wonder if he knew?

Was I scared? You bet, a dying husband, a new baby and now morphine shots. I was afraid. It was terrifying to know that he was going to die. It was frightening to have to learn to give him morphine. I was afraid of the damned stuff, but I also knew it was necessary in order to keep Dave from spending the last months of his life in hospital.

Having the baby was great, because I could lose myself in caring for him for a little while, but the fear of being a widow and caring for a baby was a heavy burden to bear.

On Thursdays I worked for an elderly Italian man who had been widowed. I cleaned his house every week. This was a huge help for us since we had no money coming in. I would get the baby ready, and give my husband his morphine shot. As soon as he was asleep, I would gather up my baby and go to my little job. Usually I would get home as the morphine was wearing off.

At twenty-one years of age, I was a mom, a nurse, and trying to be a good wife. We were unable to pay rent at this time. It was my responsibility to take care of the house, and cook the meals for our family of six. Dave's care took a good deal of time. He could no longer eat our food. I tried to feed him baby food. Dave did not want to eat and often cried when I was trying to give it to him. I cried too. He would die if he did not eat, and he was losing weight. I carried him to the bathroom. He weighed sixty-seven pounds and did not have the strength to walk.

March 19, 1957 I awoke early to find Dave up in bed playing with the baby, who was seven months old at this time. This was very unusual. I was happy to see them together and hoping that things were improving. It was time to go to my cleaning job later that morning. Dave was back in bed and not feeling good.

Dave's Mom who lived on the Sunshine Coast was visiting at her daughter's. She had come to see us as well. I called her and asked her to come and stay with him till I got back from work. I did not feel right leaving him alone that day. She did come. I gave Dave his shot, took the baby and went to work. About an hour into my work schedule, Dave's mom called to tell me that he was making some weird sounds. I told her that he often did that, to just wait and I would be home shortly. A few minutes later she called to say that he had died. He died in our bed, and I was not there for him.

I came home immediately. Why did I go to work that day? How come he died while I was away? How dare he die when I was not there? My mother-in-law was a sweet lady. Why did she have to see this? I was in shock! Now what?

This was a stressful, horrifying time.

Once again, I began to use my God given strength. I called the church I went to and where we had our son baptized. They told me that they couldn't help me because Dave had not turned Catholic. This was the way they did things, and they could not help me. I wasn't sure what to do. Now I know that God was at work, but at that time I felt He had abandoned me.

I had not yet learned that God said, "Never will I leave you; never will I forsake you." Hebrews 13:5,6.

My brain kicked in. I called the church where my husband attended Sunday school in Pender Harbour on the Sunshine Coast of British Columbia. The pastor was wonderful. He agreed to come and do the service.

This was all taken care of. The funeral was over. Now what??? I knew that my son and I had to eat, and I could not rely on my parents forever.

Past experience in office work made me press on. I could earn more money than Mom, so I went to work. I found a job real close to home and was able to come home on my lunch break to enjoy my son. Mom looked after Don. That was good, because she loved him very much, and I knew he would be well taken care of. I now paid room and board for Don and myself. That felt good.

My Thursday job became a Saturday job, so I worked at the office during the week and on Saturdays I took Don and away we went to do the house for my Italian friend. He was so good to us, always having chicken in the fridge for me, and bananas for Don.

I got $10.00 each time I cleaned Joe's house. He was so happy that I was willing to do this, and I was relieved to know that I had a little extra money coming.

I decided it was time to repay my Dad for the car loan. I opened an account in his name at the bank where they dealt. Every time I earned the housecleaning money, I deposited it into the account. I also added as much as I could from my pay check at the office. Once the money was all in the account, I had to decide how I would present it. For Dad's birthday, I bought him a nice shirt and put the bankbook in the pocket. I can still see him opening up the package and when he found the bankbook in the pocket, tears streamed down his face. He did not ever expect me to repay him, especially so soon.

I felt really great about paying my debt back. Dad was a hardworking man and always made sure that things were paid, so I knew this was the right thing to do. I felt very relieved to have that off my mind.

I missed my husband terribly. We had been together all day long every day, sharing thoughts and dreams.

I felt so alone. My son and I went to the cemetery to visit the grave every day, rain or shine. When Don was old enough to run around, he had so much fun smelling the flowers wherever they were, and I would sit there and cry. After a few months of this, I finally realized that I couldn't continue to do this daily.

That was the beginning of healing for me. We gradually stopped going there every day, and I began to feel like I would like to live again.

One thing I did learn about life is "If you don't start, it is certain you won't arrive".

My plan was to try to live and enjoy my child.

I had not yet learned that in Joshua 1:9 it tells us, "Be bold and strong!! Banish fear and doubt! For remember, the Lord your God is with you wherever you go."

My friend Eileen was now married and had a baby boy. She often invited my son and myself for a weekend with her family. We would talk and the boys would play in the playpen next to us. Her hubby, Dale was working on building their home, so he would be hammering away. My baby was not used to the noise, so Dale would stop while the boys were asleep. He would join us in a cup of coffee. I will never forget that. It is a wonderful memory.

Being left out of plans with friends was not unusual after Dave's death. I often felt like 'the third shoe' if I did get invited, or worse yet, not invited at all. I soon realized who my friends really were.

Somewhere else I read, "You not only have the right, but the duty to be happy and successful". I hung on to this one and made a decision to enjoy my life, and my son.

Mark Twain wrote: "Dost thou love life? Then do not squander time, for that is the stuff life is made of."

I loved my son and really wanted to have a great life. The following quotes are good to always keep in mind: 'If you lack courage to start, you have already finished'.

Fear is a coward. Face him and he will run.

Chapter 2
How is your Attitude?

Your mind is like a parachute. It works only when it is open.
Author unknown

Happiness is an inside job. Only with God's help can I make me happy.

My life has been a series of happenings that really made me use the God given abilities that I did not even know I had. I was either in a situation, or coming out of an episode, or going into another adventure.

I know that my story will not always stay in chronological order. There was never just one situation happening at a time, often five or more serious difficulties taking place all at the same time, often overlapping. As the story goes along, I am trying to point out the lessons learned from these predicaments. Even though things may seem out of order sometimes, they do come together.

It seemed there was no end to all that was going on. I could not understand why these things were happening to me. As you read on, in the following chapters you will see how my life has been, and the ways I learned to deal with the 'Lessons in Life'. 'Lessons in Life' is what I like to call these occurrences. If I did not think of them as 'Lessons', I would not have made it this far.

In each event, I learned some very important skills for life on Earth.

In opening up to the world, the experiences of my life and the ways I searched for help and found it, I am hoping and praying that someone, somewhere will find these contents useful in making their life worthwhile. I began seeking solutions when I was in my forties.

One of the most important things that I learned is that my attitude had a lot to do with how I handled certain events. Now I wonder, "Is my attitude worth catching?"

The best description of 'Attitudes' is what I found in a book called 'Blueprint for Progress'. A book printed by The Al-Anon Family Group Headquarters. This book focuses on problems caused by Alcoholism, but in reality it can be used in all parts of life.

It says: "Attitudes are emotional responses to situations, people, and ideas. We were not born with these feelings; we learned them from the outcome of relationships with our parents, our friends, and other past experiences. We continue to learn as we grow older, but we are not always aware that we have become conditioned to feel, to think, and to act in certain ways."

This idea of how attitudes are formed made me aware of how I handled certain situations. It also made me realize that I was the product of a home where my Dad was a controller, a perfectionist, and could fix or build anything out of nothing. We were of European background where boys were given more privileges than girls, and my Mother always followed Dad's lead.

My brother was five years younger than I. He could do most anything and it was fine with Dad because he was a boy.

Guilt is a tool for control. If our experiences have clouded our thinking with resentment, fear, and self-pity, then we need to change our attitudes. We must be willing to learn new ways.

I could not learn new ways to change my attitude till I faced reality. The most difficult reality I had to face was, that as long as I kept doing the same things over and over, the same things would happen over and over, and I would be treated the same way over and over again. To do this was not a simple task. I learned that I needed an attitude adjustment.

Every person has certain dispositions that are learned ways of trying to cope with what life deals us. Our attitudes are the ways we look at things. Actions and reactions reveal how we look to the rest of the World.

In order to help us have a good attitude, we must be willing to learn from experiences and from other people, and unlearn some of our habits replacing them with new ones. Some habits do not work any more, and must be altered. Unlearning old habits takes a lot of work; but first we must realize that we need to make some alterations. It is not easy to recognize that one needs to make changes. There has to be a willingness to do this.

A different way of viewing our world is part of the learning process. I had learned some very specific coping skills while growing up. As the learning process begins, we realize our opinions and circumstances have shaped our feelings, thinking and actions in certain ways. Some of these ideas may have worked at one time, but are now causing pain.

We have the power to change our 'Attitude', and to attain 'Serenity' in spite of the circumstances around us.

How is that possible? I am hopeful this book will help you to see that this goal is a possibility in spite of what life brings.

Realizing I do not have control over people, places or things. The only control I have is over myself. That is the hardest one to change. It is difficult to change; I don't even know why I felt I could change anyone else.

There are so many choices to make. I was not conscious of the fact that I had a choice. When I became aware of the idea that I had so many, it was exciting. There are numerous ways in which to deal with certain situations, but when we are programmed to do the same thing all the time, the results are always the same.

Recognizing God's gifts and realizing that I have an abundance of resources all around helped me to recognize that I am not alone.

I found this great story in a self-help brochure. It means a great deal to me.

John is the kind of guy you love to hate. He is always in a good mood and always has something positive to say. When someone would ask him how he was doing, he would reply, "If I were any better, I would be twins!"

He was a natural motivator.

If an employee was having a bad day, John would tell the employee how to look on the positive side of the situation.

Seeing this style really made me curious, so one day I went up and asked him, "I don't get it! You can't be a positive person all of the time. How do you do it?"

He replied, "Each morning I wake up and say to myself, you have two choices today. You can choose to be in a good mood or ... you can choose to be in a bad mood. I choose to be in a good mood."

Each time something bad happens, I can choose to be a victim or...I can choose to learn from it. I choose to learn from it.

Every time someone comes to me complaining, I can choose to accept their complaining or... I can point out the positive side of life. I choose the positive side of life.

"Yeah, right, it's not that easy," I protested.

"Yes, it is," he said. "Life is all about choices. When you cut away all the junk, every situation is a choice. You choose how you react to situations. You choose how people affect your mood.

You choose to be in a good mood or bad mood. The bottom line: It's your choice how you live your life."

I reflected on what he said. Soon hereafter, I left the Tower Industry to start my own business. We lost touch, but I often thought about him when I made a choice about life instead of reacting to it.

Several years later, I heard that he was involved in a serious accident, falling some 60 feet from a communications tower.

After 18 hours of surgery and weeks of intensive care, he was released from the hospital with rods placed in his back.

I saw him about six months after the accident.

When I asked him how he was, he replied, "If I were any better, I'd be twins...Wanna see my scars?"

I declined to see his wounds, but I did ask him what had gone through his mind as the accident took place.

"The first thing that went through my mind was the well-being of my soon-to-be born daughter," he replied. "Then, as I lay on the ground, I remembered that I had two choices: I could choose to live or...I could choose to die. I chose to live."

"Weren't you scared? Did you lose consciousness?" I asked.

He continued, "The paramedics were great. They kept telling me I was going to be fine, but when they wheeled me into the ER and I saw the expressions on the faces of the doctors and nurses, I got really scared. In their eyes, I read 'he's a dead man'. I knew I needed to take action."

"What did you do?" I asked.

"Well, there was a big burly nurse shouting questions at me," said John. "She asked if I was allergic to anything. 'Yes, I replied.' The doctors and nurses stopped working as they waited for my reply. I took a deep breath and yelled, 'Gravity'."

Over their laughter, I told them, "I am choosing to live. Operate on me as if I am alive, not dead."

He lived, thanks to the skill of his doctors, but also because of his amazing attitude... I learned from him that every day we have the choice to live fully.

Attitude, after all, is everything.

Author Unknown

Reading this article about John's attitude, made me think hard about my life and my attitude. I decided that I needed to really consider how I was living.

In Matthew 6:34 of the Bible it tells us: "Therefore do not worry about tomorrow, for tomorrow will worry about itself. Each day has enough trouble of its own. Today is the tomorrow you worried about yesterday."

Is my attitude worth catching? I'd like it to be. Willing to try to change my attitude or anything else I could to stop the hurts became very important.

Really wanting to enjoy life, I remembered reading the Proverbs in my Bible. In Proverbs 12:15 it says, "A stubborn fool considers his own way the right one, but a person who listens is wise". At the time I read this I was still struggling with trying to change things in order to make a good future for my family.

After considerable experience in the area of not having any luck with my actions and decisions, I decided to be honest and admitted that what I was doing was not helping anyone, especially me.

To the best of my ability, I will try to share some of my experiences. This may help you to understand how things got so out of control.

The Kidney Foundation bulletin had many helpful points to remember. This is one of the articles I found there.

"Happiness lies for those who cry, those who hurt, those who have searched, and those who have tried, for only they can appreciate the importance of people who have touched their lives." This made a lot of sense to me, but I did not know how to achieve such peace.

Life is like a coin. You can spend it any way you wish, but you can only spend it once. I wanted to spend my time wisely.

I discovered that 'Letting Go' was very difficult, especially if I really felt strongly about something, or loved someone deeply. I tried so many ways to 'Let Go' of difficult situations. I discovered this article on 'Letting Go', and it got easier to do if I practiced the concept. Letting Go is an Al-Anon concept.

I mailed a copy to my very dear friend, Roberta. "She has it framed over her bed. Berta and I have been friends for over fifty years and have shared much of our lives.

Since 'Letting Go' has been very important in making life worthy, I will share it with you.

LETTING GO

To "Let Go" does not mean to stop caring; it
means I can't do it for someone else.
To "Let Go" is not to cut myself off, it's the
realization I can't control another.
To "Let Go" is not to enable, but to allow
learning from natural consequences.
To "Let Go" is to admit powerlessness, which
means the outcome is not in my hands.
To "Let Go" is not to try to change or blame
another; it's to make the most of myself.
To "Let Go" is not to care for, but to care about.
To "Let Go" is not to fix, but to be supportive.

To "Let Go" is not to judge, but to allow another to be a human being.
To "Let Go" is not to be in the middle arranging all the
outcomes, but to allow others to affect their own destinies.
To "Let Go" is not to be protective; it's to permit another to face reality.
To "Let Go" is not to deny, but to accept.
To "Let Go" is not to nag, scold or argue, but instead to
search out my own shortcomings and correct them.
To "Let Go" is not to adjust everything to my desires but to
take each day as it comes, and cherish myself in it.
To "Let Go" is not to regret the past, but to grow and live for the future.
To "Let Go" is to fear less and love more.

It is so freeing to know that I have options. When I feel right about a situation, I can choose to go along with it, or I can settle on not doing a certain thing. If you put little value on yourself, you can be sure the world will not change it.

It is not enough to just think about something. People judge you by your actions. You may have a heart of gold, but so has a boiled egg.

One of my favourite pieces of literature is the Al-Anon Forum. That's where I discovered the following:

"Of all the things you wear, your expression is the most important."

Chapter 3
ANGER

Here is the first test to find out whether your mission on earth is finished.
If you are alive, it isn't.

Guilt leads to anger and anger leads to depression.

Mom and Dad decided to make the bedroom larger that my son, Don, and I
shared. It was great to have space to move around in. Now Don was older, he
had toys that needed room as well as all the daily necessities.

After the death of my husband Dave, it was strange when our friend
Donald, who my son was named after, decided that we should date. Both my
husband and I liked him, so I decided that it would be nice to go out with
someone I knew.

He was very kind to Don and myself, and we had fun together, often
going bowling, to the park, a movie or other enjoyable activities. He also made
sure that we did things where Don could come. He bought Don a tricycle.
He helped to paint and decorate the newly renovated bedroom.

I knew we had fun together and I also knew that he liked me a lot.
We went out for a short time when he asked me to marry him. That never
happened. I was not in love with him. He was and still is a good friend. He
moved on and married someone else. I continued to work and care for my
son.

In time, I began dating several different men. They were interested in
spending time with me but usually suggested that I leave Don with my Mom
or someone else. My son and I were a package deal. If you did not want him,
you didn't want me either. I was disappointed in some of the men I dated.

Many of my dates thought they would be able to have sex easily because I
was a young widow. This was not my idea of living. Yes I was interested in sex,

but not with just anyone. The person had to be my husband and these men were not interested in my future. I just gave up on meeting someone special.

Planning to take my son on a trip perhaps to visit family where we came from or maybe somewhere else, I ordered a new car. I was waiting for my new car, and working hard, when mom and dad's next-door neighbour, Bernie, asked me if I would like to go on a blind date with a man that he worked with. He spoke highly of this person so I decided to go. It was safe with Bernie and his wife Frances being there with us.

On Friday nights I worked till 8:00 p.m. It was arranged that the three of them would pick me up after work.

When I told my co-worker about this, she said, "Oh Klevie, that was her nick name for me, you need to buy a new jacket and put on some makeup". I knew I needed a new jacket so I went out at lunchtime and bought one. Later she put some of her makeup on me. I rarely wear makeup. All set and ready to go, but still had to balance my cash. I worked for a finance company where the cash was balanced at the end of each day. Seldom was I out in my cash, but I guess with the blind date, makeup and new jacket excitement, I was nervous. I got upset and frustrated. My cash was out by $10.00. I did not want to keep my friends and new date waiting. In the process I began to tear up. My partner told me, "Klevie, you can't cry. Your makeup will run". And run it did. I had to wash my face before I left.

When I met my date, he was very shy and quiet. Milt was a tall, Swedish man, with the bluest eyes I had ever seen. I still remember how I was fascinated with his eyes. He had big blue eyes. So blue you could swim in them. That evening we went out to dinner and to a golf putting range. Neither my new date nor I had ever been to such a place. That was our first and last time, although we had a good time. We were very comfortable with each other right away, and during the evening, I told him about the makeup incident. He laughed and told me that was a good thing because he hated makeup on pretty women. One point for this guy!!

When they drove me home that evening, Milt asked if I would like to go to Stanley Park on Sunday. He said, "If we go to the park, we can take Don along. He would probably enjoy that". Two points for this guy!!

We went to the park on Sunday. We went to drive-in movies, and lots of other places after that Sunday. Don came as well. I met Milt's sisters and his brother. They all seemed happy for Milt and me, and easily accepted my son. Milt's Dad died the year before I met him. At this point and time, Milt was still living in their family home with his mother.

Milt's mom had a problem with alcohol and prescription drugs. In time she sold all their possessions to a used furniture dealer, so that she would have money for her addictions. Eventually the house was sold too, and she moved in with one of her daughters.

When Don and I went on a trip to visit family on the Prairies, Milt wrote me often while I was there. He told me that he never wrote to anyone.

Milt was twenty-seven years old and ready to settle into family life. He loved me and I was in love with him. We did not think very long, because we were both sure of our decision. My parents wanted us to wait for a while longer. They felt it was too soon for such a big decision.

On August 30, 1958 we were married quietly, by a minister with Bernie and Francis being the witnesses. I was happy and very sure that I made the right choice. Milt was happy to become an instant Dad and pleased with the whole idea. Don was comfortable with the situation and I was sure Milt would be a good dad. My first husband's older sister took Don for the weekend so we could go away for a few days.

We rented half a duplex in a small community where we both had approximately the same distance to travel to work. It wasn't the greatest place, but it was clean and the rent was reasonable. We planned to work and buy our own home as soon as we could. There was a furnace in the basement of our living quarters. We had to go outside and around to the basement entrance to stoke the furnace. Don and Milt enjoyed this little ritual. Milt would go down to stoke the furnace and Don would sit by the heat vent and wait. When Milt got down there they would make crazy noises or just talk and laugh. This was so good for me to witness.

Something that I soon noticed was that every time I was not around, my hubby went to the pub, always bringing a case of beer home when he returned. I thought it was habit to go and visit with his friends.

One Saturday after a few months of marriage, I had been out doing my Saturday housekeeping job. When I got home, Milt was not there. This upset me because I was working this extra job to help us purchase a house. I had worked a bit longer than usual that day.

After I thought about this for a while, I put Don in the car and drove down to the pub. I saw his car. I just turned around and went up the hill to where my cousin and his family lived. We had a visit and they asked me to stay for supper. I got home sometime mid evening. Milt was home now. When I got in the door, there were fern plants and cut flowers everywhere. He was happy we were home, but also annoyed.

That evening we had a huge argument. I told him I did not marry to just work and be a wife. I wanted him home with us, not wondering where he was. Things got better, however he always managed to have beer in the house and one in his hand. He still went to the pub but not often.

When I read what Socrates once said, I thought he must've had some marital problems too. He said, "My advice to you is to get married. If you find a good wife you will be happy, if not you'll become a philosopher".

We continued to work and finally had enough money to start looking for a house. We began by looking at seven acres with an old house on it. The house would need some work, but the seven acres of land was very intriguing. It turned out that it cost more than we planned, and was situated in a low-lying location that was often foggy. When I told the man I worked for on Saturdays that we did not have quite enough money, he offered to lend us the difference. It was great to have such a generous employer, however we decided to buy a little house in a quiet neighbourhood in a completely different location from the previous one, and this one we could afford. The house was about 1050 square feet, in a quiet neighbourhood in an area that was not built up. The house had no basement. It was a cute little rancher with two bedrooms. We were so pleased to have our own home.

After we lived in our house for a while, we decided it was time to buy some furniture. Milt told me to go and buy what I liked. If I liked it, he would too. So when payday came, I went out and purchased a bright Chinese red sectional chesterfield, a corner table, an end table and a coffee table. They threw in a lamp with the purchase and delivered it all that evening.

When Milt got home from working afternoon shift, the furniture was in the house. I left a light on for him. We had hardwood floors that were shiny, so the light reflected the red. He was overjoyed with what he saw, and had tears in his eyes when he spoke about it. I knew that he was thrilled with my choices.

I know this is a strange place to write this, but we loved our Chinese red sectional a lot, so when it got sun bleached after about ten years, I put it outside and spray-painted it Chinese red. We could not afford a new one and there was no dye that colour that I could find. That sectional lasted another ten years. The material was so strong and took the paint well.

Milt's mother had moved out of his sister's home and was living in Vancouver in a rooming house. He hated that idea. There was nothing left of the family belongings.

I got home from work one evening to find that he had moved his mother in with us. He did not discuss or even mention this to me. I was pretty emotional and now had to re-arrange our home, moving Don into our room and Milt's mom into his. She managed to have a piano, which went into the room as well. She told us she had purchased it. The room was very small, enough for a single bed and a dresser. Somehow we squeezed the piano in as well.

We struggled with this arrangement for three months, during which his mother decided to go to the country to visit one of her daughters. Milt was still on afternoon shift, so was home during the day. A letter arrived for his mom from William's Piano House. He decided to open the letter, discovering that the piano was being rented, and the rent had not been paid. Milt decided to send the piano back to the company.

During his mom's stay up country, Milt's shift changed. Now he was working days. From then on his shifts switched every two weeks. Two weeks of days, two weeks of afternoons and two of graveyard. My mother-in-law returned from her visit with her daughter and she was angry about the missing piano. I did not get into that situation. That was between her and her son.

Glen, Milt's older brother worked at the same place as he did, so on Friday nights on day shift, they often went to the pub near the work place. Since I worked late on Friday nights I would sometimes go to the pub to see if Milt was there. Milt would then come home. I was upset because I did not feel I should come home after working late on a Friday night to him not there, or worse still, when I got home and he was there, both he and his mother were intoxicated.

On Friday nights I worked till 8:00 p.m. Upon arriving at home after work one Friday night around 9:00 p.m., Milt came outside and met us at the car. Don was asleep in the back seat. He said, "Please don't bring Don in yet". I wondered why. He asked me to come in by myself first, which I did. I found my mother-in-law passed out on the couch naked. In the corner where the new table stood was pee and puke. Wow!! Now what? I asked, "Why did you leave it for me to clean up". He then announced it would make him throw up too, if he did. I cleaned up the mess and put my mother-in-law to bed, then brought Don in and put him to bed. Of course we had a long discussion about all of this. The tension in our home grew.

Many times I used to be so upset, I felt hate for this woman who came to live with us without me even being told. I sometimes wonder if the situation had been discussed, would it have been easier? Most likely I would have consented to the matter, because it was his mother. We could not leave her out on the street.

We loved our home and got to know our neighbours. Next to us was an empty lot where the neighbourhood children spent many hours. It was a forest to the children; a place to build a fort, a hide out, or whatever they decided it would be for that day. All the neighbourhood children enjoyed this special spot.

Next to the empty lot lived a family with three daughters. Don played with the children and I became friends with the mother. When one of the girls had a birthday, Don was invited to the party. I went along to spend some time with the adults. This is when I met Roberta, my neighbour's sister-in-law. I will call her Berta. That is what she liked to be called. Berta lived up the road from us and had a son, Alan that was Don's age. The boys became chums quickly. Roberta and I also became friends.

Some pub nights, I would blame Milt's brother for not being a responsible older brother. I tried to justify what my hubby was doing. In the meantime, since the disaster we had that particular Friday night, I was taking my mother-in-law with me in the mornings. My Mom had Don to take care of, as well as my mother-in-law. Mom was trying to help in any way she could.

I did not tell my parents that my husband went to the pub or that he drank at all.

During the times that Milt would drink, he often said he drank because I did this or that, mostly accusations of things that never happened. I on the other hand, was always on the defensive, trying to get him to understand that these were not what I would do.

Eventually, Milt's mother moved in with one of her daughters. She did come to visit and when she did, she brought her pills in a bag and booze too.

One such weekend, somehow Don got a burn near his eye from her burning cigarette. It was good to know that she would be going back to her daughter's the next day.

Sometimes I felt like I could hit her hard. I am so happy that I never did, but I felt like it many times. My friend, Betty that I worked with often heard the stories of my mother-in-law. She used to tell me to just hang in there and things would get better. I on the other hand thought things were gradually getting more complicated. Resentment and bad feelings were not strangers to me. This was not a nice way to live, and definitely against everything I believed. The reason I put up with my mother-in-law was because she was my husband's mother. I never felt comfortable having Don near her after the burn episode. I made sure I could always see both of them.

The accusations of me having affairs were deteriorating our relationship. I did not understand alcoholism at that time and tried to defend myself by telling him that I would never do that. I explained to him that he, my son and our home were most important. I told Milt hundreds of times that I loved just him, trying to explain that there wasn't time to have an affair even if I wanted to.

Milt and I wanted more children, and eventually I became pregnant. We were both happy and continued to work.

There were lay offs at Milt's work coming up. I had a good boss, who told me I could work till the baby came. The only stipulation was that I did not have the baby at work. Milt did get laid off in January and was now taking care of Don while I continued to work. Sometimes he was so funny. If I called home, he would tell me that he just finished ironing the tents. The tents were my maternity tops.

To do laundry, we had a wringer washer that I pulled up to the kitchen sink. I used a tub to rinse the clothes then hung them outside on the clothesline. In the winter, I had a line strung up in the house where I dried them overnight. Milt decided to help by doing the laundry while I was at work. He ordered an automatic washing machine that same day. When I heard about that, I was concerned as to how we would pay for it since I was not able to work much longer, and he was laid off. He told me, "Don't worry, we will pay for it. I won't be laid off forever". He was right. We did pay for it and it was much easier especially with a baby coming.

Milt was a good man and a good father. The only problem was that he always had to have a beer, or some sort of alcohol if there was no beer. This was costly and after several bottles it changed his dispositon. I decided to make beer, so that the cost would be less. The beer I made was good, according to him and his nephew. I did not drink beer or much of any other alcohol. A glass of wine or a bit of something else, not much and not often was enough for me. One evening when Milt was on afternoon shift I was making beer. His nephew came over and we chatted while I prepared to bottle the stuff. Both Milt and his nephew were waiting for it to be ready. It took time for the beer to mature. They decided to sample it. I went to open a bottle and it took off and flew across the room smashing against the wall, missing his nephew by a fraction of an inch. We were surprised by this reaction, but did not take it very seriously.

One night we heard a bang. We were asleep and both jumped out of bed to see what happened. Finding nothing, we went back to bed. A little while later there was another bang. Up again, now really looking. We discovered the beer in the cupboard was exploding.

I then realized that I had sugared the bottles twice when our nephew was there. This double sugaring created bombs. Milt in his wisdom was going to destroy these explosives. He got a large garbage can with a lid, put on his hardhat, and heavy gloves. He was ready for action. A bottle of beer in one hand, the garbage can lid in the other he would drop the bottle into the can. There was a gigantic bang, and eventually the beer bombs were defused.

While these mini-explosions were taking place, our next-door neighbours watched out of their upstairs window. They also enjoyed the beer and wondered what we were doing. Two Mormon elders came into the yard at the right moment. I bet they had a good laugh after we told them what we were doing. They never came back, and that was the end of my beer making.

There were three of us friends pregnant at the same time. My delivery was to be first, however the other two delivered while I impatiently waited. Eileen had a baby boy and so did Berta. God does things when he wants to. The other two delivered. I was still waiting. I went to the doctor on Friday. He told me that if I didn't go into labour by the following Wednesday, he would induce labour. I was not anxious to be induced. It seemed right to wait till the baby came when it was ready.

On Monday I had a spurt of energy. I cleaned the house thoroughly, cut up the Christmas tree ready for disposal, and did a lot of other projects. By evening, I was exhausted. Monday night I had a horrible dream that I was sitting on top of a manure pile with terrible stomach pains. When I woke up, I was in labour. It is funny how after all these years, I still remember this dream. After calling Flo, our next-door neighbour to come and stay with Don, Milt drove me to the hospital. After an examination, I was told that I had a long wait. The baby's head was not in the canal. If I had not had a baby before, I would have gone along with this theory. I said, "the pains are only a few minutes apart and powerful. This baby is ready to come". The doctor was called. When he arrived he took a quick look, threw a smock on over his clothing and got to work. The baby was in a breach position, but could not come out. No wonder the nurses could not see the head. The delivery was a hard one and I needed an incision to deliver. Our second son was born on March 16, 1961. I wanted to call the baby Clayton. I love that name. The rest of the family did not care for the name as much as I did, so we called him Randle Clayton. He was a little fellow weighing 6 pounds 11 ounces, and a beautiful baby. He was three weeks late and his skin was dry. I could hardly wait to get this little guy home and oil him, and oil him I did as soon as we got home. Once we were home, we called him Randy.

My neighbour, Flo, who stayed with Don while Milt took me to the hospital, invited me over for coffee one morning when Randy was about a week old. We had a great visit. This was wonderful because it did not happen often while I worked. There was no time. After coffee, I was only home a few minutes when Flo called. "Didn't you forget something here?" Oh my goodness, I had left Randy there. She sure did get a chuckle out of that incident. It was over five years since I had a baby and I just honestly forgot. I sure did feel like a half-wit. That never happened again, but Flo often reminded me of it and we had a chuckle over and over again.

We had milk delivered to our home after I stopped working, getting milk for the family, and chocolate milk for Don. He was now five years old and so excited to have a baby brother. I remember nursing the baby when Don asked "Is one of those milk, and the other one chocolate milk?"

Don started school in September of the same year that Randy was born. The day school began, my neighbour Ann and her three children, Don and I all walked to the school together. I was deep in thought about the years I missed while Don was growing up because I had to work. I began to cry. Ann was melancholy as well, because she said: "Stop the tears. If Don sees you crying, he'll cry too". I realized that was true. It was just such a short time I had to enjoy him since I stopped working. My heart was sad. It was an adjustment, but I was busy being an at home mom and enjoying it.

It was so neat that Berta had a baby boy they called Ken. Eventually Randy and Ken became good friends as well. So now we had Don and Alan, Randy and Ken and Berta and me. That was a great time for all of us. We did things together while the men were at work. Berta and I did a lot of sharing during that time, but I never told her about the drinking problem.

In the summer months when the children were on vacation, Berta and I would pack a lunch and away the children and the two of us would go, often to a park that we all enjoyed. The children took swimming lessons at the pool. We had summer birthday parties there, or just hiked through the trails. There was no end to the adventures for the children at Hume Park. Berta and I could stay in the picnic area with the two younger children, if we did not feel like traipsing around, while the two older boys explored. The kids did what they liked to do. The younger boys would play in the playground. That gave them an adventure and we could visit and keep an eye on them as well. The two older boys explored the trails while the two younger ones played nearby. The only stipulation was that Don and Alan had to check in with us often. It was always an enjoyable day for all of us.

Both Milt and I were pleased to have another child, and Don was thrilled. I was still hoping that having a home and a family would make Milt happy so that he would not want to drink.

Milt began to work more steadily, but always there was the threat of strikes or lay offs. I had not yet learned to enjoy the good stuff and let the rest be. My mind was always working, thinking about the 'what ifs'.

Some of the things I thought about did come. Lay offs did happen, but not for long. Strikes did come, but not for long. I know that now, but then, I was very afraid of what would happen to our family if these things went on for a while.

The truth is that when we had 'Beer Strikes', it was more serious than lumber mill strikes. When the beer strikes would happen, Milt would drink wine. The wine made him crazy. He would make hurtful accusations that were not true. Something in the wine made him nuts. He turned into someone else.

Beginning to feel like I was going crazy, I decided to go to see a psychiatrist. At the session, I told the psychiatrist, "If I had all of the affairs I was accused of, I would have penis' coming out of my ears". He cracked up in laughter. I asked him, "What's so funny? This is not a joke". He kept laughing and told me, "I am just picturing you with penis' sticking out of your ears". After some discussion, I could see the funny side. The man laughed and told me I was fine, just too serious. "You will only need few sessions", he suggested. The cost was high. We were not rich. One appointment was enough for me. Now I was wondering if I was too serious.

I did not want to believe or even think about alcoholism. I lived in a dream world of denial, still blaming his brother and his mother. Not knowing much about alcoholism was not helpful.

Randy was a toddler when I became pregnant again. I was so thrilled. Having a family was always my dream. I so much love children.

In the wee hours of August 27, 1963 I awoke with labour pains. We called a neighbour to stay with the other children so Milt could take me to the hospital. He wished me well and dropped me off going home to be with the other two. In those days they did not want the father to be in the delivery room. Tim was born in just a few hours. Randy was two and a half and Don was seven. Mom came to stay with them while I was in the hospital so that Milt could go to work.

When I called home after Tim was born, I told Milt, "You can go and buy another pair of cowboy boots and a hat". Our boys loved their cowboy boots and hats. He was thrilled to have another son and I was happy to have another healthy baby. My boys were the most special in the world.

Mom stayed two days after I came home and enjoyed helping me with the new baby. It was certainly much different than when I brought Don home to her house after he was born. I was such a fanatic then. Don was born in August and I used to turn up the heat so that he would be warm. I asked Mom about that during those two days, because Tim was also born in August. She said, "It was so warm that a little more heat would not make that much difference". She also added, "I knew you would eventually get over that idea". I did.

I enjoyed my new baby and so did his brothers. When the milkman came, Randy was so excited to show him his baby. What a joy this little guy was. He learned to walk early and could talk by the time he was a year old. What a happy baby he was!!! He was so much fun to take on an expedition, talking constantly and enjoying everything around him.

We had a time when our house insurance, car insurance, taxes and other expenses were overwhelming. There was too much month, not enough money. Milt and I discussed me going to work part-time to help out with this dilemma. He would look after the children on day shift and graveyard. We only needed help when he worked afternoons. With a home, husband and three children, where do you find such a job? I was fortunate to find employment in a drug store nearby. The hours were ideal. I worked from 6:00

p.m. to 9:00 p.m., but I got paid for four hours work. This went smoothly for a month or two. Milt did not really want me to work. He did some strange things to make it harder. The two older boys would make a mess that was always left for me to clean up. If the baby needed a diaper change, Milt would change the baby and stuff the dirty diaper somewhere in a corner. I found one behind the drapes that had been there for a few days. Phew!! In spite of all the obstacles, I worked at the drug store for over a year, and we were able to pay our bills. I was willing to work a bit longer, but Milt did not want to cooperate.

It was rather comical my friend Berta was pregnant again when I was. These pregnancies were not planned to happen at the same time. She had a baby girl they called Colleen. Colleen and Tim became good friends and played well. It was even more fun for us now because we had another pair of friends to join us in our adventures.

After a shift of graveyard, Milt came home one morning while the boys were having breakfast. He said, "If you can guess what I have in my pocket, you can have it". Of course the boys thought of food, toys or something he may have made. Finally, he pulled out a teeny, tiny Chihuahua puppy. She was so little she fit in Milt's hand. The boys were so excited they could hardly contain themselves, and immediately named her 'Tiny'. Tiny was so adorable and special. She learned to do many things with the boys. We loved her dearly.

When Tim was about 2 years old, the boys, along with our Chihuahua, Tiny, were playing with a soccer ball in the back yard. Tiny was a cutie. She would push the ball around with her nose. Milt was on his way to the workshop and the ball was on the sidewalk. While kicking the ball he slipped and fell. Tim ran up and jumped on him thinking that daddy was playing with them. He told the boys to go and play. The truth was that Milt had been hurt when he fell. I was inside preparing lunch. Milt crawled from where he had fallen to the back door and called for me. When I asked, "What's the matter?" He said, "I am hurt. I can't stand up". I called the doctor and described what Milt had told me. The doctor said, "Call the ambulance and take him to the hospital. He has a broken hip". Oh my goodness. Now what? When I told Milt what the doctor said, Milt was upset and suggested: "Go next door and get Guenther. Ask him to bring over one of their camp cots. Load me into the back of the truck and drive me to the hospital. We can't afford an ambulance". I did what he told me to do, but it was a job to lift this man into the truck. He was a big man. Eventually we did get him into the back of the truck. We got a neighbour's daughter to stay with the children. Guenther was in the back with Milt while I drove. What a painful ride that must have been!! The roads were mostly gravel and the truck was not smooth riding even in the cab. We did get him to the hospital, and he did indeed have a broken hip. He needed surgery where they put a pin into his hip, and he stayed in hospital for a week or so.

Of course Milt could not have a drink in the hospital, so he was anxious to come home. Milt asked the doctor if he could go home. After a few days he was discharged with the idea I could take care of Milt. The doctor would come to the house to remove the stitches.

When my Dad heard all of the details, he came over with one of his paychecks to help out. I was concerned that Milt would not be able to work for some time and now we owed Dad this money. We were grateful because we needed food for the three boys and of course some beer.

A week or so later, it had been raining, so I hung the laundry in the house to dry. Just as we were about to go to bed, there was a knock at the door. The doctor arrived to take out the stitches. As he came in he said, "Oh my goodness I'm in a Chinese Laundry". I was embarrassed. The doctor thought it was funny.

I decided that three children were plenty to look after. Milt was beginning to drink more and more, but I still did not want to look at the whole picture with reality. I was wishing it was different, but it was not. I was disappointed because I always wanted six children. Milt kept saying that he would have a 'vasectomy', but that did not happen. I decided to have a 'tubal ligation' to be sure that I did not become pregnant again. Mom was happy. She felt that three children were plenty to take care of, and she did not even know about our 'Family Secret'.

The day before my surgery, Mom came with me to the hospital. She hung around as long as she could. I took several walks to the nursery thinking about my decision. Mom asked, "Why are you going to the nursery? Don't be silly and make yourself upset. Just do what you have to do". She was a practical person.

I did have the surgery and was relieved not to have to think about having more children, but I was also sorrowful knowing this was so.

Milt's Mother came often to stay with us for long periods of time. She was getting more and more agitated with living with her daughter. When she arrived, there was always a big bag with booze and pills in it. I would put the bag up out of the way. When I left the room, my mother-in-law would bring it out and put it beside her. Tim was a curious little fellow and would look into the bag. She would get angry with him. I was defensive of my baby.

One such time, I was outside hanging laundry to dry, I heard my toddler cry out. The cry, as I recognized it, was a pain cry. I ran in to check. He was visibly upset. I asked, "What did you do to him?" Her reply was, "He never leaves my stuff alone".

This was on a Saturday. Milt was home and in his workshop. I went out there with our baby. I told him what happened and said, "If she doesn't go, then I will". He drove her back to his sister's that afternoon.

Milt loved to create in his workshop. I encouraged him to make something we could sell for spending money. He began to make bunk beds. This became a wonderful outlet for him and I could use the sales techniques I had learned. Milt in turn did not enjoy the interaction with the people interested in purchasing the beds. He made them and I sold them.

This part of our lives was fun. I learned that if I got three calls about a set of beds, we would usually sell it. We would sometimes wait till we had two or three sets before placing an ad, to save on the cost. Once the bunks were sold, we had a little extra money. Milt got a case of beer or whatever he felt he wanted, and we would have fish and chips, or Chinese food for supper. Sometimes we would go to a drive-in movie. This is a great memory.

Milt had an old truck that he enjoyed. Sometimes if a customer had no way of taking the bunk beds, we would deliver. One Friday we had bunks to deliver that had been purchased during the week. During the day, I washed and waxed the floors and made a huge batch of doughnuts. When the children and Milt got home, the house looked and smelled great. After supper, we delivered the beds. Arriving at the residence of the customers, we discovered a messy, smelly home. The children living there were misbehaved and not clean. We left as quickly as we could. It was wonderful to come to our little home that smelled so good. We were all grateful.

Eventually, Milt's mother moved into a place of her own away from her daughter's home. After many episodes of self-destruction, she died. I felt sadness mixed with relief. This was a terrible feeling for me that led to guilt. I felt guilty because I felt cold about her death. When I think about it now, I think Milt felt relief as well. He did not show much emotion either way, and seldom spoke of his Mom.

Sometimes, after supper I would hop on Don's bike and ride down to Berta's for a cup of tea and a chat. Before I would even arrive, Milt was on the phone checking to see if I was there. She lived only a few blocks away. At that time she thought it was so nice that he was concerned about me. Eventually it became a ritual and we had many good laughs about whether he would call before I got there or after I arrived. I did not think it was so funny, but I never did tell her the real problem. The SECRET was safe. I did not want to spoil the chuckles. Actually we were both young with many issues and we did not chuckle, we really laughed till tears rolled down our faces.

It was so good to have a friend close by. We could laugh hard about silly things. That was many years ago and we still laugh about goofy stuff. She no longer lives near me, but we still have many break-up laughs over things while talking on the phone. We would laugh about me having an affair in the ditch between her place and mine. It was not at all funny, but when you don't know what to do, you resort to nonsense.

I was so concerned about Milt's drinking bouts, but continued to try and make a home for my husband and family looking after several children to help out. Berta had gone back to school and after finishing her schooling, she began to work, so her children stayed here as well. This was a huge responsibility, but I was home with my children. In a way it was nice for them, because there was always someone to play with.

Building memories for my little guys was my dream, but I was so emotionally involved with my husband's love of alcohol, those memorable moments were short lived. Many arguments occurred during those times when Milt drank too much, and my feelings were mixed with anger, guilt and worry.

My cousin, the one who wanted me to try smoking when we were teenagers, also became an alcoholic. She was drinking more and more. Going into treatment institutions did not help her. As soon as she got out, she drank again. I was terribly upset. She is like a sister to me. When we lived on the farm, she spent her summers with us and when we moved to Vancouver, we lived with her and her parents till my Mom and Dad bought a home for us.

I love this saying: "When you come to the end of your rope, tie a knot on it and hang on!!" At this point this is mostly what I did.

I had much to learn. I did not yet know that "An angry person stirs up a fight, and a hot head does much wrong". Proverbs 29:22

I hated being upset and angry all the time. Resentful of the way life was going, but mostly angry that my boys had to witness all this crap during the drinking episodes.

Nor did I know that I could "Be angry without sinning. Don't give the devil the opportunity to work". Ephesians 4: 26,27

Anger is a condition in which the tongue works faster than the mind. I wasn't aware of any of this and I did not understand what was taking place. Honestly, I did not know what to do!! I was very angry! My life was falling apart.

My attitude was really terrible. I was 'Afraid', and now very, very 'Angry', and getting 'Resentful'. I felt that God had abandoned me. Given up on me. Left me alone and frightened. I did not know what to do.

I had a lot to learn and I did not realize, "It is not the load that brings you down, it is the way you carry it". I definitely did not know how to carry this load.

Another expression worth thinking about: "The happiness of your life depends on the quality of your thoughts", and the quality of my thoughts had been deteriorating for some time.

Sometimes the one you think is your knight in shining armour turns out to be an idiot in tin foil.

Chapter 4

RESENTMENT

Life is like an onion.
You peel it off one layer at a time and sometimes you cry.
Carl Sandburg

Broken promises, feelings of bitterness and violent acts were becoming common occurrences in my life. I did not like what was happening and what I was becoming. All I wanted in life was to be a good wife, have a loving husband, a home and family. I had never even thought of such things as were now happening in my home.

As each chapter of my story unfolds, the order in which incidents occurred are sometimes out of order because of the point I am trying to make, and often several events overlapped. It eventually all comes together.

Milt was not an outgoing person, but one evening, he had been out with a couple of neighbourhood men. I waited and wondered what was next. Finally around 10:00 in the evening he returned. He had found a huge chair and somehow managed to bring it home. It was an ugly monstrosity and dirty. Supper was drying out. He sat down at the table. I served his spaghetti and meat balls over his head. There was spaghetti sauce everywhere. Our beautiful light green drapes were covered in sauce, as were the walls and cupboard. He just proceeded to go to bed. I felt sick, embarrassed and stupid, and was left to clean up the mess. It took a long time and lots of work to get that sauce out of the drapes.

'The whistle is loudest when the fog is thickest', was something I heard and began to think about after this episode. I was doing some pretty bizarre things. I wanted to change that badly, but did not know how.

I am grateful still that the children were all in bed when this took place. It also taught me to think before I do something stupid.

This crazy behaviour on my part really made me become aware of the fact that I was losing it. He drank and did some dumb things. I was sober and insane. I knew that I loved my husband. My children were my joy and I wanted nothing but the best for them, however, this is not what was happening in real life.

Resentment was not something I thought much about. I was not even sure what it meant. I began considering what resentment meant, and realized that I had better start paying attention to what is really going on in our home.

I continued to ride over to Berta's on the bike and Milt continued to call just as I arrived or before. I began to resent that he needed to keep track of my every move. However, I did not share 'The Secret' with my friend.

When my first husband and I were married, his friend Rolly lent us his car to go on our honeymoon. He was a very close friend, and he was one of the people who lived in the little shack that we had fixed up. Anyhow, after Dave died, Rolly was very kind to Don and me. He came to visit and spent quality time with us. He was also Don's Godfather.

Rolly tried to keep up the friendship, after Milt and I were married. Milt was fine with it when he was sober. When he drank, he accused me of many things I do not want to even think about, even saying that Don looked like Rolly. Rolly was always a great friend and I wanted to keep this comradeship.

I explained the situation to Rolly. I only heard sporadically from him by phone after that. I really did miss having him to talk to, but thought it was better this way. Now I realize that once this was out of the way, Milt found something else to torment about. At one point it was my boss that he was jealous of. Then it was another friend. There was no stopping his imagination when he was intoxicated.

Weekends came and went with alcohol being the most important part.

Being resentful was coming easily and there was more and more trouble, especially on the weekend. Long weekends were terrible and I began dreading them. Knowing that I needed help, not knowing where to go, and not mentioning this 'Family Secret' to anyone was making me sicker and very tired.

Some days life would be great, and the next day could be fine. After a few good days, I would begin to think it was all in my head. Something dramatic would happen because of the alcohol, and my mind would be spinning.

Time was moving along. Our sons were growing up quickly. We needed more room. Milt used to tease and say, "No problem, we'll just hang them up by the collar".

The empty lot next door to us came on the market. My thought was that we should buy it and build a larger home on it. Milt was sceptical. One of the neighbours was a builder and was interested in purchasing the lot. He is an honest and kind man. He came over one afternoon and put it to us this way: He said, "I am asking you if you are going to buy the lot next door. If you are not, then I will buy it and build a house there". Milt was still unsure, so Fred bought the lot and began building a house.

Eventually we made a deal with Fred and he finished the house for us. It was so great to know that we would have room to move around in, and the boys would have the basement to play in during the rainy season.

Shortly before we moved into our new home Milt's mother died. I felt both relief and guilt about her death. I was relieved that I did not have to deal with her addictions any more, and guilt because I did not feel very sad.

Moving was simple. I asked Fred to finish a corner in the basement so that I could move a little in every day. Every day I packed a box or two and took it over. In the end we only had the furniture to take over.

We moved in to our new home in December 1968. Our home was ready with everything done as promised. Our boys were now 12, 7 and 5 years old. How happy they were to have a room of their own and a basement to play in. They were great kids and just wanted to be kids. I on the other hand was obsessed with Milt's drinking problem. I was not as good a mom as I had hoped to be.

We loved our new home. For a little while, we were wrapped up in getting organized. I missed my clothesline. I did not have a place to hang laundry and it did not feel like home. When I told Milt this, he immediately put one in. It was times like this that made it difficult to come to terms with our confusing lives. There were times that seemed so right, and reinforced my thoughts that he was a good guy and really loved us.

I was reacting to stupid things. I love a hot bath. Sometimes in order to be belligerent and needing to do something dumb, Milt would turn the heat down on the hot water tank. When I went to draw a hot bath, there was no hot water. This did not make any sense to me whatever, but when he threatened to drown me in the tub, was absolutely frightening. The children told me never to have a bath when they were not home.

One thing I said I would never do was to get upset over dumb things with the children, and I was beginning to do that. This was one thing I wanted to change more than anything else. It was instrumental in my eventual decision.

Milt was obsessed with alcohol and I was obsessed with him and what he was doing. Life was awful. The reality was that I was dead, just still breathing, like a walking tree, but reacting to stuff that did not make any sense.

Plans made were rarely kept. Promises were broken and I was very overwhelmed with the way life was going. It never occurred to me to keep promises to the children even when Milt did not. I was getting every bit as sick as he was and I did not drink. The worst part was that I did not realize that I could make a difference. I really felt that it was his problem causing all of this mess. It was, but I could have done things differently if I had been more aware. I could not be aware when I was so full of hurt feelings, craving for what I believed to be a normal life.

I continued to wait for things to change. In the meantime doing the same things over and over. This was total insanity. Doing the same things over and over and expecting different results.

I was angry and resentful.

I read this in the Forum, an Al-Anon pamphlet, and it made me start to think: "If you bury your head in the sand, you **will get kicked in the butt**". I became aware that I was losing myself in all of this confusion, and getting kicked in the butt often.

Some days life would be great, and the next day could be fine. After a few good days, I would begin to think it was all in my head. Something dramatic would happen because of the alcohol, and my mind would be spinning.

I was in a dream world thinking that now we would have more privacy and things would get better.

I was a good parent. I took great care of my boys. They ate well. They had a good clean environment to live in. I took them to all their activities. In body I was there for them, but my mind was always pre-occupied with what was happening with their Dad. What was he up to now? Was he at home or at the pub? If he was home, how much had he had to drink? What would he be like when we got home? The questions in my head were endless. I was fixated with what my husband was doing.

I love to garden and often spent hours working outside. This helped save some sanity in my life.

During one alcoholic bout, I became depressed. Milt had been extremely belligerent and had pushed me down on the floor and poured beer over me. He had been drinking since Friday night and it was now Sunday. I felt like I would rather be dead than live like this. When he finally went outside, he sat down in a lawn chair in the back yard and just stared into space. I made sure that dinner was in the oven, the house was clean and then I planned to kill myself. I took some of Milt's tranquillizers and a good shot of alcohol. Soon the house was spinning and I took to my bed. How crazy is that. I sure was not thinking straight. How were my sons going to live in this kind of environment?

Tim was about six or seven years old. I had been teaching my boys what to do in an emergency. At that time our doctor would come to the house if necessary. This happened on a Sunday. When Tim came into the house and found me in bed looking awful, he took it upon himself to call the doctor. The doctor came immediately and asked me what I had done. When I told him, he checked me over and said, "You will be fine. Come and see me on Tuesday". He did not work on Mondays.

In the morning when I realized what had happened, I felt guilty and stupid. I was embarrassed to go to see him on Tuesday. When I did go, he wanted to know if I wanted something to calm me down. I promised that such an event would never happen again. I felt foolish and guilty, but that did not help the situation at home.

Milt was a 6'2" tall man. Our basement was not yet finished and he often drank down there. Sometimes I would get so frustrated if he did not keep his promise that I would become sick. I would lose my breath. Now I know that I was hyperventilating. At that time I did not know what was happening. When this would happen, Milt would become frightened and make a zillion wonderful promises. I would calm down and go back to what I should have been doing and he went back to his primary enjoyment. Within an hour things would be the same.

There were times when I would get so upset that I would grab the crow bar and chase my husband around with it. The craziest part of this is that he ran. I was so messed up that I did not think about what would happen if he turned around and whacked me with it. How crazy!! Thank God, the children did not ever witness this insanity.

Often I would turn up the heat in the house so that Milt would go to sleep. He rarely fell asleep, but I sure did get drowsy. I soon learned that did not work.

Milt seemed more agitated if Randy was not home. If Randy was over at a friend's, Tim and I would have to leave in the night and go for a walk or take the car and sleep in a parking lot somewhere. Other times, Randy would be waiting for us behind a telephone pole across the street from the house. He would be afraid to come into the house. If the bedroom window was open a certain way, it meant that their Dad was asleep, sometimes we were not sure. Not a great way to live. Randy would wait for us to come home. We would all come in together, waiting and hoping it would be peaceful, but never sure.

In order to bring in some income, I took in neighbourhood children while the parents worked. I took care of Berta's children while she went back to school. Looking after other peoples children was hard work and the pay was poor. I also cut hair for friends and neighbours for $1.00 a head. The money I earned was not much, but it did help.

After Tim started school, I went back to work for the same company I worked for before the two younger boys came along. Milt did not want me to work, but alcohol is expensive and we had three boys to bring up. I decided that it would help us in more ways than one. It would give me something new to think about. It was a lot of work looking after other children and at that time the pay was poor.

We had been in our new home for a year or two when my parents were nearing their wedding anniversary. A surprise party was planned. Our boys were excited at the prospect of having a party in our house to surprise Grandma and Grandpa. As soon as the date was set, the boys decided that they would clean the basement so that we could use it in spite of the fact that it was unfinished. They dusted and hosed wherever they could. In doing this, they discovered several full bottles of alcohol in the rafters. This was upsetting but we pressed on. The party was important to all of us.

The anniversary was a huge success and Grandma and Grandpa were very surprised. The boys were happy and content to know that they had done their part in making this happen. I was obsessed with the findings in the rafters. It was impossible for me to think about much else.

It was great to have been able to do this for my parents, however feelings of resentment were in my heart. How could he hide liquor in the rafters? Did he think I was stupid? Today I know that he did not think I was stupid. I know now that he had an illness called Alcoholism.

Not knowing much about this illness, I continued to do a lot of dumb things, liking asking him to promise to come with us on picnics, or swimming, or some of the boys games. All that I was doing was setting myself up for hurt. I did not realize that the idiotic things I did were part of the disease of Alcoholism.

Things got pretty awful. Milt was very quickly getting worse and I was angry and resentful. One night he drank and caused a lot of trouble before finally falling asleep. He was on holidays so did not have to think about work. I was off for the summer. We did not go anywhere, so he could drink till he passed out. In the morning there was a check in the mail from my job that covered a raise negotiated some time before. I asked the boys if they wanted to go to the prairies for a holiday. Don was already working and living away from home. Randy and Tim went for the idea.

We packed and left. Milt did not hear a thing. Taking the bus was fun for Randy and Tim. My mind was on other things, but I was relieved to be leaving for a break. We spent the time with my uncle who lived with us when I was a youngster. His wife, aunty Helen, and I were dear friends as well. They lived on a farm so the boys were busy driving the tractor and trying to shoot gophers. During the first two weeks we did a lot of things there. Uncle Jim lent me their car, so I was able to take the boys to the farm where I grew up. Even the old house still stood. Later on the house was torn down and a new one built. It was good for me to see it one more time. Both sets of graves of my grandparents were in two separate church cemeteries. The boys were very interested in seeing where their ancestors were buried and cleaned the surrounding areas. I answered as many questions the boys had, as I knew the answers to. My dad's parents were deceased before I was born so I did not know them. However, I knew a little of my maternal grandparents. We spent time with my uncle and aunt and we had fun. After two weeks, I called home. I told Milt I would not go to the liquor store for him any more, because I hated to do it. Milt promised that things would change. Just come home. We stayed a few more days and then came home.

Coming home by bus was not as much fun as going. We were not sure what we were coming home to. Milt met us and was happy to see us, but on the way home he stopped at the liquor store.

Never again did I go to fetch liquor for my husband. It was beer he got when I was picking it up. Now that he went to get his own, there were other problems. Milt was even more belligerent when he drank wine, or hard liquor.

A friend of Milt's was over one Friday evening. They were having a grand time getting sloshed. Milt has his stash and Nick brought more. Sitting in the basement watching television and drinking to get drunk was their mission. I decided to go out for a while. When I returned, they were still there doing what they did best. The boys and I went to bed.

Around 3:00 a.m. Milt came to bed very drunk. He said, "I think I am going to die". I was thinking, "That would help", but I said nothing. I got up and went to sleep on the couch. Around 7:00 a.m. I felt a tapping on my head. There was Nick in his underwear asking if I could make some coffee. I was used to men in underwear. I had three boys, two husbands and a brother. While we were having coffee, he said, "Last night I lost my sun glasses somewhere in the basement. I looked again this morning and still cannot find them. Can you come down and help me look?" Of course I did. While I was crawling around looking, Nick made a sexual move towards me. I was shocked and surprised. I jumped up and told him, "Get your pants on and go home where you belong. Do not ever come to my home again".

He did get dressed and he left. He called the following Tuesday night to apologize, but he never did come here again.

I told Milt about the incident. He did not say a word about it, but the friendship was over. Good thing. It was not a friendship in my eyes. It was a drinking bout each time.

Funny thing about this that still baffles me is that Milt would make accusations of all sorts, but this was real, and he never ever brought it up.

I tried hard to make this marriage work and did many kinds of work to help out financially. In the process, I sold jewellery, Amway products,

Avon cosmetics, lingerie, Watkins Products, and other things. The most fun I had was when my brother and his wife decided to sell wigs. Marion, my sister-in-law, felt I would do well and recruited me into the sales end. I had a blast with these items both with the clients and being able to show them off myself. Jewellery sales were fun too, but selling wigs was the most fun. I enjoyed wearing them myself which helped the sales end of it. These sales activities were fun and gave me a new perspective. I felt valued and enjoyed the interaction with people.

The boys were growing up to be wonderful people in spite of our ignorance and idiotic behaviour. For the most part they were the same as most kids, but very confused. They were mostly confused by my behaviour. Dad was drinking and did senseless things. Mom did not drink, but behaved like a fool at times.

After eighteen years of hidden bottles, anger, fear and now full of bitterness, I knew that I had to change something. I did not want to become a bitter old woman. I made a decision that I was going to do something to make life better for myself, and the children. I wasn't sure what that would be, but began putting ideas into the brain where there was nothing now but obsession, and resentment.

It was good to know that I could work and help with expenses, and I enjoyed my job. While I was at work, I seemed to be able to let go of the home front till around 2:00 or so in the afternoon. Around that time, my stomach would knot up and my thoughts went from work to what Milt was up to. Later on the boys admitted to the same feelings.

Milt did not want me to work. Often we had huge arguments about it. He tried to make me quit work by saying that all I was doing was giving the government more money. It would all go to the tax department. He would say, "You need to be home where you belong". I loved being at home, but I was determined to continue working, mostly because I could see the Alcoholism accelerating. I continued to work.

Eventually I changed jobs from working for a Finance Company to working for the School District. I loved my new job even more than the other one, because I loved kids and was off during the summer. It was great to have a few weeks to enjoy my boys.

After years of hearing that I was this, that and the other, and if it weren't for me he would not drink, I doubted myself. Accusations of affairs that never happened made me sometimes think, "If I have the name, may as well play the game". I learned quickly that having an affair was not hard to do. It was much harder to stay on the right track. An affair was never my idea of dealing with life. Besides which, I loved my husband, but I did not like what he had become. Even worse, I hated what I was turning into.

One Saturday evening after a whole night and day of drinking, my husband started to sob uncontrollably. I had been asking him to stop the insanity and live a good life. A life that could have been so great was all I wanted. He cried and cried, finally I asked him, "What on earth are you crying about?" His answer was, "If only he hadn't died. Oh my God, if only he hadn't died!" My dilemma was, "If only who hadn't died?" His reply was, "Your husband. If only he hadn't died, I wouldn't be in this mess". I was crushed. Why? I don't know. He wasn't speaking with a clear mind.

Milt worked swing shift. From 2 weeks of days, 2 weeks of afternoons and 2 weeks of graveyard. For a long time the afternoon shift was best. He slept most of the morning, got ready to go to work, only drinking after work. However as time progressed, he began having a drink or two before going to work. That always concerned me. His position involved being in charge of many men. He worked in a Mill where there was dangerous equipment and he needed to be fully alert.

Sometimes during a bad spell of drinking, Tim and I would go for a drive, during which Tim would pretend to be a lawyer defending me in court, making me laugh, but I was dying inside.

The two younger sons played hockey. It was early on a February morning that we were at a rink. I went to the concession for a cup of coffee, meeting a friend that I had known for a long time and that I had worked with at one point. Audrey merely asked me, "How are you?" and I broke out into a sobbing, blubbering mess. Of course, she did not know what was happening in my home. It was a 'Secret' – no one knew except the children and myself. However, it turned out that my friend also lived with the 'Secret'. Audrey asked me a few questions. Then she asked, "Would you like some help?" She knew just the place for me to go.

My first Al-Anon meeting was in February 1977. I am forever grateful for being introduced to this wonderful program.

After eighteen years of a marriage on a merry-go-round, I decided to attend Al-Anon meetings. These meetings are for people whose lives have been affected by someone else's drinking, people who are family or friends of alcoholics.

All I could do was cry for the first few meetings. I soon learned that I did not cause this problem, could not cure it and definitely could not control it. Whew!!! What a relief.

Being in Al-Anon made me realize that everything I had been doing for eighteen years only made the problem worse. Only one month later, I knew that I had to do something to stop the insanity.

This is when I began tossing ideas around in my head. Our eldest son had moved out, but came home often to see how we were doing.

Tim was ready to move with me, but Randy was not. Milt seemed to be more patient with Randy than he was with the rest of us when he was drinking. Randy told me to go and he would bring us money and whatever he could. He felt that his Dad would give him these things so that he would stay. I told him, "Either we all go, or we all stay".

I realized that Randy was not as brave as he sounded. He often went to his friends. There were the times he would stand behind the telephone pole across the street from our house and wait for Tim and me to come home before entering the house.

Tim and I had gone out to visit friends one evening. I used to feel I had to stay home to keep an eye on things, but I learned in Al-Anon to just go, nothing different will happen whether you are there or not. When we got home, Randy had asked his friend, Glen, to spend the night. The boys had a hockey practice at 4:00 a.m., so we needed to sleep. Glen played hockey on Randy's team as well. He would come along with us. Tim often played on Randy's team when they were short a player, so he practiced with both his team and theirs.

I went to bed and so did Tim. Milt was in the basement enjoying his stash and was pretty drunk. We just went to bed, leaving Randy and his friend up. My younger boys were now eleven and thirteen.

When I awoke at 3:00 in the morning to take the kids to hockey, Randy said, "I am ready to go whenever you find a place". I wondered what made him decide this. He told me that Milt had been pounding on the ceiling of the basement. I slept so soundly I did not hear it. Milt would do things like that when he drank. Randy went down and asked him to please stop. They could not sleep when he was hammering, then came back upstairs.

Milt became angry, came up after them and proceeded to try to throw both boys through the living room window. There were two of them so they managed to push him down on the couch where he passed out.

We were ready to move. Don came over to visit one day and I told him my plan. He was relieved, telling me, "Mom, try and get a place big enough for all of us. I will come and live there too". I was so pleased that he was willing to do that. When Don's roommate found out, he also wanted to join us. The idea was now in progress. Don and Gord would pay room and board, which would help out financially as well as being great to have Don back with us.

I had to come up with a plan. We had a nice home that was comfortable and big enough for all of us, yet we had to move. I knew that Milt would never leave without a war, even if he were ordered to do so. He might have left, but not without a continuous fight, and I did not want to fight any more. I was not sure how to go about this. Working full time, and shuttling the boys here and there took a lot of time. There wasn't much spare time to be looking for a place to live or going to lawyers, and I was very naïve.

The resentment continued to build. I was angry that we had to leave our home. I was frightened about the move and the changes that would take place and so very concerned about how we would make a go of things. Of course, I did not share this with the children. I wanted their transition to be as smooth as possible.

Working full time, transporting my boys wherever they needed to go, and trying to keep things going at home was enough without thinking about moving out of my precious home.

My thoughts were everywhere. Maybe he would stop drinking if I told him what I was planning? He should be the one to leave after all; it was because of him that this was happening. Where will I take my children that will be home?

After much thinking, planning and looking around, I finally found a house not far from where we lived. I really did not want the children to have to change schools, and I also wanted them to eventually see their Dad. The rent was far more than the payments were on our family home. The rental place was a homey house, with a room for each of us, and Don and his roommate would share the larger room in the basement.

I read in Proverbs 13:4 in my Bible: "Lazy people want much but get little, but those who work hard will prosper and be satisfied". I was not lazy, so set out to make a new life and try to prosper and be satisfied.

Will Rogers said: "Even if you are on the right track, you'll get run over if you just sit there".

I really got a lot of help from these quotes, and have put them to work in my life.

A while ago I received this little parable from a friend that made perfect sense to me. It goes like this:

One evening an old Cherokee told his grandson about a battle that goes on inside people. He said, "My son the battle is between two wolves inside us all. One is: Evil, Anger, Jealousy, Sorrow, Regret, Greed, Arrogance, Self-pity, Guilt, Resentment, Inferiority, Lies, False Pride, Superiority, and Ego.

The other is Good: It is Joy, Peace, Love, Hope, Serenity, Humility, Kindness, Benevolence, Empathy, Generosity, Truth, Compassion, and Faith."

The grandson thought about it for a minute, and asked, "Which wolf wins?"

The old Cherokee replied, "The one you feed".

I can totally relate to this little story. It makes so much sense to me now. It is much like one of my favourite Bible verses: "When the Holy Spirit controls our lives he will produce this kind of fruit in us: Love, Joy, Peace, Patience, Kindness, Goodness, Faithfulness, Gentleness and Self-control." Galations 5:22

It made such a difference in my life when I realized these things and began working on changing my thoughts. The old Cherokee may have learned this from his culture and was passing down a great message to his grandson, or he may have learned it from the Bible and was using it in a different context. It doesn't really matter. If we feed the right wolf, life gets better.

Life just gets more valuable and more precious as I continue to learn new ways.

The Value You Place on People

The value you place on people determines whether you are a **Motivator** or **Manipulator.**

Motivation is moving together for mutual advantage.

Manipulation is persuading or even subtly coercing people to do something so that you win and they lose.

With the **Motivator,** everybody wins.

With the **Manipulator**, only the manipulator wins. And to that, I might add that the victory is temporary.

Manipulators are losers who produce resentment and discord.

Author Unknown

I know both motivators and manipulators. From my own experience, manipulation produces resentment and causes lots of trouble. Sometimes recognizing the difference can save tons of heartache.

The following statement is so true:

The heaviest thing you can carry is a grudge.

Chapter 5
SELF-ESTEEM

Motivation is like nutrition.
It must be taken daily and in healthy doses to keep it going.

There was plenty of nutrition, but I needed all the motivation I could muster. My self-esteem was not good. I knew that trying to put myself to sleep forever was not normal.

Life was full of turmoil, accusations, stuffed feelings, and thinking about the kind of parent I had become. It was tough to be motivated with little self worth.

Self-worth is a fragile thing. I worried about what other people thought about me, not even considering the fact that most of them did not even know what was happening, and they had their own problems. Often the opinion of others was so important, because I no longer had a good opinion of myself.

Working full time, transporting my boys wherever they needed to go, and trying to keep things going at home was enough without thinking about moving out of my precious home.

My thoughts were everywhere. Maybe he would stop drinking if I told him what I was planning? He should be the one to leave after all; it is because of him that this was happening. Where will I take my children that will be home?

Much thinking, planning and looking around, I finally found a house not too far from where we lived. I really did not want the children to have to change schools, and I also wanted them to see their Dad.

I was still angry that he had a home, and we did not. Some attitude adjustment needed to take place before I could do much. I was angry, fearful, and resentful. I did not have much self-worth left, but knew that I had to move on.

51

Another quote from Al-Anon sources came to mind, "The biggest troublemaker you'll probably ever have to deal with watches you in the mirror every morning".

I continued to work. Working at times had it's own problems. My boss was a confused man who tried to control every situation, consequently making some mistakes that upset the whole system.

We needed a new Head Secretary at the school where I worked, and I still do not understand how he did this, but he did. He hired a young woman without going through the Union. He ordered a new typewriter for her and treated her as if she were a diamond. I will call this person Sally, not her real name. The rest of us did not understand what was happening, so we just worked, waited and wondered.

Every time our boss, who was the school principal, left the room, Sally complained that she did not know what to do, how to do it, and that he expected too much from her. There were four of us in the office at that time. She continued to ask me how to do this, that and the other. She asked questions about every task. It was evident to everyone concerned that she did not understand the procedures required by our system. I already had enough to think about, I just helped her along and continued to make plans about my family situation. I really did not want anything more to think about.

Two of the other employees were off Monday. One was sick and the other on her day off. There was a phone call for Sally. After the call was completed, she told me she was quitting her job. Stunned and confused, I was secretly happy. There was much going on inside my head and I did not know what to do or say, so I just continued to do my work.

Sally went in to the boss, quit and left immediately. I wondered what would happen next? Did I need more problems? What will he say to me? I remembered that I read somewhere or someone told me, "You cannot plough a field by turning it over in your mind".

I did not have much time to ponder. He came out and called me into his office. I was the only one there. There were three phone lines ringing and people to attend to at the counter. Not to mention the rest of the work.

He told me not to worry and just come in to his office. Next came the question, "Do you think you can handle this position?" My reply was, "I have been handling this position". I could not believe what came out of my mouth. His next question was, "What do you mean by that?" I proceeded to tell him how she talked when he was not around, explaining that she asked me how and what to do. "Of course I can do the job. There is no doubt in my mind", I told him. This whole thing amazed me, because I suddenly became quite sure of myself again.

He explained that I would now be doing the job until it was posted, and that I should apply for it when it was. Wow!! Planning to leave my home, starting a new job and being the Head Secretary of this office. The first thing that came to mind was that I would be making more money. That would help. There were no doubts about being able to handle the position. I somehow felt better about the whole situation. Once again my God given abilities began to return.

After the initial shock, I told him, "I will take the job and do it well", but you must promise me something". "What is that?" he asked. "Well", I said, "I want you to promise me that you will treat us all the same with no favourites". "I guess I had that coming", was his reply. Funny I can still picture that whole dramatic scene. He promised me he would be fair and thanked me for being honest.

I then explained my home situation. He was very supportive, as well as surprised. It was all unfolding. My move from my home, and my job advancement were happening all at the same time.

I made it clear to my sons that we would not have much money left over to buy extras, so any treats would have to come from their own money. That was fine with them. The two younger boys often babysat or cut grass. They had their own money, and Don had a full time position.

I was trying to keep things on an even keel as much as possible and did not tell the boys much, except that I was looking for a place. Arrangements were made for the moving truck to come at 5:30 in the evening of April 1st, 1977. The truck would take all the things we could not. After Milt left for work that night, I told the boys we were moving. "When?" they asked. "In two hours", was my reply. They were frightened and excited all at once.

As we were packing up, I was crying. The boys wanted to know why I was crying. I tried to explain that this was not what I really wanted. The telephone rang several times. I did not answer. Many months later, Milt told me that he did not feel right at work and that he called home a few times that night.

We threw all our personal belongings into garbage bags and put them in Don's car and mine. When the moving truck came, we put our beds, dressers and larger items in the truck. The boys decided to take the television from the living room. Milt had one in the bedroom. I was not concerned about the TV. I was in a trance.

The move went well. Everything went into the basement in a heap in our new home. We managed to put the beds together enough to sleep the night, with the plan to do more the next morning. At 11:00 p.m. or so, I was having a bath when I realized that I had left all my underwear and socks in the drawer of the dresser at the house. I called the boys and they said, "Just enjoy your bath, we will go and get the stuff". I tried not to worry about what could happen there, in case Milt decided to come home early. All went well and they returned with my belongings. I was really relieved because I could not afford to purchase much at that point. My bed was ready, and I was tired. Once again a saying came to mind: A woman is like a tea bag. You never know how strong till you put it in hot water. Well I was in 'Hot Water'.

I heard someone once say at an Al-Anon meeting, "Thou shalt not worry, for worrying is the most unproductive of all human activities". Another thing I was told, "Worry is like a rocking chair. It gives you something to do, but doesn't get you anywhere". I hung on to these expressions.

It is so interesting how some sayings or Bible verses come to my mind when I need them.

I really began relying on prayer while taking Christian Counselling. One of the things that helped me a great deal was repeating some positive thoughts like "I like myself unconditionally, because God loves me unconditionally!" Daily I would repeat the things the counsellor suggested would help. "I enjoy the special and unique person that I am", was another.

The counsellor told me to remember that the Love of God would set me 'Free' from the past and the mistakes of the past. How much I needed to hear those words. To hear them was good, but to put them into practice took some time.

Finally, "I can do all things through Christ who strengthens me".

When the counsellor's suggestions combined with what I was learning in Al-Anon were put to good use, things began to improve.

Al-Anon taught me I can't control another human. It freed me. I became much more detached.

We were living away from our family home. I hated paying rent. It took some time for me to get over that we were paying much more in rent than my husband was in house payments. Not to mention that there was not much owing on our family home. I spent a lot of time thinking about this. In the meantime the house the boys and I were living in came on the market. I decided that I should try to purchase it. I did a lot of research before making a decision. I did not earn enough to qualify for a regular mortgage. Don told me that he would buy the house with me, if we needed to do that. I didn't want him tied to me while making his way in life. Another good thing I had learned.

After much research and contemplation, I was able to figure out a way to purchase this house. The payments were sky high, but at least I was not paying rent. Somehow that made more sense to me and relieved my mind somewhat.

After several months of taking the Christian Counselling, the counsellor asked me if I would be willing to speak at a gathering of people, to share some of my thoughts and feelings. There was a large group of people in attendance.

I was nervous at first, but that passed as I began to talk. I was pleased with how well it went. As I prepared to do this sharing, I realized that time heals almost everything, if you are willing to wait, and work at getting better.

While Don was growing up he was always excited about his dream of becoming a policeman. He would take a scratch pad and walk up and down the street writing down addresses and pretending to be a policeman. Milt encouraged him by obtaining several posters of Mounties on horses or with dogs, which Don put up in his room.

While waiting for a response to his application for becoming a member of The Royal Canadian Mounted Police Force, Don had a full time job. He was interested in becoming a member of the Force, but if that did not work out, he planned to try out for the Fire Department.

After being in our new home for a few months, Don was accepted for training with the Police Force. Once Don was notified of the acceptance, he only had a short time to give notice of resignation to his employer, and get together what was required for his new adventure. While he was getting ready to leave, we had a barbeque in celebration with family and friends. I was happy for him, but sad as well. My first-born son was leaving home probably forever.

Don was happy to be doing what he dreamed of. We missed having him around. He called home every weekend to let us know how things were going and telling us what had been added to his collection of equipment. He came home for weekends whenever possible.

One weekend, Don had been home having a great time with his brothers. We got him to his flight on time for his return to depot. Upon arriving home, we discovered he left his running shoes behind. He had been telling us about how they ran every morning so we knew that he would need them. Randy was working for a courier company at the time. He bundled the runners up and took them to his work place. Somehow he managed to get those runners to Don in time for his run in the morning.

Milt found us after a while. He was still drinking and doing some very peculiar things. He purchased a German Shepard pup. After several weeks he realized that he had made a mistake and turned the pup over to the Royal Canadian Mounted Police for their use. They told him that the dog would be returned if it had a hip problem or could not be trained.

One morning as I arrived at my job, the telephone rang. I answered it. Milt was on the phone and told me that he was going to kill my parents and blow up my boarder's truck. Don's roommate had purchased a semi-trailer truck. He still lived with us after Don left. He drove his truck long distances and was not always home.

I found I had a new approach to this dilemma. I was so surprised at what came out of my mouth. I told him, "You do what you have to do". All the while praying that he would smarten up. I had learned in Al-Anon to stay calm and not re-act to the alcoholic's threats and accusations. After that phone call, I decided that I needed to get a legal separation. I was not sure how to do that, but I would figure it out. I decided it couldn't be as hard as moving out of my home.

I called what was then 'Unified Family Court' and made an appointment. The advisor there had me complete the papers required for a legal separation. He told me that the papers would go to Milt that day.

A few days later, I got another phone call. Milt was distraught. "Why did you do this? I don't want a legal separation." That's when I told him, "I can no longer live this way and the threatening phone call cinched my decision". He was totally in shock. He could not believe that I would want a separation. Of course I did not really want it, but it was something I needed to do.

Another appointment was made by Milt, for counselling for us with the Family Court establishment. Milt, the counsellor and myself met. The Legal Separation papers were ready for signature. Support payments had not been discussed yet. The counsellor brought the topic up.

Randy and Tim both played hockey. The fees were high. Milt had not contributed any money since we left.

Support money for Randy and Tim was discussed and agreed upon. There was to be monthly maintenance for each. The counsellor asked, "Do you want the payments to go directly to you, or do you want Milt to pay it to us and we will forward it to you?" I told him it would be better if Milt paid it to them. Milt was not pleased with this idea. I only wanted support for the two younger boys. I did not ask for any money for myself. The 'Separation Agreement' was signed by both Milt and myself and witnessed by the counsellor. While the counsellor went to make copies of the agreement, Milt said to me, "So is he moving in?" "Is who moving in?" I asked. "The new guy", he replied. This disturbed me. Although it was not a new thing, I did not expect to hear that especially considering where we were and why we were there. Once again I realized that nothing had changed and that I needed to continue.

Several times the counsellor called me to tell me that all Milt wanted was for us to get back together and for us all to come home.

It would be senseless to go back to the same situation. I also knew that Milt could be charming and cunning when he really put his mind to it. I told the counsellor this.

Several weeks passed. We were legally separated, when more insanity began.

One evening I got a call from Milt. He was totally inebriated. He began by calling me everything possible, and threw his wedding ring against something that clanged. I could hear it. He then hung up. Later that same evening, he drove up and put a letter in my mail slot. In it was his wedding ring and some money. The letter accompanying all of this was very mixed up.

It was a lovely summer evening. I put the ring away, as well as the letter, crying all the while. As I was getting ready to go out into the yard, my sons asked, "Going out to see your psychiatrist mom?" "Yup, I am", I told them. This time they suggested that I bury the wedding ring and plant a garden. I got my gardening tools and went to the back yard and began to dig. I always felt better after spending some time outside in my garden. I dug and I thought about the whole thing. By the time it was bedtime, I had made a decision to take the letter and see the counsellor again at Unified Family Court, as soon as possible. He read the letter, and looked up at me saying, "Oh my goodness, this man suffers from Alcoholism". Hello!! What had I been trying to tell him for months?

Nonetheless, this letter was the key to the court counsellor's belief in what I had been trying to communicate. I felt better knowing that someone understood what our family was dealing with. He called Milt and spoke with him. Arrangements were made for us to meet again.

All of this was the beginning of some hope for sobriety, or divorce and freedom from this devastating situation. Milt did not want to hear of divorce. I was both pleased and frightened. I was pleased that he did not want a divorce, but frightened about what was coming next.

Somewhere in the midst of all of this commotion, two of my neighbours from our old neighbourhood gave me some disturbing news. They had seen a blond woman going into our house with Milt's sister. I was both happy that my friends were looking out for me, but also upset. This particular sister did not ever want to hear about our dilemma. She remembered Milt from his boyhood, and did not want to understand or believe what was happening. She once did suggest that I attend Al-Anon, but that was as far as it went.

When I heard this news, I was physically sick to my stomach, but knew that I could do nothing about it. We were legally separated, and what could I do in any case? Not much, I realized.

One Saturday night I could not sleep. My night was listless and I could not put my finger on why this was happening. I did not have trouble sleeping since we moved. Milt was on my mind and I kept tossing and turning till morning. Just after seven in the morning, the phone rang. It was Milt. He began by crying and telling me that he had gone to a dance with his sister, her husband and this woman. I never did ask her name or who she was. He told me that it was a terrible evening. All he could do was think of me, and the boys. In turn, I told him I could not sleep all night. We talked for a while and decided to go to Squamish for a weekend.

While we were away Milt apologized for his behaviour, "I am so sorry for taking off my ring and throwing it. I will never take it off again, if you let me have it back". I asked, "What makes you think I even have it?" "I don't know", he said, "I'm just hoping". "Hold on a minute", I said. I went to my travel bag and took out the ring. I gave his wedding ring back. He was happy and cried. At that point, we made a decision to work hard on restoring our marriage.

My husband was trying desperately to stay sober. He joined Alcoholics Anonymous. He went for counselling to a Christian Counsellor who was associated with 'Burden Bearers'. I was taking counselling there as well. This was all helpful to both of us.

During the counselling sessions we took part in a Marriage Retreat on Orcas Island. It was a beautiful Island and we enjoyed the weekend. We learned a lot and were very encouraged.

The boys and I were still living away from our family home.

Three months later, Milt started missing AA meetings. He said the counselling was enough and he would be fine. He wanted us to move back home. I was not keen on doing that just yet. There were too many signs of relapse for Milt. I also had a lot of bad memories from living there. Milt said he could re-do things to look different and it wasn't the house that was at fault, however, if I really did not want to come back to our family home, we would sell it and buy another.

We looked at other homes to buy. Milt was a lumber worker, and he loved to build things. The houses we looked at were poorly built, and as Milt said "Just thrown together". Our house was well built. We lived next door and watched how it was done. Fred used plywood, not chip board and proper framing, as well as cedar siding that we both loved, so we decided to keep our home and fix it up.

Milt came to stay with us when he began to fix up our family home. He added a porch to the front, changed the kitchen and finished the basement. Things were going well. I was pleased that he was busy with the house. This gave me more time to see how his sobriety went. He did more work on our home in one year than in many years before the split.

A cousin of Milt's and his wife came to visit. She and I stayed at my house while Milt took his cousin to show him what he had been busy doing.

A while later I got a letter from the cousin's wife telling me that Milt was overworked and having a hard time keeping up. Could I let up on him? Once more, I was upset. I had to reply to the letter. I wrote and asked, "Do you understand the disease of Alcoholism?" I also told them that I felt what we were doing was in the best interest for all of us, and that this arrangement would get our home fixed up, but would also give us time to see how Milt's sobriety went. I was angry that Milt had discussed all of this with his cousin, but decided to leave that alone. Much to my surprise I got a reply admitting that they did not understand the disease and wished us well.

Randy, our middle son was now seventeen years old. He had been seeing his girlfriend for several years. Diane only lived a few blocks away so they had known each other since they were youngsters. I was concerned about them. They saw each other daily. I loved this girl like she was my own. She was often at our place. The kids spent many hours just being kids. Baking cookies, playing games, and helping around the house. Both Milt and I loved her. They started by being friends and then began dating. They were inseparable. Diane was at our house when he was not at hers. It was like she belonged in our family. We enjoyed her and everyone was reasonably happy.

I was concerned that she would become pregnant even though Randy and I discussed birth control and he assured me that everything was fine.

Just a few days later, while Diane was sitting at my kitchen table, she began to fall asleep. I asked her if she was not feeling well. She told me, "I am just so very tired all the time". I then asked, "Could you be pregnant?" That is when everything came out. She told me that she wished she wasn't but it was a possibility that she was. Arrangements were made for her to see a doctor. It was confirmed that she was indeed pregnant.

Milt and I decided to go away for a weekend again. Orcas Island was our destination. We needed to get this pregnancy through our heads and we needed to do some serious talking about our future.

On our way to the ferry, Milt said, "I wonder if they serve drinks on the ferry?" My stomach went into a knot and I felt sick. While on the ferry, he spoke of drinks. I do not remember if he had a drink or not. I just remember that all he talked about on the way to the hotel was how he would have a drink. I really was upset to hear this and scared of what I would do if he did. Something in me triggered and at that point I said, "Stop the car. I am going back home." We had been driving about five minutes so I assumed we were not too far from the ferry. He stopped the car. I got my suitcase and he carried on down the road. I had most of the money in my purse. Now I was on a mountain road with a suitcase and my purse, and it was hot. It was the middle of summer and really, really hot and humid.

I continued to walk back toward the ferry terminal, sitting on my suitcase to rest and wondering how much further I needed to walk. As I rested, I looked up and saw a beautiful home tucked in the mountain. Low and behold, there was a lady washing her windows. Do you think this was a coincidence? I know it was God taking care of things. I shouted up to her, "Can you tell me how far it is to the ferry". She replied, "It's about five miles from here". Oh my, five miles and I was already hot and tired. I asked her if she would be able to drive me there if I paid her. She told me she wasn't planning on going anywhere that day, but yes she would drive me there.

We drove to the ferry. I could not believe the distance we had gone. It did not seem so far when Milt was driving.

This lady would not take any money. I explained the situation to her and told her what had happened. She told me that she attended Al-Anon on the Island and she understood perfectly. We exchanged addresses and wrote to each other for many years.

As I was walking on to the ferry, I saw Milt waiting in the line up. He had not seen me and I was wondering what to do when we did see each other. I walked on, got a comfortable seat and just waited to see what would happen. He was totally surprised to see me on that vessel. He came over and asked, "What are you going to do? I replied, "I just want to go home". He suggested that we ride home together.

It was a quiet ride and when we got home to my place, he said, "I need that lamp that's in your living room". I remember going into the house, gathering up all of his belongings, putting them in a garbage bag, and throwing them out the door. I did not give him the lamp. It seemed every time he wanted to get drunk, he would find something to use in order to cause a commotion so that he could justify it.

Finally I was getting the whole concept of this being a 'Disease'. How could it be anything else? This intelligent, handsome man would become this unbelievably, difficult person. Off the poor man went one more time, to have another drinking bout. The difference this time: I knew it had nothing to do with me and that he had to experience once again what this horrible disease was doing to all of us, especially him.

It was a great feeling for me to know that God was in control and we would be fine. I was doing a lot of kneeling and praying. One of the church sermons that I had heard was really making a lot of sense now. "He who kneels before God can stand before anyone." I was starting to feel stronger.

Milt came back to my place sober. After three weeks of drinking, he did not look well. His eyes were sunken, and his colour was grey. He asked me if I would make his lunches. I told him I didn't mind making the lunches but he would have to supply the fillings. It was a huge help financially. He brought enough filling for all of our lunches.

Every morning he would come to the house around 6:30 to pick up his food on his way to work. I had all the lunches made by the time he arrived. After a few weeks, one particular morning he said to me, "How long is this going to go on for?" I asked him what he meant. He asked again, "How much longer is this going to go on? Us living like this?" I told him, "I don't know. Depends on how long it takes you to quit this drinking nonsense for good".

At this point he announced, "I am ready to start again". I told him that if he did that, " please do not involve any more children. Enough children have already been hurt". "Oh I will start a new family", was his reply. I was furious. "Get out of my house, and don't come back". I threw his lunch at him. The bag opened and the sandwiches went flying one way, the fruit another. He left without anything.

When I arrived at work the phone was ringing. "Well are you over your mad?" My first thought was that I wanted to kill him. Once again I needed to use what I had learned in Al-Anon. Stay calm. Do not react. I kept talking to myself. Then I said, "Milt, I do not want to talk with you here at work, and I have nothing more to say. You were the one who said you want to start a new family, so I am accepting that". Dead quiet on the other end. He hung up.

I had become stronger because of what I was learning.

So many things were happening.

My cousin that I lived with as a teenager became an alcoholic as well. She had been in treatment many times only to start drinking again after each release. Receiving a call from her at work was quite normal. A few times I left work to stop her from attempting suicide. I would then have to make up my time at work. I was already over exhausted from the stress in my life without this added to it.

In Al-Anon I learned about enabling, so the third or fourth time she called I told her, "I am at work. It doesn't help when I do come, because it is only a temporary fix. You do it again and again, and I am left to make up the missed time at work. I love you but I cannot help you right now". The calls to work stopped.

Her husband tried moving many times, to various places, so that it would be more difficult for her to get her supply of alcohol. She was asked to leave a job that she loved. Her children began to ignore her and her husband. She would hallucinate and talk to people who were not there. Nothing was as strong as her craving for alcohol. This wonderful, smart woman is now in a nursing home, diagnosed with 'Alcohol Induced Dementia', unable to walk and barely able to feed herself. What a devastating illness. This cousin of mine was a great cook and homemaker. She had a lovely singing voice and was very social. Everything went spinning out of control because of Alcoholism.

Once more I was grateful for having Al-Anon support in my life, and for having learned what this terrible disease does to everyone involved. Not much of a future for folks with this disease, nor for the ones living with it unless they reach out for help.

I knew that my self-worth was beginning to improve. My Mom made Easter dinner for all of us every year. This particular Easter Milt decided to give me some perfume. I was pleased, and decided to put some on before leaving for my parents. My brother and his wife were already there. When we arrived, the first thing my brother brought up was, "What is that smell?" I did not reply. After an hour or so he once more asked, "What do I smell?" Then again he asked the same thing. I decided to answer. "Milt gave me some perfume for Easter." With some choice words he said how I knew he hated perfume, etc. etc. I am not sure what he expected, but I said, "Well I guess you will just have to stay away from me today". Gosh it felt good to not react. We had a good day.

Our son, Randy quit school and went to work, eventually finding out that it was not so much fun to work with no education. His girlfriend was pregnant. They moved out to try living together. I did not like the idea, but they were adamant. They felt they were too young to marry. I could not argue that point. They were only seventeen.

Some weeks later Randy came home and said, "Mom, is it ok if I come back home? It isn't working out with us living together." I told him, "I did not want you to go in the first place and the rules are still the same."

Randy and Diane decided that the baby would go up for adoption. Milt and I offered to keep the baby till they were old enough to care for it. When I mentioned this to Randy, he said that the two of them felt that if they left the baby with us, there would be lots of added problems. If we did something they did not like, they would be upset. If they did something we did not approve of, we would not like it. So they made the decision to give the child up for adoption, because they felt they were too young to care for a child, and because of the experience they had living together. They felt this would be better for all concerned. This was probably a wiser decision than I would have made. I was quietly hoping that once the baby was born, they would decide to keep it.

September 21st, 1978, Randy was with Diane when she gave birth to a baby girl. The Christian Agency that Milt and I had gone to handled the adoption. It helped a little knowing that our firstborn grandchild would be raised in a Christian home.

My heart was broken. I found it difficult to even look at the two of them, much less make conversation. Randy asked me, "Mom, what is wrong? How come you won't talk to me?" I was careful to explain that it had a lot to do with me processing what had happened and to just let me go through my grieving process. He seemed to understand. I am sure he was grieving as well. I was selfishly thinking about how I was feeling.

It was difficult for the kids to understand why I was so quiet. That is not my nature. They were not used to me being silent. I was afraid of what I would say. It was difficult for me to accept that my grandbaby was in someone else's arms. How I wanted to hold that baby. I so badly wanted to see her. I wanted to steal her and run.

It took three weeks to slowly be able to be civil to them, and eventually I was fine. The sadness did come. Of course each time I thought about that little girl, my heart would break. To this day my heart breaks for what we missed. As I went through this, I began to be grateful that they gave her up for adoption and did not abort her. She had a chance for life, and they could move on with theirs. Once that idea came to me, I told the children what I thought and that helped with the healing process. This granddaughter is now in her thirties and I think of her very often. I wonder where she is, what she is doing? Is she healthy? What are her parents like? Did she have a good childhood with loving parents? Does she have children? Who does she look like? Is she happy? I have many thoughts. My one consolation is that she has had a chance at life. If I am meant to see her, God will see to it that I do.

Learning I had no control over people, places and things helped me to sort out my own thinking.

I grieved for the loss of my granddaughter, my first grandchild. I thank God for giving Randy and Diane a mature decision to give her up and **not abort** her. Had they chosen to abort there would be no future for her and heartache for them. In spite of their age, they decided this together. I realized it was a wise decision.

Many times I asked the Lord, "Keep your arm around my shoulder and your hand over my mouth".

Well into December of 1979, we moved back to the family home in time for Christmas. It took us about three weeks to move back in, opposed to the two hours it took us to move out. My emotions were mixed. I was happy to be home. Christmas was coming and there was a lot to do. The boys were also happy.

Randy had once again decided to finish school, and was adamant that he would succeed. I was very pleased about the choice he made.

This was a good Christmas. We were home again and everyone gathered at our house once more. Milt was not drinking and life seemed to be moving along smoothly.

I will end this chapter with this quote:

I am not afraid of storms, for I am learning to sail my own ship".
Author Unknown

Chapter 6

LOVE

"I've never quit loving you and I never will.
Expect Love, Love and more Love!!!"
Jeremiah 31:3

Love cannot pass through a heart that is full of fear or resentment.
From Al-Anon's Blue Print for Progress

Falling in Love is easy. Staying in Love is something very special.

Resentment was my middle name, but I was working hard on releasing it.

I did not want resentments to take over my life, nor did I want to keep living like a 'Walking Tree'.

A 'Walking Tree' is how I used to describe the way I felt. That was slowly changing as I applied what I learned at Church, studying my Bible, and attending Al-Anon meetings regularly.

I also know that life would have continued to get worse if I did nothing.

I read somewhere, "If you want God to guide your footsteps, you must be willing to move your feet". That sure did make sense to me after I had reached the point of having to do something. I am also sure that sometimes we have to die a little before we really live a lot. What you focus on increases.

Love is an endless act of forgiveness, either forgiving yourself or someone else. Once I learned to forgive, and 'Let Go' my life got better. Gradually I learned to love myself and began to live.

By March 1980 we were settled back in our family home and everyone was busy. Randy completed his Grade 12 in March and was very happy. His plan was to apply for acceptance in the Royal Canadian Mounted Police. He was so pleased that his brother chose to do that. He wanted to do the same.

There was something happening that was not easy to understand. In March 1980, Randy began having flu-like symptoms, terrible headaches and nausea. His back hurt. Seeing the doctor three or four times for this problem did not seem to help. The antibiotics that were prescribed would help for a week or so and then the problem would return. We bought him a new mattress thinking maybe that would help. The problem continued.

On a Sunday morning at the end of May, I found him sitting on the stairs crying. He told me his head ached and his back was very sore. When I looked directly at him, I could see his skin colour had turned yellow. I knew something was terribly wrong. Milt and I immediately took him to the hospital emergency, where they treated him for Hepatitis. He was in the hospital for four days with no improvement. Asking for a specialist to check on him, it was discovered that his liver had been damaged, but now it was the kidneys that were failing. He was transferred to Vancouver General Hospital right away. The prognosis there was serious. He had 'Haemolytic Uremic Syndrome', a rare condition that only happens about five times a year in the Continent of North America.

Randy was prepared for surgery to insert a shunt into his arm so that he could have dialysis to cleanse his blood. We learned that the liver had healed, but the kidneys were in serious trouble. After the dialysis treatment, he was very sick and nauseated. This seemed to happen every time he went on the machine. We were told it was because it all happened so quickly and his body had no time to prepare for it.

Tim was a teenager. He was working and driving. He was involved with a girl who was a neighbour as well. Being so young concerned us. We did not want a repeat experience. I went over to the neighbours many times trying to reason things out. Tim would come home, but would go back again. The girl's mother would let him stay there as long as he wanted, whenever he wanted. I tried to explain to her how we felt. She didn't seem to understand.

So much for Peace and Serenity!!

I explained my dilemma to my Mom and she told me to keep trying, but to realize that there wasn't much one could do. The bee goes where the honey is. Mom was so practical. One thing we did not need nor want was trouble and decided that we had to leave things alone. We were very weary and concerned about our sons.

Having Randy sick and Tim as a teenager, working full time and living with a man who was hanging on to sobriety by a thin string, was difficult. Without my Al-Anon Program, I am sure things would have gotten quite out of control. Learning that I only had control over what I did, really helped me.

Just shortly before Randy got sick he had purchased a car. It was a red Nova SS and next to his girlfriend, his car was the light of his life. When he purchased the car it was very costly for him to get insurance on it, so it was put in Milt's name which made the expenditure much more affordable. He hadn't had the car very long when he ended up in the hospital. We just left the car parked in the driveway and waited to see what the future would bring.

Randy was very weak, nauseated and in very delicate condition. When I arrived at the hospital, he was lying in bed and very agitated. He had been telling his Dad that he should just give up and die. Milt communicated this to me when I came in. It threw me off guard for a few minutes. When I realized that Randy needed to have something to think about besides his sickness, I said to Milt, "Well if he is giving up, there is no point in keeping that car. We may as well sell it". I had taken a chance that the car was pretty important. Milt clued in right away and replied, "I think that is what we will do. At least we won't have the car to think about".

Randy sat upright, like he was on a spring, "No, you will not sell my car. I want to be able to enjoy something when I get better". The conversation became more positive.

This did not stop the frustrating things that were happening. Randy was sometimes delusional from all the medication. His girlfriend was often at the hospital, which he loved. His kidney functions did not return. Randy was now on dialysis permanently. The medications sometimes made him see things that were not there, and do things he would not normally do. Like the time he told us that there were bugs all over the wall by his bed. Another time when he was asked to sit up, instead he tried to get out of bed. Many times he did the opposite. This was very disturbing to all of us. The nurses told us to tell him that we did not see those things. Eventually this stopped.

In February 1981, the year after Randy became sick, on Valentine's Day he said to me, "Mom, now I know what love means". I was surprised by this statement and asked him what it meant to him now. "Well I used to think that love was a romantic thing. Now I know it is more than that. I know that when you really love someone, you do almost anything that you can to help the person and to be there. You and Dad have been here every day since I got sick. Even Dad, who gets sick crossing the bridge, comes every day. I realized that Randy had grown up very quickly and understood many things that probably many adults do not. This conversation with him helped me many times when I was exhausted.

Milt had an anxiety disorder. He would get sick when crossing bridges. He never did get over this problem, but eventually just felt the anxiety but did not get physically sick. Having to cross a bridge each time he went to visit Randy at the hospital made his days very difficult. Being with a crowd of people did the same thing.

During Randy's illness, the manager where Milt worked was very kind to us. It was arranged that Milt worked straight afternoon shift. That way he could go to the hospital in the daytime and I went after work. If we were lucky enough to have Randy home, then someone was home all the time. I was off work at 4:15 and Milt left for work at 3:30 in the afternoon, so there was approximately an hour when no one was home.

Besides being a stressful time in our lives, it was also very costly. There were parking expenses, gasoline, wear and tear on the vehicles and the meals we ate out. We also had to supply Randy with whatever he needed. We were feeling the impact.

There was always food in the house for Tim and for us, but sometimes we just grabbed something on the run. Most days, I did not even go home after work, just went right to the hospital. I tried to make home as normal as possible for Tim. I knew it was not an easy time for him. Having your brother so ill, and being a teenager with millions of changes going on, was a rough time for him as well.

Don came as often as he could to visit his brother. His job was demanding and he was now married with a family. It was a big undertaking to come for a few days. I was always pleased when he would come. It was a change from the regular visitors for Randy, and it was good for us to have a change of focus for a few days.

Tim handled his brother's illness in his own way, often visiting Randy after hours when no one else was around. I am not sure how the staff at the hospital felt, but I had enough to think about. Once again I was grateful that we all loved each other and cared. I could not think about another thing.

My friend Nellie often came to the hospital after work by bus and rode back with me. Later I asked her why she did that. She told me, "I was afraid that you would fall asleep while driving". At the time I was too wrapped up in the circumstances to think about it. Looking back, I realize what a wonderful gesture that was. She showed me real love. As Randy was learning about real love, I was experiencing it through Nellie and other dear friends and family.

Nellie was right. I was very tired after working all day, then going to the hospital. We lived approximately an hour's drive away. Sometimes I had to pull over and snooze for a few minutes before heading out again. Other times I would put my head on Randy's bed and have a rest. He did not mind. He was happy I was there.

My friends were great at coming to see Randy. They all liked him. He could be so funny even when he felt the pits. They were also very kind to me.

On Saturday mornings I would get up early to get my house in order and cook something for us to eat. My thoughts were that Milt and I would go to the hospital together, and maybe have lunch together, only to find that he had already gone. I was disappointed. In the Al-Anon Program I learned to be grateful for things even when it did not seem possible. I would then talk to myself: "I have a car, I can drive, I have a job and a pay check, so just get ready and go". Often, by the time I got there, Milt would have already left. Now I realize that he did not want to talk with anyone, nor have to deal with anything or anyone, except be there for Randy.

I thank God for helping me get through those times. It was a concern having a teenager at home, and trying to do all the necessary every day things.

Randy had been ill for several months. His first hospital stay was from May to September. It was raining the day he got home in September. Opening the back door, he took a long, deep breath and said, "Oh God Mom, that smells good". I have not looked at a rainy day the same since, and I live where there is lots of rain. Every so often, I open the door and take a long deep breath, enjoy the smell and think about Randy.

Surgeries had to be performed. Randy pulled the shunts out of his arm in his sleep or in a delusional state. There was surgery to remove a vein from his leg and try to make an apparatus to do the dialysis. This was a huge incision. He had 54 staples in his leg. Staples had just become the things to use after certain kinds of operations. The time came for the removal of the staples. The nurses on duty had never taken them out. One nurse was assigned to this project. Randy read the instructions and she did the snipping. They both laughed and when she was done, they hugged. He had become so courageous. From someone who was afraid of an inoculation, Randy grew to be very brave. He was quite helpful to the medical staff and comical. Needles became part of his day.

After a while when the nurses were trying to draw blood from Randy, a regular procedure, his veins were on strike. No blood could be taken. A nurse that was exceptionally good at this was called. He knew her well. I will call her Nancy. Nancy arrived, worked on Randy's arm a bit and lo and behold she got the blood. As she went to lay the needle and vial down, it accidentally spilled. I do not remember exactly what happened, except that the next thing I knew, Nancy was crying and Randy was telling her it was ok. "Just try again". I was so proud of the strength my son had, and concerned about his future all at the same time.

Several times, I would just get into bed after the trip home from the hospital. The phone would ring. "We need to do emergency surgery. Randy is not able to sign. You have to sign the consent form. Please drive carefully, but come as soon as you can". Going back there in the middle of the night after just falling asleep was scary. Many times, it was hard to remember how I got there and back, but God knew.

Mom kept telling me to rest and take care of myself. I told her, "Mom I have to do what I have to do. Randy is really sick right now and he needs our support". "I know that. Randy has people taking care of him. I am concerned about you", Mom said. It felt good to know that she was thinking about me, but I realized there was not much could be done about that.

Dad on the other hand was forever reading his medical book trying to find a solution. It kept him busy. He would often come to visit Randy and suggest a laxative to solve the problem. He was very upset over Randy's dilemma and was only trying to help. It gave Randy something to chuckle about for a minute or two.

Randy used to enjoy this interaction between him and Grandpa and he would laugh about it for a long time after. My Dad loved his grandchildren and did not know what to do to solve this problem. Dad was a practical man. He was trying by reading his book, making suggestions and bringing Mom to visit Randy as often as possible. They were getting old and had just moved to be closer to us. It was hard for Dad to believe that this strong grandson of his who just helped them to move into their place a short time ago, was now so sick and unable to do much. Dad often described how Randy carried a table all by himself.

The hospital called around 11:00 p.m. one night just as I was falling asleep. They needed my signature for another unexpected emergency surgery. As I arrived I heard Randy shouting, "Ok, let's get the show on the road". In his drugged state he did many things that were not normal for his personality. I was frightened, stressed and tired. I really think I just moved in whatever direction was needed without much thought. Once more I was kind of numb.

At one point, they had to do a blood cleansing procedure on Randy. They were separating the good cells from the bad, so there was blood everywhere and needles. The smell of blood was very evident. Never before had I thought about the smell of blood. I was concerned that it hurt while this was being done. Telling Randy how I felt and how it looked to me, smiling he said, "Mom, that is one time I did not feel anything".

Randy had to have his kidneys removed, because they were causing him problems not functioning. They were also in the way of a possible kidney transplant. He asked how long he would have to stay in hospital for this procedure, and told that he could go home as soon as he could eat and walk.

The day of the surgery, I planned to stay home after work. I was so sure he would not wake up till the next day. When I called to find out how he was, I heard him shout. "Hurry, I am waiting for you." As I arrived, I saw him sitting up. He was home in four days. Being able to come home was so important to Randy.

Two of my friends were concerned about my safety because I was so tired, so they decided they would drive in to see Randy at the hospital together. One would drive my car home and I would ride with the other one. I am still not sure what that was all about, but knowing that the tide could turn at any given minute, I felt I needed to drive my own car home so that I could return in a hurry if I had to. They were trying to be helpful. I appreciated it then and still do now.

I tried to make Randy's hospital stays a bit homey. I would bring him flowers. He would ask, "Did you buy these?" "No son, they are from our garden at home." "Good Mom", he said, "I only want flowers from home not from the store". It was nice to know that he enjoyed that. Toward the end of summer, there were no more flowers to bring except marigolds. I dug some out and put them in a pretty pot and took them to him. He was so pleased and every day he asked, "Mom, did you water my garden?" Or, "Mom, don't forget to water my garden".

Milt's sister, Myrt, and her hubby came to the hospital often. They came to see Randy, but they also wanted to be sure that I went out for exercise and something to eat. Myrt also grew fresh green peas for Randy. He could have a few peas, and was always so pleased that his aunt remembered how much he loved them. It was good to have this kind of love. Exercise was not something that was on my mind at the time, nor did I plan to go out to eat.

Randy was on the list for a kidney transplant. We had a consultation with the surgeon. The doctor explained the whole procedure. Explaining that he would have to take medication to keep the kidney from being rejected by his body. He was told that sometimes the medication needed makes patients lose their hair. Randy was noticeably upset about that. He had very dark, thick, curly, healthy hair that he enjoyed taking care of. The doctor realized this very quickly and said, "Randy, God only made a few perfect heads. On the rest he put hair". In the process he bent over to show his bald head. We all had a good laugh. Then the Doctor said, "Randy, you know that worse things can happen than losing your hair". On he went with the explanation of the transplant surgery.

Randy was having seizures and there did not seem to be any reason for them. He would get very frightened when this happened. Physicians were baffled and were trying to rectify the problem.

This son of ours was a strong individual. He seldom complained and endured whatever came up, however he did have three bad times of wanting to terminate his life. This was depressing for his dad and myself.

About this time, Randy's girlfriend decided that she was not able to take the pressure any longer. She was young and this was a tough time, especially after all they had already been through.

I had been going up to the hospital daily. Milt had taken a week's holiday from work and went up to see Randy during the day. One morning he suggested, "Why don't you go home after work and have a hot bath, and relax? I will go see Randy and stay a bit longer". Oh my, that did sound good. I was finished work at 4:15 in the afternoon.

Around 3:30 Milt called me at work and said, "Please come up. Randy is giving up". I went to the washroom, had a good cry and completed my day. I left the school and went directly to the hospital.

As I came into the room, I could see Randy punching his pillow and crying. "What's up?" I asked. Milt got up and left the room. "I have had enough, and so has everyone else. My friends don't care and my girlfriend doesn't want to be with me any more. I will just refuse dialysis and that will be that. What am I supposed to do?" All the while he was pounding on the pillow and even the wall.

After several minutes of this behaviour, I said, "Randy, listen carefully. I will support any decision you make. I am sure you are sick and tired of all of this. It isn't me going through what you are, but I sure am tired, so you must be exhausted." He stopped for a moment and looked at me with disbelief. "Mom, what should I do?" I said, "Randy, I know that if you stop dialysis, you will have about 21 days to live. If you choose that, I will be here for you. The choice is yours, however, if after two weeks or so you should change your mind and it is too late to do anything, how will you feel then? Once you make this decision, you may not be able to reverse it should you change your mind. It could be too late." He continued to cry out, "My friends hardly come to see me. My girlfriend is gone. I just want to give up." Randy was totally exhausted and disillusioned.

"Randy", if one of your friends got what you have, how often do you think you would go to see them? They come to see you quite often I think. They have jobs and are busy as you were when you were fine."

We talked for about half an hour. He expressed what he was feeling and thinking, and then settled down. I was just going to get him something to drink when I heard four of his friends coming down the hall. What perfect timing that was! I left and went home. He felt better. I was exhausted. The timing for their visit was perfect. God gives us what we need at just the right time, not a minute before and not a minute after.

This is how it went until August 31, 1982. Surgery, hospital stay, a little good spell, then more surgery and so on. He had approximately twenty-six operations or more in this period of time. Randy had been at home for a few days until that day in August, which also happens to be my birthday.

The phone rang and it was for Randy. He had been dozing on the couch. I called him to the phone. After the conversation, Randy was beaming and full of energy. I had not seen him like this since before the illness began. Running around the house shouting, "Oh my God, Mom. Now I will be able to coach minor hockey. Now I can go fishing". Although it was great to see him so exuberant, I was still wondering what the call was about. He finally settled and said, "I have to get ready. There is a kidney for me." Off we all went to Vancouver General to prepare for this surgery.

Before Randy's illness he played hockey. The last season he played, he received the 'Most Inspirational Player Award'. He knew he would never play hockey again, but he planned to coach or referee minor hockey. He spoke of this often.

Randy was well known throughout the hospital. He had been in nearly every part of it for all the various surgeries. While he was being prepared for the operation, he had visitors from all over the hospital. These nurses, interns, cleaning staff, and even patients all arrived with well wishes for him. As he sat on the toilet, people were shouting their wishes, and everyone was in a joyful mood. Milt and I were overwhelmed by all this 'hoopla', but it did help to make us excited and less anxious. Randy was just a 'Ball of Fire' getting ready. The surgery was to take four to five hours, so when Randy went into the operating room, Milt and I went home.

Finally the call came. The operation was successful. The kidney was functioning. All we needed to do now was wait for the recovery. Whew!!

Every day the liquid intake was measured, as was the urine output. We were all so happy to have this surgery out of the way. Who ever thought that looking at someone's pee in a bottle could be so fascinating and exciting. We found out that the donor was a young fellow who was killed in a motorcycle accident, and the family was happy to know that someone else could live even though their loved one died.

The young woman who received the other kidney was in the bed next to Randy. Her kidney was being rejected and medications were being changed to help. I will call her Kate. She and Randy were comrades through this rough period. He was constantly asking how she was doing, and very relieved that he was getting better.

So many people were praying for Randy. A young boy who was in the room next to him asked his priest to come and pray over Randy. Randy got a little frightened when he saw a priest there, till I explained what was happening. We were all touched, and we too were praying for our son.

There were fun moments during this time. A group of interns came in one day to study Randy's surgery and discuss things with him and the doctors. Kate was full of ideas and she posted a star on the door of their room with a sign saying 'Randy, Star of the Day'. These kind of things made their time pass more cheerfully and quickly. Things were moving along nicely. Kate's situation improved and she was soon able to go home. Randy on the other hand had issues that needed to be dealt with. Many of the levels that should have improved did not, and he had to stay in the hospital. It was now October and he was still there. The kidney was functioning but something was amiss. Kate came to visit and was doing fine, so that helped make it easier to wait. She was preparing to go back to work.

This was when we got to know a young woman by the name of Maureen who was a kidney patient as well. She had a transplant that her body rejected, so she was still on dialysis. Maureen came to sit with Randy to help pass the time. We got to know her parents and soon became friends. Maureen's parents lived quite far away so they were only able to be with her once in a while. She was lonely. Living in a basement suite with small windows did not help.

Kate's visits became less frequent as she went back to work. Randy was still in the hospital. By October more problems became evident and now we were told that he had 'Dialysis Esepholopathy'. This meant that his brain was swelling.

November 9, 1982 we had a snowfall. Milt had been in bed for over a week and just could not seem to be able to get up. This was the day that I went in to him and said, "I want to go and see Randy and I do not have the snow tires on the car". As I got ready to leave, he got up and changed the tires without my knowledge. To this day, I am grateful for this and even more grateful for having learned how to be thankful, even if it isn't done the way I would like.

I went to visit our son, and Milt went back to bed. I remember staying with Randy till quite late that evening. He was enjoying the snow, and I read and dozed. He just wanted me to be there.

Randy told me, "Mom I saw death today". Oh my God, I did not want to hear that. "What do you mean?" I asked. "Well I saw this beautiful tunnel and there was a light at the very end". Instead of asking more about what he had seen, I really just wanted him to think about something else. He was adamant about what he saw. This was very distressing for me and I did not want to believe it. I suggested that maybe a doctor or nurse had shone a light in his eyes. He just laughed and said, "I think I know the difference now, Mom".

We talked about a trip to Hawaii after he got well. I was hoping it would get his mind off of the light and the tunnel, as well as mine. How I regret that day. Why did I not listen to everything he had to tell me about that experience? I have regretted this so very much, however I cannot bring it back so have had to let it go.

There have been many people sick that have died since that time, but not one of them has told me about such an incident. I have been listening so hard. Maybe it will never happen again? I am sure that he wanted to tell me more. It was just too painful for me to hear. I will forever regret this missed opportunity.

I slept well that night and when I got to the hospital the next day, Randy was not able to talk and was crying. I knew he must have had a seizure. When that happened it always took a few hours for things to return to normal, however he did not usually cry. Two or three hours later he told me what had happened. He had been going into a seizure and called for the nurse. We knew Delores, the nurse well. We often said she reminded us of a sergeant major. Delores came to the door and said, "Randy, you know I can't do anything so why are you calling me". He told her that he was afraid and just wanted someone there. She turned and left the room. There were only two patients in the ward at that time, so I knew that she had the time.

It was hard enough that my child was having seizures. It was a long way home, and I needed to know he was safe when I did leave. My mind was scattered and I was angry, disappointed and frightened. I needed to be able to go home and sleep and not worry for a few hours. Just then the hospital pastor came in to see Randy. He and Randy had become good friends and he was very kind. He often visited and they talked. Again, God provided at just the right time.

The pastor asked why Randy was so upset. He was still having difficulty talking. I explained what had happened and that I did not know what to do, but I needed to do something so that this kind of thing did not happen again. Both Randy and I were both visibly upset, and crying. "Ok", said the pastor, "I will take you to someone who will help". Off we went to see someone. It was one of the most emotional times in my life. Up to this point, I was leaving the hospital without reservations, knowing my son was being cared for. I also knew I could not be there all the time. We spoke to the head person of the department taking care of Randy at the time. I explained as best I could. She promised me that she would take care of the situation.

For two or three weeks we did not see Delores. Eventually she returned and could not do enough for Randy and myself. She tried to make me comfortable as well as Randy. Later on I found out that she had been suspended for a while. In the meantime, Randy's seizures began to happen often and then very often.

On November 21, Randy was in a bad state. The seizures were coming over and over, without much rest in between. I knew I needed to stay overnight.

I had already arranged with my job for a Leave of Absence till January. Milt knew how things were going. He could not get out of bed. I called my parents to let them know. Mom immediately came to be with Randy and I. We notified the family that things were not looking good.

Mom and I stayed that night. The seizures came one after the other with no lull in between. That had to be the most horrific thing for my son to endure. It was horrific for his grandmother and me. It was like a demon going into the head and working its way down through the body and out of the feet, then in and out again over and over. Randy was frightened and worn out. I knew he was in bad shape. Things were looking grim. Even the thought of what lay ahead made me cringe. I was scared too, and I am sure Mom was as well. We were trying to be strong for Randy, and I could not keep from crying. I tried to not show my grief to Randy and would turn away when the tears came. The seizures just did not let up.

I asked the staff if there was some way to at least slow the seizures down. They told me that if they gave him anything else, it would cause his heart to stop. We knew he was dying. You did not have to be a rocket scientist to see that he was not going to make it. I asked what the reasoning was behind all of this. A doctor was called and he prescribed something. It stopped the seizures, and Randy was quiet. Just shortly after 5:00 a.m. on November 22nd, 1982, our son Randy died.

Mom and I cried, and said our good-byes during that horrific night. He hung on to us with his hands. He cried, but did not speak. He squeezed our hands to let us know he knew we were there. There was no way he could speak with seizures coming and going, starting and ending over and over again. I am grateful that we were there. We could do nothing else, but we were there. I hope that gave him some comfort. I'm sure it did.

I do not know why our son had to suffer all that he did, but I do know that God does work in strange ways. The most ironic thing was that Delores was working that shift. She was there when our precious son died. I did not even look at her for fear of what I would say or do.

Mom immediately began cleaning up around the room, putting things in a bag, just trying to do something. I asked her, "What are you doing?" Her reply was, "He doesn't need any of this now".

I just sat and hung on to my son, wondering what else we could have done.

Mom and I stayed with Randy till they came to take the body.

God grant me the serenity,
To accept the things I cannot change,
Courage to change the things I can,

75

And the Wisdom to know the difference.

In spite of all of this sorrow, I hung on to my Prayer. In times of stress or decision-making, I find it very helpful and calming.

There was a lot to accept at this time, and not much I could change. I knew I had to go home and tell my husband and the rest of the family the sad news, and then try to have the wisdom to do the necessary preparations for our son's final resting place.

Many thoughts and memories came to me on the drive home. My first thought was, "Milt might start to drink again". Then it was, "How can I tell him and then comfort him?" I knew he would be torn apart. Randy's brothers would need comfort as well. Mom and Dad would be mourning. My parents were so supportive during Randy's illness and considerate during the grieving period. They too were full of sorrow for the loss of their grandson.

How was I going to let my son go and stay sane?

It was hard to think of God in a positive way at this moment. How could He take our precious son after all he had been through? In spite of everything, as I drove home, I was able to think of a verse that calmed me for the moment.

"Be strong and courageous. Do not be afraid or discouraged, for the Lord your God is with you wherever you go". Joshua 1:9

Mom and I were silent.

Hug the ones you love today. Tomorrow may be too late.

Chapter 7
RESPONSIBILITIES

If you want your dreams to come true, you mustn't oversleep.
One thing you can't recycle is wasted time.

Arrangements were made for Randy's funeral and because he and I had talked about what we wanted in the event of our deaths, it was less difficult to decide what to do. He always told me that if and when he got married, he would have a stream of decorated cars honking for miles before going to the reception. He also told me that if he died before I did, to be sure that the drive to the cemetery was a good long one. "I will only marry once and I will only die once. I want it to be known that I lived. There should be a long stream of cars with their lights on, leading to the final resting place", he told me many times. All of this was done. As the entourage drove to the gravesite I was silent and in deep thought about my son and what he endured. I was in a trance. It was an unbelievably desolate feeling. I was grief-stricken. I could hardly believe this was happening. It was a nightmare. However, when I looked at the cars behind us with all the lights on, I wondered if he was looking down on us.

Tim had a teacher who was extremely kind to him during this sorrowful time. He spent the whole day with Tim and spent a lot of time talking this through with him. I appreciate this even more now that I can think straight again.

Don and his family were here. Everyone was handling the situation in the way that best suited each person.

After the trip to the gravesite, everyone came back to our home for lunch and an ending to this terrible day. Don had a tickly throat. There were many people here and the front door kept squeaking loudly. I could not think where I kept the oil that would fix this problem. Everyone was busy talking and eating so I went to the cupboard and got the vegetable oil. I put some in a jigger and handed it to my son, Don, to put on the hinges. He was very distraught at the time and just drank the oil. Well we all got the giggles. This was a great way to change the atmosphere of the day. Somehow that incident made the way for people to begin sharing stories of Randy and his wonderful nature.

During this sharing time with our guests, my eldest son, Don, commented, "Mom, it isn't fair". "What isn't fair son?" I asked. He replied, "When my brothers were little, you were always home. When I was little, you always worked". "Son", I said, "It isn't fair, but you and I we had a problem". "Oh ya", he said, "What problem?" I said, "We both liked to eat". We all had another good chuckle. The door did not squeak any more after the second dose was put on the hinges, Don's throat seemed fine after he drank the oil, and somehow we made it through the day. It felt like the longest day of my life.

I am grateful to those folks for coming to the house. It really did help our family.

This wonderful article has continued to help me through the years. My hope is to pass it on so others can learn from it.

A Winner Versus a Loser

A Winner is always a part of the answer.
A Loser is always a part of the problem.

A Winner always has a Program.
A Loser always has an excuse.

A Winner says "Let me do it for you".
A Loser says, "That's not my job".

A Winner has an answer for every problem.
A Loser has a problem for every answer.

A Winner says, "it may be difficult, but it is possible.
A Loser says, "it may be possible, but it's difficult.

A Winner does as much as he can.
A Loser does as little as he can get away with.

A Winner sees a green near a sand trap.
A Loser sees 2 or 3 sand traps near every green.

A Winner is constantly trying to improve.
A Loser knows everything and fights any change.

A Winner makes decisions.
A Loser avoids them.

A Winner will always try to find out what caused a problem.
A Loser will always blame someone else.

Be a winner – the Rewards are numerous.

Written by Glen Turner

A huge measure of my problems stemmed from the fact that I felt responsible for most things. Not just my husband and children, but for my work, my parents, my friends, and whatever else was happening at the time.

Once I learned what my responsibilities are, and when I need to M.M.O.B. (mind my own business), my survival improved. I had to work hard on sorting things out. What is my problem, and what does not belong to me? This is not an easy task. I began to concentrate, and realized that I am responsible for my own happiness. No one can make me happy except God and me. I am not responsible for the happiness of anyone else. Once my children became adults, the responsibility for the lives they lead is theirs.

The Lord knows I tried to make my family happy, and did what I thought was right. I made many mistakes. When I heard that the only people who do not make mistakes are the ones who don't do anything, it helped a little. As my life moved along, I realized that much of what I was doing was making life more complicated. This made me realize that I need to use my favourite Al-Anon slogans much more: "Keep it Simple" and "How Important is it".

Often I said things that I did not mean, and did not follow through on what I said. This was confusing to everyone involved, especially me.

Once I realized I was doing this, I was able to start making changes slowly. Another important life skill I learned in Al-Anon: "Say what you mean, and mean what you say". I have added to it, "but don't say it mean".

I began with small things, like not picking up the boys dirty clothing before doing the wash, or not going to pick them up past a certain time. With Milt, the circumstances were different. However, I soon learned to 'Say what I mean, and mean what I say', gradually increasing from small areas to larger situations and eventually it became habit. This is one of the most important

79

lessons I cultivated, to make more sense out of this life I was given. I think that the whole family realize that I say what I mean, and mean what I say.

When I say I was given this life, I now realize that this was a gift to me from God. God gave me life. He also gave me my own will. I have a choice in how to live my life. That was a profound lesson.

Buying the house we had rented became even more difficult after we moved back into the family home. Milt did not like the idea. Once things settled again after Randy's illness and death, he began again to bring up selling the rental home. For two years we discussed this regularly. One such time, I told him that no matter what happened, I would not sell that house. It was good to know that I had somewhere to go if I needed to. I told him "There is a God, and you are not He!" By this time, he had figured out that I said what I meant, and I meant what I said. Eventually, we came to an agreement. He told me, "Don't expect me to go there and do things, because I will not". He never did anyhow. My next question was, "You mean to tell me that in retirement, when I buy groceries with the rent money, you will not eat?"

We did not discuss this any further, and the subject was dropped. I never did ask him to do anything there, and he did eat when I bought groceries with the rent money. That was fine because I felt secure.

I went to 'Drug and Alcohol Counselling'. The counsellor was very aware of the devastation of Alcoholism. He helped me sort out some areas including the house I purchased. I told him that Milt did not like the fact that I had purchased the house that we were renting out now. He said, "Lots of people do not like a lot of things. Is this house hurting anything?" "The only thing it hurts is the fact that he will not let go of it". The counsellor then suggested that I just stick to my plan, and Milt would either eventually get the idea, or he wouldn't. Either way, I would be fine.

Over the course of several years, I had been having attacks of pain in my gut. This distress was like no other I'd ever had. I would double up in excruciating pain and was sure I would not live till morning. Most often it struck during the night. X-rays did not show anything. Doctors kept asking me if I had pain in my back. I did not. It was December 1979. These attacks came nearly every week. I was always so exhausted after an onset that it took at least two or three days to feel right again. Just beginning to feel better – it would happen again. Each time I went to emergency, I was given a shot for pain and sent home. One such time a doctor on call asked me, "Are you an emotionally secure woman?" I wanted to slap him, but did not. On December 20th, I had a violent attack. I called my doctor at home in the middle of the night. He told me to go to the hospital and he would call ahead and have them keep me there till the problem was solved. The following day an internal specialist was called. He ordered an Ultrasound. It was discovered that I had gallstones. I needed surgery immediately. Surgery was booked for the 22nd. I was very happy that the problem was discovered. I was not excited to have an operation, but I was relieved that the problem was discovered. This was not a good time for surgery. Don and his girlfriend were arriving on the 27th. We had not yet met her. She had a little girl who would be turning one on the 31st. I did not want to be in hospital while they were here. Christmas gifts were sitting at home unwrapped. Milt was concerned about what the boys would do for Christmas with me in the hospital.

The surgeon was a very approachable fellow, so I asked him if I could go home for a few hours, since the surgery would take place in the morning. When I told him why, he told me not to say anything except that I had business to attend to. He let me go.

As soon as I got home, I wrapped the presents, put them under the tree, and then went back to the hospital. When I returned, the staff all laughed and asked, "Well did you get it all done". They knew why I needed to go home. I was so relieved that the pain would end. Never did I think I would be so happy to have surgery.

The operation was done in the morning of the 22nd, where they found a stone the size of the top half of my thumb. The pain was caused when this stone blocked the duct. They sent half to the laboratory and gave me the other half. Milt came to the hospital and had Christmas dinner with me. Tim went to my brother's and Randy went to his girlfriend's. Mom and Dad went to my brother's as well. Usually we all had dinner at our place.

I asked if I could go home, to be there when Don, his girlfriend and little girl came. The surgeon let me go home on the 26th, if I promised to stay quietly in bed for another week.

We met our daughter-in-law to be and her little girl for the first time. When they arrived, I was so happy to see them. My new granddaughter slipped off her shoes and climbed into bed with me. That was the beginning of many years of good times with my granddaughter. Mandie became my granddaughter immediately. We celebrated her first birthday on the 31st, and I know she was a gift from God. We lost one granddaughter and gained another. The kids just stayed a few days, and I was able to get around enough to enjoy the birthday and say good-bye to them when they left. They got married six months later, during the crucial time of Randy's illness. I will explain more about this later.

Randy insisted that I go to the wedding. He would go if he could. I did go and so did Tim. I made up my mind to enjoy this special time, which I truly did. I was very happy to have a daughter-in-law, and also a granddaughter. They have added three grandsons to our family. All of them are adults now.

Many situations over the years were difficult, but many more were wonderful. Once I learned where my responsibilities are, I could enjoy the good stuff and discard the rest, or at least put it to rest. I had to learn that what the boys did or did not do was none of my business. They were adults now. I had to concentrate on what was mine.

During Randy's illness, Tim and his girl moved in together and just after Randy died, they informed me that I would be a grandma again. It was hard to put that thought into my brain. I was still mourning the loss of my son. I was happy, but also sad as I really wanted them married and settled. However, I decided that my responsibility was to love them and enjoy being a grandmother.

Their son was born the following September and they named him after his uncle. It was hard to accept that we had another Randy at first, but now I am happy about it. It is amazing how many characteristics he has similar to his uncle. Tim has some characteristic similarities to his brother, but it is noticeable because of the namesake. Sometimes I tease my grandson, Randy, about it, "You know you are spooky. Your uncle would have done that, or said that, or whatever it happens to be". He doesn't mind, and actually seems to enjoy it, especially since his writing is nearly identical.

Tim and his girl friend had a baby girl about 18 months later. She was so welcome in our family. The parents were having many difficulties. They did eventually get married and had a tumultuous relationship. I am not going to say any more. That is their story to tell.

We had the children most weekends and enjoyed them to the utmost. They were very comfortable with us. I was attending church regularly. These two special little people joined me every Sunday. It was fun to have them with me.

Eventually after much turmoil one particular weekend, Tim came over to pick the children up and told us that he and the children were moving away from here. The children were already in bed and asleep. We had to wake them. Randy was visibly upset to be leaving, but in his little grown up way said, "Well, if I have to go, I better get dressed".

We did not see them for nearly two years. I felt like a death took place. After having the children every weekend since they were born, I felt the void. I had learned to 'Let Go and Let God' take care of them. In the meantime I was busy with life. That does not mean that I didn't miss them. I missed them terribly. They had become so much a part of our lives. It would have been unbearable had I not continued to work, garden, take care of our home, Sunday school and church activities, sponsorship and whatever I could do to help in Al-Anon. I am very fortunate to have many good friends as well.

There was an announcement one Sunday at church. They were looking for people to work with the children in Sunday school. Loving children, I attended this meeting even though I was a bit nervous. When I came in to the group the following day, a lady named Margaret invited me to sit with her. I began by being her helper. After a year of helping Margaret she moved away. I began to teach the Sunday school curriculum and loved it.

So many things were happening in life.

I eventually transferred from working at a Junior High School to an Elementary School. There were several changes of principals during the duration of my years at the elementary school. The school district transferred principals after several years in one location. After three or so years of being there, we had a switch in principals.

I enjoyed working with the new principal. Lloyd was understanding and easy to work with. He seemed to value my input and was a hard worker. It is easy to work hard when there is someone in charge who has a similar work ethic. It was fun to do the correspondence for this man. There was tons of paper work to do. It made sense to do what I could to help lighten the load. To make it simpler, I made a folder for him so that when he had time to sign the letters and forms, they would be in one place and it could be done quickly. Often after reading these letters and signing them he would come out and say, "Boy do I write good letters". Or, "You did a good job, thank you". Sometimes just a little note attached to my work made me feel that someone appreciated what I did. He is younger than I am by several years but he called me 'kid'. What a kid I was, because I so much enjoyed that nickname.

Part of my duties at work was doing the financial accounting for the school. This was a time consuming duty and very important to be accurate. It was difficult to concentrate sometimes. There is much activity in a school. I once said, "I should try to do these books faster. It seems to take so long". His reply was, "Kid, you can't go any faster". Knowing that he understood was encouraging. In all the years I worked there, I never had a bad bookkeeping audit. The audits were always error free.

One lunch hour, a little girl had been standing in a classroom doorway with her hand in the opening between the door and the frame. The wind blew the door shut and her finger was in the way. The tip of her finger was taken off. She came to the office holding up her hand. I could see right away that the tip of her finger was missing. Everyone was interested and getting excited. It was a job trying to keep the adults calm as well as the youngster. I wrapped the hand somewhat so that no one could see it. The little girl was very calm. She just held her wrist up. What a brave girl she was. In the meantime the principal came in and asked what happened. My motion toward his office was understood right away. I went in and asked him to go to the classroom and see if he could find the piece of finger in the doorjamb. He went and found the finger end and took the girl to the hospital. They were able to stitch the finger back on. I often wonder if she still has her finger.

Working with this man made time go very quickly and I often whistled quietly while I worked. He used to say, "Kid it sure is good to hear you whistle".

Another time, we had a little boy who was from a sad situation. He was a very sick little boy one day, and messed himself. The teacher sent him down to us. The smell was terrible. Lloyd asked me to go to the 'lost and found' and get some clean clothes for the boy. Then proceeded to have the boy take a shower. I suggested that I go along in case of a future problem. I just stood in the entrance. He thanked me for thinking of that. It was times like this that made me grateful to have him to work with.

Principals were only at a school for a certain number of years. When he learned that he was being transferred, he told me. I cried. He reassured me that I would be fine with the new administrator and would like him. It was weeks later that he came over to me and said, "Hey kid, it is good to hear you whistling again". I was not even aware that I had stopped.

Work was always good, but working with this person was best. He encouraged me in my writing skills, in my dealings with the children, and with life in general.

There were several different principals during my duration at the school. I had no problems with any of them. Some were easier than others to work with. All were fine.

At this point in time, a young woman in my church was pregnant. Her husband had drowned while on a fishing trip. I was upset for this young woman, but I did not know her. However, I had been in her shoes at one time, and I felt the urge to write her a letter, which I did. I told her that if she felt the need to talk, I understood and would be willing to help in any way possible. It felt good to reach out.

Much later, a substitute teacher's assistant came to the school where I worked. I took all the information, picked up the keys required, and began walking her to the classroom. She said, "You don't know me, do you?" I had to admit that I had never met her. "I am the person you wrote the letter to when my husband died." That was quite a way to meet. I was so happy that I had followed my instinct when I wrote the letter. I found out that she had a baby boy. Later on he was in my Sunday school class. Life is so interesting.

By this time, I had become a member of my church, and was teaching Sunday school. This was so good to do. Not only did I enjoy the children, it was good to be busy, and I was learning a great deal both from the volunteer position and from the children.

There was a family at my church with four children. The mother was suffering from breast cancer. I did not personally know the parents except to say hello and goodbye when the children were dropped off and picked up. First I had one of the boys and a year later his sister. While the five-year old girl was in my class, the mother died of her illness. I was very upset for the children. I did not know the two older siblings, but I knew they were only a few years older. My heart went out to those children, and their dad. He is of Ethiopian background and I wasn't sure if he had family here or not. I knew she had a brother many miles from here.

What to do? What to do? What to do? I sat down and wrote the dad a letter telling him I would not be at the service for his wife because I did not know her, however, I would like to help him with the children wherever he needed help. I just knew I had to try to help this family somehow. The children ranged from five to twelve years of age.

Several days later, the dad called to tell me that he appreciated my offer and that it would help a lot, since there was no family here. He also told me that there would be a 'Tree Planting' in memory of his wife in the complex where they lived. Would I be able to attend? I went. Little five year-old, Abby took my hand and did not let go till the evening was over. I was hooked now. I had to do something to ease the pain for these little ones.

I was working but I had every Thursday off. One evening the dad called and asked if I could come on Thursday and stay with the children while he attended to some business.

That first Thursday was the toughest. The children were visibly upset, but trying hard to be strong. Jessica, the eldest was trying to do laundry. Elliot, the second child was outside. The two youngest were supposed to put the dishes away, after which we would play a game. Nathan was around seven at the time. He was doing his share of the dishes. The little one disappeared. When I went to find her, she was standing on her head on a chair in the living room. I suggested she come and do her chores, she said, "I don't want to". "Fine", I replied, "when Nathan is done, we will play a game. I guess you would rather stand on your head than play". A few minutes later she came in and did her share.

I enjoyed these children. They had different personalities and seemed to enjoy everything we did. Often we walked in the park near our home taking our dog, Prince, along. These children did not have a dog, so thoroughly enjoyed this part. On one such expedition, Nathan counted how many times the dog peed. He did not know that dogs do that to mark their territory. We also took along a plastic bag and some picker uppers and gathered garbage as we walked. Abby and I made up songs, played games and we talked a lot. The two older children were trying hard to be strong individuals, but enjoyed being kids. Jessica and I would sometimes play a game and chat or go somewhere enjoyable. Elliot loved to talk about building and asked for some nails and some pieces of wood to add to the supplies needed for a fort he was building. He also enjoyed games. Once he drew a wonderful picture for me of our back yard that included clothes on the line. We did this for five years after their mom died.

Somewhere in the fifth year of my time with these four children, my Mom got very ill. Dad went to take his driver's test and lost his licence because of his poor eyesight. My Thursdays now consisted of taking my parents for their appointments, going grocery shopping for them and us, and doing what needed to be done here and there. It broke my heart, but I had to cut down on seeing these four children.

I had my grandchildren as well as these four children. My life was changing once again.

Don and his family from Alberta came as often as possible. That was always enjoyable, and those grandchildren were growing up fast.

We missed Tim and his family. Tim and his wife got back together. Eventually they did come to visit. It was so good to be able to see them again. They lived a fair distance away, so the visits were far apart. During this time they had another little girl, Keshia.

Several years later, Tim called from his home in central B. C. He had been having trouble with his back for many years. He grew too fast for his spine to keep up and ended with Sherman's Disease. It is a gradual deterioration of the spine.

Specialists in this field were suggesting that they take ribs from his rib cage and fuse them to his spine. There was no guarantee about the outcome. He was confused and asked what he should do. At this point he was in his thirties with a family. I thought about this situation for a while and told him that this was something I could not advise him about. If the surgery went well, that would be great. If the surgery failed and he ended up in a wheel chair, I did not want to be responsible even a little. He was an adult and had to make the choice. I would always be supportive of whatever he decided. He chose not to have the surgery at that time. He said, "I am still walking and can do some things, I think I will wait".

It is upsetting to know that my son is suffering, but also very rewarding to see how he handles this. He does what he can, when he can, and the best part is that he hardly complains. I am proud of the way he deals with this part of his life.

I do not know why we had two sons with medical problems, and a grandson who is developmentally disabled. I do know that God has a plan for each and every one of us that all work together for good. All I need to do is be supportive and believe!!

I sent tickets for the grandchildren to come and visit when there was a school holiday, so we got to see them all. Both sides of grandchildren came as often as was possible. We enjoyed them growing up and develop into wonderful adults, in spite of the usual difficulties of growing up.

Moving back to our family home brought with it another dilemma. The grocery money had now become an issue. It was always important for me to have plenty of groceries in our home. There seemed to always a problem with grocery money. To me, it was clear as a bell. When we lived in the rental home planning to come back Milt suggested that he would be contributing a certain amount and I would put in whatever else was needed. This worked pretty well because I bought what was necessary, having to add much more than he contributed, but I said nothing. It was difficult but it worked out. I was trying hard to make things go smoothly. We often had people over and the grandchildren were here every weekend. Making the grocery money stretch was a challenge. Milt was harbouring resentment in regards to the rental home. There was nothing I could do about that.

Maureen was our son Randy's friend who had been in the hospital while he was there. She would often sit with him and keep him company. After he died, she remained our friend. She would often come and spend a day or two with us, and one such time she asked if she could come and live with us. Having a transplant that was rejected and had to be removed, and living in a dark basement suite was lonely. She needed moral, and physical support. I suggested that she come and just stay with us for a while, to see if she would be content here, but to keep her own place. I told her that things were not always wonderful here either. Eventually she moved in. Milt did not mind her being here, and she stayed with us till she got married almost three years later. She met her hubby while they were both on dialysis.

While she lived here we had some good times. She and I played crib every day. The loser put in $.25 each game till we had $25.00. It was a fun thing to. It was especially exciting when we had a playoff for the pot. I enjoyed this as much as she did and we did that till she married.

I tried to get her to do a few things while she was here. Once I asked her to clean a cupboard. I put a note on the counter saying, "Do it like it was your own". She in turn cleaned the cupboard and added to the note: "It is done. If it was my own, I wouldn't have bothered".

Maureen did not often go out however one evening she went somewhere. It was about 11:00 p.m. when she returned. I was standing against the counter in the kitchen when she arrived. Opening the door she went "Agh" really loud. I asked, "What?" She replied, "Have you ever stayed up this late before?" She could be funny.

During the time that Maureen came to live with us, she paid less than

Milt gave toward groceries. He decided that he would contribute the difference between what she paid and what he used to give, and all would be well. He had in his head that I was saving money from this. The truth was that I was having a struggle and did not know what to do about it. Maureen was on a handicapped pension and could not pay more. I was making payments on the rental house and all the other expenses involved with that house, which was Milt's biggest concern. I was paying my share where we lived as well. Milt was earning double what I was and the family home was now paid for. We also had the German shepherd that ate well. There were three of us now, a big dog and the same amount of money. Milt was testing once again.

I spent a lot of time thinking about what I had learned at the Drug and Alcohol Abuse Centre, and what I observed and heard at Al-Anon. At church, we always learned about various life lessons. After much deliberation, one Saturday I had my opportunity to try something. It would either work or something else would take place. I was ready to take a chance and make another change in our lives.

Milt's friend, Joe, was a machinist. He was coming to fix Milt's planer after a golf game. Milt told me that Joe had a good appetite and would be here around 10:00 in the morning for breakfast. Milt told me that he liked about four to six eggs, and toast. This was all arranged a week in advance. Now I had to put my strategy to the test.

It was humbling to put my plan into action. Much to my embarrassment, and I am sure to Milt's surprise, this is what happened.

Joe arrived and they went to repair the planer. My instructions were to make breakfast. When the men came in, breakfast was on the table. Milt only wanted coffee. I fried two eggs, made two pieces of toast and poured the coffee. Milt said, "Joe would like more toast and a couple more eggs". I said, "I am sorry but that is all I have". The look on both their faces was shock. On the other hand, I had to act as normal as possible. Then Milt said, "Pour him another coffee". My reply was, "This is all we have in the house". As I write this, I can still see their faces. Milt was visibly shaken, and told his friend, "We are going shopping this afternoon". This was news to me.

I am sure Joe was happy to leave, and I was waiting for Milt's reaction. I did not say a word until Milt did. And, what he said was surprising. "Are you ready to go shopping now?" I replied, "If you are, but I can't afford to pay for everything." He told me he would buy what we needed. At the grocery store I made sure I had all we needed and then some. On the way home, I asked him, "Is this what I have to do for the rest of our lives, so that you will understand? Can we come up with a plan?" "What do you want to do?" he asked.

This is when we decided to each put so much money into a 'kitty' and use the money till it was gone. The first of the month each of us put in the same amount. We came up with a fair amount and thus began our plan.

I was learning more and more about the disease of Alcoholism, and the effects of all the other diseases that my husband suffered from. I learned that the disease of Alcoholism is present even if the person is not drinking. There is a definite uneasiness with life in general.

I was able to relate to something I read once again. "If you want to get somewhere, you have to know where you want to go and how to get there; then never, never, never give up".

Sometimes it would have been easier to give up. "Thank you God, for making me able to push ahead, and not give up!!!" I wanted us to be a family. I wanted our children to enjoy their dad, for the grandchildren to have a grandpa.

The grandchildren were all growing up. There are seven of them: Mandie, Charles, Anthony James (A.J.), and Nicholas (Nick), are from one family. Randy, Victoria and Keshia from the other family. It was discovered that one of the boys has some difficulties and no one seems sure exactly what he suffers from. The name doesn't really matter, but the disorder is difficult for everyone concerned. One of the girls was born with many allergies, also difficult for everyone concerned.

Milt was a mill supervisor. The job situation became stressful. His place of employment closed and moved to a different place and he was unemployed. At this point, he asked me about his retirement and how he should take his pension. I told him that if it were my decision, I would take the pension for life. He then became very irritated and said, "I am not going to live to 65, and I need the money now". One thing I did observe about my hubby is that he seemed to want everything now. He asked what I thought, and I made my suggestion. The rest was up to him. There will be more about this in a later chapter.

In the middle of all of this, Milt was going through terrible depression. I could do nothing right. If I was cleaning the deck, I did not do it right. Driving the car was never to his liking. I was not doing anything right. No matter what I was doing, he was critical.

Eventually the depression was treated with anti-depressants, and his anxiety with anti-anxiety medication. To this he added whatever he could get over the counter. He slept a lot. Milt's doctor also prescribed Tylenol Threes for pain. He became addicted to the codeine in them.

Milt also suffered from Diabetes. He did not eat the way he was supposed to so that did not help the situation. It was a blessing that the Diabetes medication seemed to work pretty well for him.

During Milt's early teen years he had Polio. This illness was devastating to him as a youngster and it left his body weak on the left side. His left arm would twitch or jerk unexpectedly. I learned very early in our marriage that I only filled his cup three quarters full.

In spite of all our differences, and hurdles, we loved each other. We were loyal to one another and deeply cared about each other.

In July 1991, nine years after Randy's death, Milt's sister and I had made plans to clean out our freezers. We had been at her place the day before and did hers. She and her hubby were coming early the next morning, so I asked Milt to call me since he often was awake before me. When he came in to call me, he looked like he had soaked his head and face with water. I thought it was hot outside since it was July 1st. I asked, "How come you're soaking wet?" He said, "I have a terrible headache, and I am going to bed". Milt often had migraine headaches. After he went back to bed, I made sure the drapes were pulled to darken the room and then went about my day. I checked on him before we started to clean out the freezer and he told me to go ahead, that he was fine. I wasn't so sure. It seemed more severe than usual.

After we finished cleaning the freezer, I went to see how he was. Realizing he was much worse I said, "I am going to take you to emergency". His reply was, "You can't". I asked, "Why not?" He then told me, "I can't lift my head up off the pillow and I feel like I am going to throw up".

I called the ambulance. They took Milt to Surrey Memorial Hospital. It was discovered that he had a brain aneurysm. He was moved to Royal Columbian Hospital where they had doctors and equipment to deal with this situation.

Being July 1st and a holiday, we had to wait till the next day for decisions to be made. The aneurysm was a slow leak. I was told that this was a very serious problem. If it burst, he would probably die. They had Milt strapped to the bed and gave him a shot that put him to sleep. He had to be very still. I came home and called our sons. The boys reassured me that they would be here as soon as they could.

Interesting how I dealt with this. I called everyone who needed to know and then proceeded to clean. I scrubbed everything in the bedroom, did all of Milt's laundry and then went outside to work in the garden. It was late at night. I was just doing something to keep from going crazy. I dug a flowerbed in the shape of a grand piano right beside Milt's workshop with just the back yard light on. I was very tired, but could not sleep.

The next day I had a meeting with the surgeon and two anaesthesiologists. The surgeon told me that I needed to sign the permission for surgery. There were several ways it could go: Milt could have a stroke on the operating table. He could die during the procedure. He could be a vegetable, or could be fine, but surgery had to be done. I said, "There really is not much choice, is there?" "Not really".

I signed the papers. We had to speak with the anaesthesiologists. There were two of them. Milt was present. They told us what they would do, reassuring Milt that they would take good care of him. They told Milt that he should not smoke because that could cause more problems. If he smoked, he could have another aneurysm. They assured him they would monitor the situation while the operation was being done. We listened, then I went home, while Milt went in for the operation.

Tim arrived during this time. We waited for the outcome of the surgery. Don was on his way as well. I felt better knowing that my boys would be here with us. So we waited, and waited. Finally the call came. The surgery went well, however there were two aneurisms not one. There was one on the side of Milt's head and one in the middle. It seemed like Milt would be fine, but time was what was needed.

We went to see Milt when we felt he would be coherent. As soon as we walked into the room, he asked Tim for a cigarette. I could feel the anger rising up in me. I did not want to do something stupid, and I was very tired. As carefully as possible, I told Milt, "I did not sleep at all while waiting for a decision regarding your surgery. I am very tired, and you cannot think of anything to say except that you want a cigarette. I am out of here. I may see you tomorrow." With that I left and went home. When I got home, I made a big bowl of popcorn, got a glass of juice and went out on the deck to enjoy the sunshine and my hammock. Ate the popcorn, drank the juice and slept all afternoon.

Tim later assured me that there was no smoking done and that his dad was doing well.

When I went back the next day, the nurses brought in a lazy boy chair and I slept again. No more mention of a cigarette.

Don arrived. Both sons were here. It was great to know that they were around for support and also it took some of the pressure off the visiting schedule.

My parents did not understand what was happening. Milt and my dad did not see eye to eye very often, so there was always that underlying tension. Besides they had never heard of an aneurysm.

I was so grateful to have two caring sons. As much as I missed Randy, I was happy to have two more. I began to think that God gave him to us for a short time for a reason, and I had better deal with it. I started being grateful to have had him for a short time, and that I still had two more. Many people never have any children.

The surgery took place on a Tuesday. The following Sunday morning when Don and I went in to see Milt, on the side of his head was a big lump about the size of a coffee mug. Another set back. Milt told us that there was a leak in one of the clamps, and that they would have to reopen the incision and fix it. They had been taking the blood out with a needle and would do it again that day, and operate on Monday. Milt did not seem upset about the idea, so that helped us all.

Monday, the incision was reopened and the problem repaired. Now we waited to see how it all went. The boys left for their respective homes after a few days. After three weeks in the hospital, Milt was discharged and home.

The going was rough after Milt got home. He could not do much. When I cut the grass, he watched me through the window with sadness. After the job was done, he would tell me how to do it right. I was just happy I could do it. This part I could understand. Cutting the grass was always his duty or one of the boys. Now it was my job. It wasn't long before he was able to cut the grass slowly. He was happy and I was relieved, because there were many other duties that he could not do.

In the first few months of recovery, Milt could not drive. Every time we had to go to an appointment or somewhere else, he constantly criticized everything. "Why did you go this way?" "How come you are in that lane?" "You and your short cuts!" "You always go home the wrong way." "It takes too long if you do this or that." I was frustrated and yet did not know how to stop this constant complaining. I was trying to be understanding and kind, and did not know if this was always going to be. There had to be a change and I needed to do something different.

"Life is too short to dance with ugly men", came to my head. Somewhere I read this and although Milt was far from ugly, I was beginning to feel resentful. No more resentment for me, I must do something.

I also read: "For something new to begin, something must end", and "You never know how strong the tea bag is till you put it in hot water". Well I was in hot water and wanted to cool it down.

These changes do not come easily and I thought about this one for a while before deciding what to do. I told Milt how his complaining made me feel and that the next time he started, I would turn around and bring him home. He did not reply. Once again I had to, "Say what you mean and mean what you say".

Well it was only a few days later that we were going to his sister's for supper. He really did not want to go, but we got ready. As soon as we pulled out of the driveway, he started telling me I was turning the wrong way. He always went left, and I went right. I said, "Milt, remember what I said. I know where to go, I've been there many times". He was quiet for a few minutes. About four blocks away from home, he began again. As soon as I was able,

I turned the car around and headed home. He asked, "Now where are you going?" "Home".

Nothing more was said. This was a hard thing to do, but it did work. From then on it began to improve. I only had to do that one more time, or maybe two. After that he said things like: "You know your way around pretty good." "I didn't know that we could get here this way." "You sure do know different ways to go places, don't you?" Wow!! What a relief and how enjoyable our trips were. He began to enjoy different scenery.

I realized later on when he could drive again, that he only remembered one way to go certain places, and that he had forgotten many things.

Gradually things kind of came back to normal, whatever that is. I began to notice that Milt's tremors became worse and his walk was different. He always had slight tremors, and I thought it was from the Polio after effects, or the drinking. I mentioned these things to Milt's doctor, who told me it was from many things including the Polio, Aneurisms, medications, and other things. Milt was taking a lot of medication and Tylenol Threes were his top priority, as were the anti-anxiety pills. Together they made him sleep a lot.

Eventually I began reading things about tremors, mumbled speech, slow walking and other things I began to notice. I read about Parkinson's disease. Once again, I mentioned it to the doctor and he dismissed it.

Milt's doctor became ill so Milt had to make a change. He chose one and started going to him. This doctor was much younger and quite approachable. Again, Milt seemed to be deteriorating and asked me to drive him to the doctor. While we were there, I mentioned my suspicions about Parkinson's. He watched Milt for a while and asked a few questions, then said, "You know you could be right". Wow, finally someone was listening.

Milt was referred to a specialist in the area that dealt with Parkinson's. This lady was not only a specialist she was special. When we arrived and she met us, she was so pleasant and gentle, that we both felt safe and comfortable. She went through the procedure slowly and carefully, asking many questions of Milt. After about one hour, she confirmed that he was definitely dealing with Parkinson's, and prescribed many medications. Milt was so used to taking pills, this was not a problem for him. I was concerned. He not only abused medications, he really was not able to dispense them properly and did not want anyone else to do it. Added to his array of pills were 12 more. Oh my, what were we going to do?

Thank you Lord for leading me to the Al-Anon Program, and back to church. I learned so much. I don't even know where to start. "Let Go, and Let God" and "One Day at a Time" were two good slogans for this situation. I offered many times to help with the pill predicament, and each time Milt told me, "I am doing good with the pills".

Diana Holt

Life moves along. Approximately 1990, Don and Tim were both having some difficulties in life and one day Tim called to talk. We were having a deep conversation when he told me that I did not understand. I was a bit upset after the talk was over, but it gave me the incentive to write the following poem:

<u>Dear Son</u>

I'll share some of my life with you now,
And I hope that it will help you somehow.

It was the spring of 1954.
I married, I loved,
I thought about it no more.
That was a strange year, and all was so new,
But I soon learned what I had to do.

It seemed real soon, we were in the second year.
Now a growth on hubbies knee did appear.
The story was endless,
It seemed so somehow.
The doctors said, "Off comes the leg, right here and now!!"

And, so another adjustment there was to make.
He thought a life without him I should take.
Because I loved him for 'Richer or Poorer',
'In Sickness and in Health',
I proceeded now to adapting myself.

From hospital/homebound he did go,
No leg to walk with, so he was slow.
As time rolled along, and he grew a bit stronger,
He could stay up a whole lot longer.

Well now I found out I was a month overdue.
I was happy, but worried, with what would I do?
No question, not even a doubt,
I had my first son, who soon was about.
When the boy was about one month of age,
There was more cancer,
Now in the last stage.

94

He soon died, and my son and I,
Were left to cope with Life and **Death** too.
I was 21 years old,
I wasn't so sure what I should do.

I thought I'd never get over this terrible blow.
But I did,
Because on with life I had to go!!
After another year went along,
I began to enjoy life and even a song.

Then one day, my neighbour introduced me to **your Dad**,
I liked him real soon, and I was so glad.
I wanted to feel alive again,
Oh just so bad.

I had been through a lot, and I was so sure,
That no matter what happened,
Any crisis I could endure!!

I was so sure that I was now holding the ball,
But 'God, He knows me, the very best of us all.
He knew that I needed, to humble and turn over my life.
I could not have done it without any strife.

So I cried, and I screamed, and I did a whole lot.
That only added more grey hairs to the ones that I've got.
Life had so many burdens to bear,
And holding on tight, got me absolutely nowhere.

About twelve years ago, I made a big choice.
I 'Let Go' of everything,
And listened to 'God's Voice'.
Whenever a problem to bear came across,
And you know real well, how many there was!!

Don went into the forces during this time.
Now my first born son was gone down the line.
Your Dad was having a lot of despair,
My 'Hanging On' did not get me anywhere.

You were a teenager and very obsessed,
With being independent and with this I was blessed.
Your brother, my son number two,
Was dealing with being a teenager too!!

Now his girlfriend was pregnant,
We were all in distress.
Our family was split, and Christmas was coming.
Oh, what a mess!!!!

I was feeling the pressure, and couldn't do much.
So, 'I Let it all Go',
And with God got in touch.

And, as time went along, I kept trying to 'Let Go'.
The tension was heavy, the 'Letting Go' slow!!
As time passed by, I started to see,
That 'Life will be, what it will be'!!

Now the girl gave the baby away!
I thought I'd surely go crazy that day.
I wanted to see her, and hold her,
And listen to her coo.
And I know that you wanted to cuddle her too.

Then your brother got sick, and what could I do?
His illness was long, with surgeries and pain.
He never was quite the same.

His pain he endured,
And through this matured, far beyond his years.
Together we shared much pain, and much joy.
And I shared with him many tears.

In the end he did leave us, without any fuss.
He never did question his lot in this life.
He accepted and endured all of his strife.
I know that he also learned to 'Let Go'.
Of this I am sure, for he told me so.

I have now learned and have started to see,

That life, like a string crumpled tight in your hand,
It stays in a twist, like a tight rubber band.
And if you release it, and then pull it around,
It follows you everywhere, as you travel the ground.

I've tried to do this a lot in my life.
But every so often I 'Hang on too tight'.
Then everything mounts up,
And I usually fight.

Then I Pray and 'Let Go', and soon I can see.
There is light in the tunnel,
And again I am 'Free'.
It is a lifetime of error and trial.
By the inch it is simple,
And hard by the Mile!!

This poem was written for both boys with only a few differences, since they had different birth fathers.

In spite of all the things that happened, I am so very grateful that I have always had lots of friends. I have enjoyed so many varieties of people ranging from newborn to 102 years old. Friends are what kept me from being crazy. I have always been able to laugh, cry, console, tease, or just listen. Although listening quietly has always been a problem, but if you ask some of my friends, I really can do this sometimes.

My neighbour, who lived across the street from us, was heading for 100 years of age, and a real sweetheart. Oh she could be cranky sometimes, but who can't be. She used to call on me to open her pill bottles, find her cane, which she called a stick, or take her grocery shopping. I would often take some of my writing over for her to read or read it to her. She seemed to like it when I read to her. It was difficult for her to see.

I was over at her place when she handed me a piece of paper that she had cut out of a magazine. It was an entry form from "The North American Library of Poetry". She told me, "I think you should enter your poetry". Wow, I was pleased and surprised, and took the entry form home.

This lady was so interesting to listen to. She had some very neat stories and she could also be very funny. 'Humour', she told me, was what helped her to live to 100, and 'Oatmeal Porridge'. I enjoyed visiting her.

She once told me the story of when she and her husband lived on a farm on the prairies. She was pregnant and was not feeling well, and wanted to go to see the doctor in town. Her husband told her to go, as he had work to do out on the field. Off she went to town. The doctor examined her and said she should go home and lie down, that she would be fine. She said she felt awful and had cramps. When she got home, she felt pressure and then the babies came. There were two of them and they were both dead. There was a boy and a girl. I asked her, "What did you do?" She said, "What could I do? Jim was out in the field, so I waited till I was strong enough to clean myself up. Then I found a shoebox and lined it with a towel and buried them in the yard". "We were poor", she said. "I felt it was the best thing to do. They were gone anyway".

Once again I was grateful for her friendship. She taught me many lessons. Sometimes she was demanding. I spoke of this with my parents one day. Dad told me, "She is the oldest of us all. She is the boss". I said, "Dad, age doesn't make a person a boss". We had a chuckle and that was that.

My brother had come to visit the same day that my neighbour gave me the entry form. He was here from his farm about five hours away. He was a cranky man, and did not ever get excited about anything I did or suggested. I learned to just go with the flow and not get into anything, so I showed him the entry form. He then asked about the poem.

I had actually written two poems at the time and showed them both to him.

One afternoon I sat in my rocking chair and watched our huge cedar tree in the front yard. It was windy and the branches seemed to be dancing in the wind. I was grateful that we had gone to the effort to plant those three little cedar trees many years before. This is when I wrote the poem about our Cedar Tree.

Oh Lovely Cedar

We got you from a demolition sight,
And worked to plant you day and night.
There were three of you all put together,
And you have stood all kinds of weather.
The three of you have now become one,
Reaching higher and higher to the sun.
In winter the wind is blocked by you,
And there are many other things you do.
The ferns and flowers make you shine.
The little birds sing, "you are mine".
The squirrels they scramble up the tree,
Seemingly saying "you can't catch me".

And when the summer sun is scorching hot,
Sitting beneath you is just the right spot.
You are home to bird and beast,
And a comfort to us, to say the least.
Your boughs they seem to shelter the flowers,
And we are proud that you are ours.
Oh lovely cedar up so high,
It seems you nearly touch the sky.

These two poems are totally different. I like the 'Train of Life' better. Although they are both from the heart, I felt that the Train of Life had more feeling involved. My brother on the other hand thought that 'Oh Lovely Cedar' was the better one. He was very outdoorsy and into hunting and fishing.

After a bit of discussion about which one to send, I said, "You know, I think I'll submit them both". Here is the other one.

My Train of Life

I believe that life is like a train,
With folks 'a comin' on, and getting off again.
Some stay with me my whole life through,
And some must do what they must do!!
My children were but chosen gifts, for me to Love and Hold,
But they too, must go and do some things untold.
And for those years, and they were precious ones
I was blessed with three most wonderful sons.
They've grown, and gone to live their days.
They'll choose their errors and their joys in many different ways.
*These boys, they've given me more, these precious **Three**,*
Than the whole world put together.
And I'm so pleased that I'm still here, Their loving, caring ways to see!!
Except for one, who was 'on loan' for only twenty-one years.
We shared so much, I learned from him, and together we shed many tears.
I miss him so, but in my heart I know we're really not apart.
And as my train goes chuggin' along, There's many a joy, and many a song.
Some friends come back along the way, some never leave and never stray.
I love them all, they are all so Dear.
At times they're far, and then they are near.
No matter if they are off or on, my train just chugs from morn' till dawn.

And if I LET THE LORD ABOVE, take charge of all I care about and Love,
My train will one day end its ride,
And there will be 'GREAT PEACE' inside!!

Not even a week later I found an entry form for 'The Canadian Library of Poetry'. I decided to submit both of these poems to them as well

After I mailed the entries, I completely forgot about the whole thing.

Ironically, my brother was here once again when I got a letter from the North American Library saying that the poem 'My Train of Life' had been selected for publishing, and would automatically be eligible for a prize contest. I was excited when I read the letter. My brother, much to my surprise, nearly jumped out of his skin. He said, "Do you realize how many million poems they must have?" I actually had not given it much thought and I told him that. "You know what? I am going to build a cabin on my property. You can come up and write where it is beautiful and quiet."

My thought was I wrote these at the kitchen table, it isn't necessary to build a cabin. However I was so tickled that he was excited for me for the first time in our lives. That was enough for me, cabin or no cabin. I was also more pleased after he mentioned how many entries there must have been. I hadn't thought about that part.

A few weeks later, I received a letter from the Canadian Library of Poetry notifying me that 'My Train of Life' had been selected for publishing with them as well. I was very elated about this. I called my brother. Another burst of joy arose from him.

Never in these conversations did he ask me which poem was selected. He may have read the first letter, but I do not recall if he did. Maybe it did not matter to him. I will never know. He only lived about a year after that.

This is the best memory I have in my heart of my brother.

I am so glad to have learned that changing myself takes up most of my time. I have no time to think about trying to change any one else.

**Don't wait for someone else to change. Lead the
way by making changes in yourself.**

Chapter 8

COMMITMENT

Don't be afraid to face the facts.

The difference between 'involvement' and 'commitment' is like a ham and egg breakfast. The chicken was involved – the pig was committed.

Commitment to me means a pledge to carry out my responsibilities to my loved ones, my job and to my friends the best way I know how. Wherever and whenever, I pledge to do my best to fulfill a promise. I am the world's most committed human being.

When it got to the point in life that I was over committed and overwhelmed, I was also disappointed in myself. So many things were happening so quickly and I was overcome with sadness. The disappointment and sadness came in waves and I had many facts to face.

I had to face the fact that my parents were aging and needed lots of help. They were from a European background, and did not easily accept that fact. My parents were from the times, parents were looked after by their children, especially by the eldest son. My Dad always felt that because he had a son, they would be looked after.

The truth was that my brother had moved far away from where we all lived. After he was diagnosed with Leukemia, his idea was that if he moved into the country, all would be well. It appeared he was trying to recreate the atmosphere we had when we were youngsters.

He was hard to deal with even when he was well, however now it was worse, much worse.

When the diagnosis was made, the whole family was disturbed. Our Dad was especially confused. To him, his son was powerful. This was not a good thing for my brother, and especially not good for me. Many times in our lifetime, it would have been much easier to deal with my brother if Dad had been solidly and consistently firm with him. Dad was not consistent. Sometimes he was too kind to him and sometimes too firm. During our growing up years, it was very evident that David was the apple of his eye. I grew up with that being the way it was, and I only had one brother. He was special to me too. Mom always tried to be fair, but Dad was the boss.

A flashback to when we were growing up. It did not matter what happened, how it happened or why it happened. I was the older one and that made it fine for my brother to throw the cards when he lost the game. I could not skate around on our little homemade ice rink. Being the goalie was my part, so he could practice shooting the puck. The puck was a frozen horse bun. There is no need to get into more. You get the idea.

I remember a time when my brother David was a teenager. Mom had made lunch and when he sat down to eat he said, "I am not eating this s_ _t". Dad told Mom to make whatever he wanted, and from then on, my brother became even more difficult. From the moment that those words came out of Dad's mouth, I vowed that if I ever had children, never, ever would I make something different for anyone. And, I never have. That day I learned a very good lesson.

When my brother married, we were all happy. We loved his wife. Dad bought them a house almost immediately. It was a fully furnished home only a few doors from our parents. All was well for a period of time. My brother and his wife decided to sell that home and purchase another in a different location.

In time there was trouble. My brother was acting out. We did not know the details at the time, however there was eventually a divorce. I was overwhelmed. I loved his wife like a sister. I could not understand why they had to break up. Later I learned from my sister-in-law that David had been abusive to her and was running around with other women. She still has a hearing problem from a blow to her head.

Even after the split, I kept in touch with my sister-in-law and we continue our friendship to this day – and I still miss her. It is always an honour and a joy when she comes for a visit. She remarried. Her husband is wonderful to her and they have one son.

My brother lived with another lovely lady. She is a good person, who put up with a lot of unnecessary nonsense. They lived together for ten years and then married, making a total of approximately thirty years.

Back again to when I was first married, I became instantly friends with my first husband's nephew and his wife. His wife, Rowena, and I became very close and we spent much time together. Because of her husband's job they moved away for a while. During their absence, it was discovered that she had

Multiple Sclerosis. Rowena became wheelchair bound in her early thirties. After several years, they came back to live near me again, which made us both very happy.

Much happened after they came back to live here. I remember they often came to visit with their five sons. I would make a huge tub of popcorn. It was amazing how much popcorn eight boys could eat.

As if five boys, Rowena in a wheelchair suffering from M.S. attacks wasn't enough. Her husband began suffering from terrible headaches and had no patience with anyone especially the boys. Tests were done and the prognosis was brain cancer. This was a tough time for all of them. I did what I could to help out. He died in a very short period of time.

Eventually the boys became men and moved out on their own. Rowena sold the family home, and bought a condominium. Rowena could still do some things, even drove her car, but she used a wheelchair. We continued our friendship. Eventually she could not drive her car. A friend of mine bought the car, and Rowena purchased a scooter. I often picked her up, put her wheel chair in the trunk and we would go for a drive or to a park, often taking a lunch along. As time progressed it was more difficult for me to lift the chair into the trunk, and it was hard getting her into the car. Pretty soon she only used the scooter. I could not handle the scooter so she would meet me somewhere. We would have lunch together and a visit. Often I just went to her place.

When I remarried she was living in her condominium. We continued our relationship. After a short time she also remarried, rented out her condo and moved into her husband's house. She was devastated when the marriage did not work. The break up was because her husband could not deal with her illness. Luckily she did not sell her place and was able to move back into it. In spite of everything else, we continued our friendship.

This lady was special. Even when her world was falling apart, and she was very sick and on a lot of medication, we spent as much time as we could together. We met for lunch, played games; her favourite being scrabble, at her place or we just talked. She seldom complained and only three times did she call because she felt like ending her life. Each time she called, I went over to be with her and we would end up sharing something that made her laugh. She did die at the age of sixty-four from complications caused by her illness.

Rowena was a wonderful lady and I was blessed to have known her. She once gave me a card that said "As long as I have you in my life, I will never be lonely". When I was hurt and could not walk for a year, she was so kind and considerate.

I gave the eulogy at her memorial with no problem because I knew her and her children well. At her service her five sons stood in order of birth and each told a memory of their mom.

My dear friends Eileen and Dale had four sons. Our children all grew up together, so we knew each other well.

As adults these boys would often come by for a letter they needed typed, or talk something over, or just a cup of tea. I loved it that they were comfortable enough to come when they felt like it. Neither Eileen nor I wanted to be called Mrs., so our boys called us 'Aunty', an endearing term and we enjoyed it. They also called Dale and Milt 'Uncle'. It was much better than Mr. or Mrs.

In July 1999, Brian, the second youngest of Eileen's four boys called me and asked if he could take me out to lunch. I was elated and accepted. He picked me up one morning early and we drove out to White Rock. It was a beautiful summer day so we walked along the ocean and chatted. As we were approaching the car on our return, we could see the meter reader checking the cars for parking violations. Brian took off like a bullet to reach his car before the reader. I had a good laugh and told Brian I had never seen him move so fast. He put more money in the parking meter and away we went to lunch. It was a special day indeed.

That September Brian was rushed to the hospital with a brain aneurysm. There was surgery and many days of waiting to see how things would go. Brian was in a coma for several weeks after the surgery. Nothing changed and Brian died on September 28, 1999.

Brian's parents live by a beautiful lake, where there is no church. The Pastor from my church officiated at Brian's Memorial Service. They were very grateful for his help. I was able to share at Brian's service. Brian was the same age as Randy. I knew him well. This was a very stressful and depressing time for my dear friends, and I was happy to be able to help.

Ron, their eldest son was the same age as our son Don. I wrote earlier how Eileen and I enjoyed our boys when they were babies. Ron never failed to call me at Easter, on Valentines Day, any special occasion or just for fun. I had a special spot in my heart for Ron, and he for me. Ron would drop by for a visit periodically.

Ron was a diabetic and had trouble staying on the diabetic diet. Ron was very sick a lot of the time and eventually had to have a third of his foot amputated leaving the big toe for balance.

During a phone call Ron told me he found a wooden wheelbarrow. He knew I loved the old wooden wheelbarrows. "This one is for mother", he told me. I will look for another one for you. Another call from Ron came telling me that he found a wheelbarrow for me. It wasn't a wooden one, but it was a nice one for the garden. "Can I come over and bring it?" Ron asked. "I also have something else for you that you will love". "What is it Ron?" "It's a secret. You will see."

"Great! When are you coming?" Ron said, "Can I come now?" "Sure".

Ron was a huge, burly guy with bushy reddish hair and beard. He arrived in his truck and immediately pulled out the wheelbarrow. I loved it right away and that afternoon I planted flowers in it laying it partly down on a low stump in the front yard. Mostly I loved the idea that he remembered about the wheelbarrow. He went back to his truck and brought out a little brown paper bag. It looked funny, this big guy with this little paper bag. However, there he was. He came in the house and I made tea. All this time, Ron was holding this little bag. I knew he was waiting for me to ask about it, but I just let him wait a bit. As we were having tea I asked, "Ron, what's in the bag?" He giggled and said, "Aha, I knew you'd be wondering", and handed me the bag. What a surprise it was!! Somewhere he found this huge napkin ring with a clear stone in the shape of a diamond in it. Did I have a good laugh? Wow!! I said, "Well Ronnie, I guess I will never again get a diamond this big". We had a great visit and I still have the napkin holder.

Approximately two years later gangrene set in and Ron had to have his leg amputated below the knee. The knee was left in order to be able to fit him for prosthesis. This was another terrible time for my friends.

I often visited Ron in hospital. Depression had overcome Ronnie, and he was not interested in his personal hygiene. Often I washed his hair as we talked, trying to encourage him, while he told me some of his problems. Ron was a kind man, but lonely and feeling sad. When he was able to get out of his room, we often went outside where he fed the birds the crumbs he saved. The birds seemed to know, and he so much enjoyed that part.

In 2004, Ron developed a heart condition as well. He was in and out of hospital a great deal, and was not able to care for himself. His parents took him to their home to look after him. Eventually he was back in the hospital and suddenly on November 22, 2004 Ronnie died of a Heart Attack.

In spite of the seriousness of Ronnie's condition, it was a shock for Dale and Eileen to realize that their forty-eight year old son was gone.

I knew the devastation of losing one child. This was their second loss. I was grateful to be able to be there for my friends to help them through a situation that is indescribable. It was so wonderful when I asked my pastor to help out, and he accepted. Once again he officiated at the funeral. Dale and Eileen were relieved to have this part taken care of. I was able to share some stories about Ronnie at the service, because I knew him from the day he was born.

Once again it was wonderful to have a church that I call home, and caring pastors that are willing to help.

In 1996, I retired. My Mom was so happy; I thought she would jump out of her skin. She just beamed at my retirement party. For sure she was much more elated than I was.

For almost seventeen years I was Head Secretary at the school, and I loved the job and the people I worked with. Retirement did not happen easily for me. Much thought and planning went into it. Probably more thought went into my retirement than any other huge decision. My work brought me much satisfaction.

I knew retirement was necessary, as I was feeling very tired with all the other obligations. This was the biggest decision I have ever made. No matter what happened, my job was consistent and made sense when other things did not, and they paid me. Often I received compliments and little perks.

I was overwhelmed at the wonderful retirement party the staff made for me. There were many people there with whom I had worked and many family members as well. Don surprised me and came to the party from his home in Alberta. Milt attended, although he really was not very well. His two sisters were there, my brother and his wife, my cousins and many friends. Mom was beaming. This is a wonderful memory.

During the weeks prior to my retirement there were many signs in the school of the upcoming event. Often I delivered materials throughout the school. Many times I watched the children making flower posters. I just assumed it was an art project. It was a surprise seeing the gymnasium walls covered with flowers that the children had made in art classes on large sheets of paper. I was not prepared for the song the staff sang on that day. They had been practicing this for ages. It was made up to the tune of the song 'My Diana', and the words were so well done that I both cried and laughed through it. How touching that was to my heart!!

There was an assembly in my honour on another day. One of the boys that I had taken under my wing and tried to help came to fetch me for this occasion. It was an emotional morning for me. Each classroom had been practicing a song. On this day, they all sang it together. I was overwhelmed and cried through it all. The song and the flowers covering the walls were overwhelmingly wonderful. Then the presentation of the pull-tabs was very warming. The young fellow who came to get me stayed beside me throughout. I have written more about this occasion later. I kept the flowered paper and used it as wrapping paper for gifts. It was too lovely to throw away.

After Randy died, I volunteered with the Kidney Foundation for over twenty years. There were many positive things that happened during that duration. I put my best effort into obtaining donations for this worthy cause, always thinking that I may help someone. It was very comforting and interesting.

I decided to do something different after twenty years. It still is my chosen charity, but I began spending time doing other volunteer duties, and taking care of immediate family needs.

For years I was asked to sponsor a group of teenagers. After retirement, I made a commitment to sponsor an 'Alateen Group'. This involved teens that had lived or were living with Alcoholism. Once again, I was committed to these kids. There was preparation for the meetings to make sure that they ran smoothly, and I needed to be with them every Wednesday evening for an hour. At least two hours a week went to these kids for ten years. It was with sadness that I resigned that volunteer position, but felt I it was time for someone else to experience and grow from this wonderful opportunity.

Twenty years or so after my brother's second marriage his Leukemia diagnosis came. I later found out that my brother blamed his wife for the disease and more trouble came. This is when they split and he moved up country. Their home here was sold. She bought a condominium and the marriage was over. This was another disappointment for the family, especially Dad.

Now my brother was living five hours away. Our parents needed help with everything. Milt was also having many health issues.

It was at this time that I had to stop seeing the four children whose Mom had died. I enjoyed the children, however, gradually I saw them less and less. Their Dad understood, and the children had grown and were moving ahead with their lives. There was not enough time to take care of my husband, my home, and now Mom and Dad.

On Sundays after church, I always took my parents out for lunch. We would often go for a drive after lunch or back to their place for a game of cards. Dad was not always keen on going for a drive, so I would tell him to just go to sleep and we'd wake him when we got home. This worked.

Most of the time, prior to Dad losing his licence, they would come to our place for Sunday dinner. After the loss of his licence they relied on me to take them everywhere. Eventually Dad gave me his car. The day of the transfer is still clear in my mind. Mom was very happy, Dad was very quiet and I was crying. Mom asked, "Why are you crying?" I told her that I felt terrible taking the car, and the fact that they had lost their independence. She said, "Just take the car and enjoy it. I feel better knowing it is not in the garage. I always worry that he will just go. You know your Dad". This did make it a bit easier to accept that in the big picture this was better.

None-the-less I now had their car and sold mine. We went everywhere together even before that. I used to park my car in their yard and transfer to theirs. Dad always insisted that we use his when we went out.

It was on my agenda that Wednesday and Sunday were days to spend with

Mom and Dad, or any other day that they had an appointment or needed to be taken somewhere. It did not matter the day, Dad always insisted that we have lunch out. Often I was gone for long periods.

Milt was very understanding. He did not want to go out much, and we had a German shepherd who was a great companion for Milt. He was a good watchdog, and it helped to know that Milt had company.

I began helping out with the children at my church very shortly after I started attending. This has always been a joy, however, sometimes it was difficult for me when everyone was sick around me. Going to be with the children for an hour and a half each week really has been wonderful. Somehow children have the ability to put me at ease and they can be so delightfully funny.

On a Sunday in 2003 after church, I went over to Mom and Dad's. Dad was sitting at the kitchen table reading his medical book. Any time someone in the family was not well, Dad would diagnose the issue. He was very often right.

This particular Sunday, Mom was not around and Dad was sitting at the table alone. I asked, "Where's Mom?" He said, "She's in bed". Mom was in bed and deathly sick. One look at her and I knew she was in trouble. She had thrown up and could not clean it up. That was definitely not her style. I talked while I cleaned up the mess, so that I could assess the situation. Then I said, "Mom, shall I drive you to the hospital, or call an ambulance?" "Call the ambulance", was her reply.

Dad was visibly upset and did not know what to say or do. Soon the fire trucks arrived followed by the ambulance. Off we went to the Royal Columbian Hospital. Usually they take the patient to the nearest hospital, but this attendant asked me to which hospital I wanted them to take her. I knew that this was the place to go.

It was a busy weekend at the hospital and the attending nurse on duty was upset with the ambulance attendant for bringing Mom there. We were only there a few minutes when Mom said, "I need to go to the bathroom". We were in the hallway at the time. I went to the paramedic and told him. He immediately took Mom, in the stretcher, to the bathroom and helped her to get inside. He then left and told me to call if he was needed. What a wonderful man he was. I appreciate it even more now.

It was only a few seconds after Mom sat on the toilet that she began to throw up and go the other way all at once and it was black and very stinky. I called for Help!! "Oh my Goodness", the paramedic said. "This is all blood". I do not remember much of the next few minutes. I know the smell was very offensive, and I knew Mom was very, very sick. She had a bed immediately and was soon settled. Eileen was in town so I called her to pick me up and take me back to check on Dad and get my car. I had gone to the hospital in the ambulance with Mom.

Dad was waiting for me, but this time he did not have a diagnosis. All I told him was that we would go and see Mom the next day, and to be sure that he had a good sleep. There was no need to frighten him. I went home.

Arriving home and seeing that everything was in order, I proceeded to call my brother and our sons.

The next few days were very frightening. Mom had been given blood transfusions and she was resting. On Sunday night the doctors taking care of Mom told me that she would likely be gone by Wednesday that she was only alive now because of the transfusions. They said they would stop giving her blood, because it was going right through her and was a waste. I begged the medical people to keep the transfusions going till the family arrived and could say goodbye to our precious, Mom, Grandma, and Great Grandma. They assured me that would be done.

By next evening many of the family were here. My brother, and Tim and his children had already arrived. The other son and family were on the way, but had much further to come. They would arrive a day later. There were a lot of people here, and Mom was deathly ill.

Tuesday, as I was sitting beside Mom, she removed her rings from her fingers and gave them to me. I asked her, "Why are you doing this?" She told me, "Where I am going, I will not need them. You wear them and enjoy them". This was tough to take.

Now everyone was here and we all needed to eat. Every day I made the biggest pot I had full of something, soup, spaghetti, stew or whatever. Each evening I had to think of something else for the next day.

One evening I was at home with all the grandchildren, Mom's great grandchildren. They called her 'Baba'. One of them asked, "Is Baba going to die?" I replied that I did not know, but it did look like that was a possibility. Then one of them asked, "Why don't we pray to God and ask him to make her live". Praying was something the grandchildren and I did together. We gathered around in the living room, and prayed. I explained that God would do what was best for Baba. I explained that she was old and maybe it was better for her to be with God. I was afraid that if she died, they would give up on prayer. We had a wonderful time of prayer and then went about our evening. The rest of the family were with Mom.

When Don, Virginia and the family from Alberta arrived, they brought with them a little Maltese/Shih Tzu puppy. She was adorable. Virginia wanted me to play with her, take her outside and to bed, saying that I would get bonded with her. She kept asking me questions like, "Do you like her?" "Why don't you give her a bath?" I told her I did not want to bond with her. "If I bond with her and you go home, I will miss her". Then I asked her, "Why are you asking me all of these questions?" "Well, when I saw her she had your name on her." Oh my. All I had in my head was Mom's illness, Milt's inability to do much and what to do with Dad.

Milt was in bed. I went in to him and asked him a few questions about the dog. He said, "She is a cute little thing, but why all the questions?" I told him that the kids brought her with the idea that we would keep her. She had her shots and was ready for us if we wanted her. Milt told me that if I wanted to keep her, that was fine with him. So now, the decision was mine. The kids had named the puppy 'Taylor'. I was not keen on that name. She was too cute for such a non- descriptive human name.

I asked Virginia, "Do you think I really need a dog right now?" To which she said, "More than ever". We decided to keep her. I told my daughter-in-law, "We have to keep her because she matches our rug and our furniture".

When I went to see Mom again the next day, she told me: "I am not going to die you know". I asked her, "How do you know?" She said, "I had a dream that I needed to be here for a while yet. There are three things that I need to do here. One is to be here for my husband's surgery". My Dad had pending heart quadruple bypass and valve replacement surgery coming up. "Secondly, I need to be here because your brother is sick". I asked. " What was the third thing", to which she replied, "I don't know the third one".

This was good news indeed, and she began to improve. She also wanted me to bring the pup in so she could see it. I asked the nurses if this was okay to do. They told me to be sure there was no one in the room with allergies. That afternoon, I brought my puppy into the hospital to see Mom in a pillowcase. The whole room was energized by the presence of this little baby. Mom and I discussed a name and we decided that I would change it after the kids left.

Thursday everyone left, and Friday Mom came home. It was discovered that she had a tiny pinhole in an internal organ that would need to be cauterized real soon. In the meantime she was home. Whew!!!! I gave her rings back.

At the hospital they told us Mom should be using a walker because she was pretty weak. Dad and I decided to stop and pick one up on the way home. Mom kept telling us, "I am fine. I don't need a walker". However Dad said, "We'll get one anyway. Sooner or later one of us will use it". Mom never did use the walker, but Dad did.

We renamed the puppy 'Chiki'. When I held her, she felt soft as a chick. That name felt right, and she became part of our lives right away. She wanted to please me and I enjoyed her. Chiki and I became a team. I taught her to do some tricks and because she had a wonderful disposition, I became interested in taking her to visit the sick children at the local hospital.

I decided Chiki was a perfect candidate for visiting sick children. After an interview, Chiki and I went for training enabling us to visit children, schools or rest homes. We could take part in such activities after all the necessary steps were taken. After this we became involved once a week visiting the sick children at the local hospital. What a pleasure this was. The experiences there are so precious. I will tell you about a few incidents: A little boy had been hit by a car and was in traction. Every day his bandages had to be changed. When the bandages were being changed, the traction was removed then replaced again. When this was done, it really hurt. While we were there one day, this procedure was being prepared. The little guy was crying knowing the pain that was coming. As soon as I realized what was taking place, I said to the little fellow: "Chiki and I will wait till you are done. We'll come back and she will do some tricks for you". He smiled through the tears. We went back into the room after his bandages were changed and the traction replaced. He kept pointing to the traction and telling me it hurt and would I be sure Chiki did not go near it. I reassured this little boy that she would not go near there. He smiled and asked to pet her. I lifted her onto the bed and he stroked her for a while. She licked his tears. He then said, "Can she do tricks?" We did our little performance and the little guy was happy. Chiki seemed to sense things like traction, stitches, or fresh bandages and stayed clear. She never once went near a surgery area.

Another time, there was a young fellow who was seventeen but looked like a twelve year old. He had Cystic Fibrosis and was going through a rough time. I asked him, "Would you like to see what Chiki can do?" He replied, "Yes I would, but I cannot be near animals". I told him she was a dog people with allergies could be near because she had hair not fur. He was very curious as to what she would do. We went into the room, did our job and were going out the door when he asked, "Could you please come back and put her on my bed?" We did this. I pulled up a chair and sat down. He stoked the dog and talked for over an hour, telling me all kinds of things. He told me his parents had split up after he got sick, and that his mom had to give his cat away. We cried and laughed through a lot of different stories he told us while stroking Chiki.

One Thursday we walked into the children's ward and began our rounds. We were in a room with a little girl who was excited to see the dog. She looked very familiar to me so I asked a few questions. It turned out that she was a child from my church. I did not recognize her in the different setting and she was not well. She enjoyed it that we were there and we spent quite some time with her. Chiki was at her best always in that setting.

When we were done at the hospital, I would then take my 'baby' to visit my parents, who totally enjoyed her company as well.

This little dog became a very essential member of our family. She made the children at the hospital laugh, even when they did not have much to laugh about. She entertained them, loved them and performed for them. Chiki always seemed to know where the incision, traction or any other obstacle was and avoided that area. The kids loved and adored her. 'Chiki' gave my parents great 'Joy' as well as the children. Especially Mom. Chiki is a willing student when I present a new idea for her to do, and she is always happy.

After a bath and grooming, I would send Chiki in to show Milt. "Go show Dad how pretty you are". He enjoyed praising her. He would say, "Oh you look nice, such a pretty girl". Both Milt and Chiki enjoyed this part. She has never been a lover of being groomed, but loves the compliments afterwards and the treat.

Every time I went to visit my friend Tam, her dog 'Pepper' would come and cuddle up to me. She was a very loving creature with tons of energy. One visit, I mentioned, "If ever you have to give Pepper away, try me first. Never was there even an inkling that it could happen.

We had Chiki about a year when Tam called to tell me that her son was allergic to Pepper. She was upset and cried, "I know if you had her, she would be looked after". I spoke with Milt and explained the situation. He was not well and could not do too much, however I wanted to know what he thought and how he felt about taking on another dog, especially a Border Collie/Blue Heeler cross and full of life. Milt enjoyed bigger dogs, so was not opposed completely. He was a thinker and could come up with things I did not think about. He said, "Why don't we bring the dog home for a week and see how it goes". "What a brilliant idea. Why didn't I think of that?" Off we went to pick up the dog. We had given our doghouse to this friend, because we did not plan to have another animal.

Into the truck went the doghouse and the dog. The doghouse seemed heavier than when we gave it to her. However, we just wanted to get them home. It was February and cold outside. When we got home, we took the doghouse up onto the back porch. Milt took Pepper to the workshop while I washed and disinfected the doghouse inside and out. When I took the mat out of it, it was dripping wet. No wonder the house was heavy. I scrubbed and dried the doghouse which was made of vinyl material, then set it under the roof of the back porch, put in a nice warm piece of rug and went to get the dog. She took one look and went into her house. It looked like she was already happy to be with us.

The problem we wondered about was how would she and Chiki get along?

In the morning, I carried Chiki outside to meet her new sister. Milt said, "Chiki has 'Homestead Rights' so if it does not work, Pepper has to go back".

Well Chiki just shivered and shook. Pepper tried to play and when she went to the little one, more shivering and shaking.

For four days we went through this performance. One day I decided to try something. I had a little wooden switch and when Pepper pawed toward Chiki, I smacked her lightly and said, "NO". When Chiki shook and shivered, I also smacked her lightly and said, "Stop it. She is not hurting you". That ended the problem. They became sisters and are still best friends. There is only one problem and that is when there are other dogs around, Pepper is very protective of the little one, so we have to separate them by putting Chiki inside.

In time I taught Pepper to do the same things that Chiki did. They have exercise and so do I. Pepper did not want to learn to 'speak' and Chiki was afraid to jump through the hoola hoop, so they each did one special thing that the other one did not. They learned to sit, sit pretty, dance, roll over, lie down, play dead, and stay. They can jump hurdles, go through an obstacle course separately, and with Chiki leading the way they play follow the leader through the obstacle course. They can fetch and return with the ball, and shake a paw. Pepper jumps through the hoola hoop and Chiki speaks. In the end, Chiki gives me a big hug as well. What a pleasure this has been.

In good weather I often took the dogs to visit my parents. One such day we were sitting on Mom and Dad's porch. Dad said, "The dogs must be thirsty. Get them some water". I went into the house and brought out a large cottage cheese container of water. Dad remarked, "That is too small. How can they have a drink out of that?" This was a time for Dad to enjoy something new. "You think that's too small. Watch this, Dad".

There was a milk jug on the porch that Mom used to water her plants. I filled up the jug and the cottage cheese container, and then put them down side by side. I sat down with Mom and Dad and said, "Now watch". Pepper immediately went to the milk jug for a drink. There was much laughter. It just happened that way unexpectedly the first time and of course after that, it was a normal procedure for us. Dad never got over that one and told everyone. Such simple pleasure is wonderful to watch.

Dad eventually had his open-heart surgery in the summer of 2001. The first surgery was cancelled when he was already by the operating room door. Dad called me from Vancouver General Hospital. "Come and get me. I am ready to go home". I was shocked. He was still groggy when I picked him up.

The second surgery was cancelled by phone. Two waits for surgery took their toll on Dad. He finally had a quadruple bypass and valve replacement operation. This procedure made a noticeable change in Dad. He was not an easy man to deal with at the best of times, but this was worse than normal.

After the surgery was done, he was very agitated. He climbed over the rail of his bed and tore open the stitches in his leg. He was angry with Mom and threatened to hit her. He demanded that I bring him his clothes so he could leave. I did not understand this behaviour and was upset when he threatened to hit Mom. She did not deserve that. He was eighty-six years old and this was a huge operation, not to mention the medications he had to take. What concerned me about his behaviour toward Mom was that they would be home together upon his discharge from hospital. I decided not to get that far ahead of things.

Many times I had to stop him from this destructive behaviour. "Dad stop! This is nonsense. Mom does not deserve to be treated this way." He would usually stop for a few minutes, before asking, "Bring me my clothes. I want to go home". I would reply, "Dad, they are in the other car". "Ok then, bring them tomorrow". Or I would say, "Your clothes are in the car but it is raining outside, I'll bring them later". These things seemed to settle him down for a while. On several occasions it was necessary to have him tied down so he would not crawl over the rail. It seemed to settle him. I asked the nurses to tie him so he could move but not get out.

After three weeks Dad was discharged. Although his heart was working fine, he was very agitated. It was here that we learned he had an infection in his leg and had to be readmitted to hospital. He was not a happy camper and he was exhausting to deal with. Dad's nephew Terry was visiting him at the hospital. I guess Dad complained that he wanted to be home. Terry called me from there and told me that Dad wanted his clothes so he could go home. I told Terry, "We don't want him home till he is well enough to stay home". Once Terry understood the situation, he helped by telling Dad some things that quieted him for a while.

It was a difficult situation for Mom. She was old as well, and dealing with this was wearing her out. These hospital visits were often short. It was important for Mom to rest while she could. After some time, Dad was discharged again and slowly healed.

My brother's ex-wife had a cousin living in England with a wife and two daughters. They had visited here several times while David and his second ex-wife were still together. The cousin, his wife and one daughter came to visit again in the fall of 2000 after the divorce, going to see my brother in his country home for a week. After returning back to David's ex-wife's place, the daughter decided to go back to the country for another week by herself.

During that week while the daughter visited in October 2000, my brother and this young woman decided that she would return the following month and live with my brother.

David, my brother moved this young woman from England in with him in November of 2000. By February 2001, she had him change his 'Will'. This was no surprise to us. What was upsetting is that she was in her early thirties and he was in his sixties. We all knew there was a plan there. To make it worse, she was the daughter of his ex-wife's cousin in England. She had come to visit and carefully planned this whole thing ahead of time. He was excited about the idea that she was young enough to be his daughter. We all knew that this was not a normal situation. Not only was he old enough to be her father, he was also very sick. When I mentioned this to him, he got terribly angry. He would not listen; his ego was in the way. I had to leave it alone, and 'Let it Go'.

In October 2001, my brother David died. My Dad's world was shattered. He was very irritable and totally unpredictable.

We tried to get back some of the money that my brother owed Mom and Dad, but it was very costly and Dad was not able to stand up in court. Mom and Dad had three break-ins at their home, where their paper work had been stolen plus many other valuables. Some of the paper work included cancelled checks and other information. There wasn't much official proof that Dad had given him all this money and purchased things for him. We all knew of the vehicles Dad had bought him. Two new trucks for sure, a backhoe and riding tractor. There were many other things that Dad purchased for him, like a boat and other toys.

This was a bad time for my parents, and not great for me either. I only had one brother. Now he was gone. His estate was lost. The loss of money was not such an issue for me. I had worked and had my own pension, however, it was very disturbing for my parents. All the work, money, and effort were in vain. It was especially distressing when we got a letter from the woman's lawyer saying that we were invited to attend a "Celebration of Life" at my brother's farm. It was by invitation only. Mom did not want to go and neither did Dad. They were very upset that they needed to be invited to their own son's funeral.

This woman became very rich, very fast. My brother was a collector of silver, coins and gold. He had acreage and new vehicles. He had boats, and many other toys. My brother worked for many years and had a good pension. She had arranged all the pensions and bank accounts to go to her in the event of his death. He was so sure he was going to live, that he did what she asked. He also bought her a car. By the time this woman left to go back to England, she had well over a million dollars. She had been with him from November 2000 to October 2001.

This further destroyed Dad's living abilities and he became deeply depressed. During this period of time I realized what the third reason was that mom lived. She was totally honest about the money, equipment, vehicles and everything else that they had given my brother.

Late December of 2002, Mom took a turn for the worse and went to the hospital.

Dad was not able to drive any more, so every day I went to fetch him and we would go to see Mom. One day when I went to pick up Dad, he was waiting for me with a little bag in his hand. He looked like a little boy who would get into trouble. I knew immediately that he was taking a laxative to Mom. Laxatives were Dad's cure for everything. He felt that if you could 'poop', you would be fine.

Mom had problems with her stomach and I was concerned that this would make things worse. I told him, "Dad, if you give that to her, she may blow up". When we got to the hospital, he gently handed her the bag and said, "Ask your doctor if you can take this. I think it would help". Mom just took the bag and handed it to me. "Put this in the locker."

The family came to see Mom once again.

The afternoon of January 6, while I visited with Mom, she said: "Save your energy. You're going to need it". Then as I was leaving to get supper for everyone, she asked, "Are you going to come back and put me to bed?" I told her not to worry. I would be back. I still get a chuckle out of these last words that we spoke. After supper I went back to put her to bed. She was very quiet. I took her to the washroom, helped her to brush her teeth and tucked her into bed.

About 3:30 in the morning the phone rang. It was the hospital saying that Mom had taken a turn for the worse. The family should come. Don was with Dad. I called there asking if they wanted to come with me. Of course they came.

When we arrived, Mom was labouring hard to keep breathing. She was not really coherent. I remember thinking, "Does she know we are here?" She seemed to know we were there because she held on to my hand. Her heart gradually beat slower and slower, till it stopped. I could not help but remember the last night she and I spent with Randy, and the many other special times we shared.

In the morning of January 7th, 2003 after three weeks in the hospital, Mom died of an aneurysm in her stomach. Dad, Don and I, were with her.

I was devastated. I lost my Mom, my mentor and best friend, and now I was left to cope with Dad. I was frightened and unsure of what to do. First we had to deal with Mom's death.

I asked Dad what he wanted done. His answer was, "You do what you think is best. Just be sure when we go to the cemetery, you put a picture on the marker of her and I together. When I die, I will go there too." My heart ached for my Dad. He was completely lost.

My church family came through for me during this upsetting time. Many of my friends attended the service. Pastor Kevin had been away on business, but returned the day before and was able to officiate at Mom's funeral. I had forgotten to ask the Worship Pastor to come and lead the singing. He came without being asked. How I needed them there. Just knowing they were there made me feel more secure. I still think about that. How wonderful it is to have a church family.

My family was all here. They all loved their grandma. The grandchildren called her 'Baba', which she was always pleased about. That is the endearing name for grandmother in Ukrainian.

We had Mom's funeral. Dad was very disturbed. He kept saying quite loudly during the service, "I didn't know she was sick. She never told me she was that sick". This was Mom. She never made a big fuss.

During Mom's stay in hospital, I prayed to the Lord that if it was time for her to go that He would take her quickly with as little pain as possible.

In the book of James, Chapter 1:5 and 6 it says: "If any of you needs wisdom to know what you should do, you should ask God, and He will give it to you. God is generous to everyone and doesn't find fault with anyone. When you ask for something, don't have doubts. A person who has doubts is like a wave that is blown by the wind and tossed by the sea".

My prayers were answered and she did not suffer. Mom only had pain for a little while and only at the very end. There had been an aneurysm in her stomach. She just got weaker and weaker.

My Mom was always there for me. This was my last tribute to Mom:

Catherine Karenko
November 22, 1914 – January 7, 2003

Our Mom, Catherine was born November 22, 1914, in Alberta to Sam and Maria Florkow. She lived on a farm with her parents and three brothers. Her brothers all predeceased her by many years.

In July 1934, Mom married our Dad, Nick Karenko, and they had been married for 69 years.

We all loved Mom dearly (each for our own reasons).

In October 2001, my brother died. Mom suffered the loss quietly and tried to help Dad through it.

Mom very seldom forced things except on rare occasions. She always loved us and let us learn from our own mistakes.

Rarely did Mom say anything bad or negative about anyone. If she did, we listened because there had to be a good reason. Mostly she always had kind things to say or said nothing at all.

It was very comfortable to just be with Mom and not talk at all. We just enjoyed being together.

Everyone was welcome at Mom and Dad's. She loved company. We could always bring our friends over even now at 88 years of age.

Mom was the boss in her home and if I went to wipe a cupboard or a canister, she would say, "What are you doing now?" "I can do that myself." I would just tell her I had nice soapy water and that was it.

Mom was so practical.

Plans had been made, prior to her being so sick, for Dad to have oral surgery at the end of January. One evening at the hospital I said, "Maybe we should postpone Dad's surgery". She said, "What for, he has to eat".

She had lost weight and her rings were too big for her. One day she said, "I'm afraid I will lose my rings, they are too big". I told her, "Mom let's get them made smaller". Guess what she replied? "Then they won't fit you when I go". "Never mind that", I said, "I will make them bigger". So we did have them made smaller.

She could be so funny.

I personally enjoyed my time with Mom. She loved to go for a drive. We used to do that often, Mom, Dad and I. Sometimes we would look for bargains, sometimes groceries. Sometimes we went to Cloverdale and had lunch and bought Ukrainian sausage. Other times we just went for a drive and then home to have a game of cards or marbles. Mostly she just liked to be with family.

Mom was a good, kind, thoughtful and loving person. She was a good listener. She seldom got angry and if she did look out.

Mom learned the 'Art of Letting Go' and never took things personally. She never held a grudge that we knew about. Mom was a quiet, private person. She seldom complained, so when she did, we knew it was serious.

Mom taught me the Joy of Gardening. Many hours she spent outside in her garden.

Mom died like she lived, quietly without a fuss. She was a wonderful Mom, Grandma, and Great Grandma. She taught all of us. She let us make our own mistakes and was there throughout.

If I had a problem, Mom's favourite saying was "Don't stir the poop (she used the other word) or it will stink. Many times that saved my day, at home, at work or wherever.

Mom was my best friend and I will miss her terribly.

James 1:4 says: "Endure until your testing is over. Then you will be mature and complete and you won't need anything".

See you later Mom!!!

A quote I think fits here now: "You can finish school and even make it easy. However, you will never finish your education and it is seldom easy". Author Unknown

First my brother's illness, then Mom's, the heart surgery and the death of both my brother and Mom put Dad over the edge. After my brother's death, Dad became demented and suicidal. After Mom died, the situation escalated. Dad was at the stage where he could not even dress himself. He was obsessed with killing himself, and was 85% blind with Macular Degeneration. I wondered, "What do I do now?" He could not be left alone. Milt was going downhill.

Milt was not well, but supportive of whatever I had to do to help Dad, which was helpful as my dad and my husband did not see eye to eye for years. Our boys did not live here, but came as often as they could. I am forever grateful for this.

In order to help Dad, be with Milt and our dogs, and keep my own sanity, here is what happened:

After Mom's funeral, the boys stayed for a few days, which gave me time to think about how I would look after Dad. I talked this over with Dad, and he agreed that it could work.

Every night I slept at his house. In the morning we would have breakfast together after which I would help him get dressed. He would have a snooze on the couch while I did his laundry, cleaned up and whatever else needed done in his house. We would then come to our place. It would often be close to lunchtime.

Dad enjoyed our dogs. He loved to sit on the deck in the good weather. As he would snooze on the deck, the dogs would be on each side of him. He was very much obsessed about where I was all the time, so I tried to be within hearing distance. That was not always possible because there was plenty to do around home. Milt was not able to do anything besides get himself organized for the day.

This plan worked for almost a year. There were days when Dad did not want to come to our place. He just wanted to stay home. I knew how he felt because I am twenty years younger than he and I wanted to stay home too. There was no way I could not go home. Milt was not well and we had two dogs.

It was difficult for the dogs as well, and for me to have to see them so upset. When Mom died and I began going to stay with Dad, the dogs would come to the gate and watch us get into the car. As we did this they would cry and hang their tails. Then they would go up the stairs to the back porch. As they got more used to the idea, they would watch, hang their tails and go.

Finally they would look to see if Dad was with me, then turn around and go. Amazing how they learned to understand. They would howl and cry with joy when we came back. I felt badly for them, but that was the way it was. I was grateful that Dad enjoyed the dogs. It gave him pleasure and it helped me a little.

This would have been an unbearable year if my cousin Harvey had not been generous with his time. I told him how difficult it was for me to get to church on Sunday mornings. Milt would come over to stay with Dad while I went to church and Sunday school, where I worked with the children. Some Sundays Milt was hardly strong enough to make it over on time. He would get rattled and lock himself out of the house and his truck. Our neighbour had a key, but that all took time. It was a struggle to make it to church on time. Harvey told me that he would come over around eight so I could go. He did this for the year. When I got home from church, Dad, Harvey and I would go out for lunch. What a huge relief that was for me to know that Dad was okay. Dad and Harvey would sometimes sleep while I was gone, one on the couch, the other on the floor. It was neat to come into the house and find them both asleep. It helped me so much to continue to go to church, not just to be able to go, but to hear encouraging words was great.

For a whole year, I did this. Going to Dad's after supper, getting him ready for bed, tidyng up what needed done and going to bed. Dad did not sleep well. Often he would be awake in the night. Mostly he would wake up because he needed to use the washroom.

Many times he would not make it to the bathroom in time. Consequently the rug or the bed would then need cleaning. I put a cover on the bed so that only the sheets would need changing, but the floor was another story. I asked him if he would use an ice-cream bucket and leave it for me to empty, to which he agreed. He used the bucket and then tried to carry it to dump in the toilet. Many times he fell and spilled the bucket. Oh my!!

We progressed to a five-gallon bucket. That did not work either because he would miss the bucket and pee on the floor.

When I suggested adult pull-ups, he agreed and then as soon as I would leave the room, he'd remove them. There was no solution to this problem. Not all nights were bad, but we had more accident nights than not.

At around 1:30 a.m., one night I heard water running. I listened to hear if I could pin point where it was coming from. When I got up to investigate, I found Dad in the bathtub enjoying a bath. How he got there is beyond my understanding. He needed help to get in and out of the tub, but this night he got the strength and courage to be able to do it. I was quite surprised to find him in the tub. I just let him enjoy his bath. After that we both went back to bed. All was well for the rest of the night.

Never having a good night's rest was hard for me. I am used to having over seven hours of good sleep each night. With Dad, I doubt I ever had more than four.

Another night I remember waking up to lights on, so I got up to find Dad sitting in his favourite spot at the kitchen table. There was cereal all over the floor. When I asked what happened, he said, "I tried to get myself a bowl of cereal and it spilled". I cleaned up the spilled cereal; poured him a fresh bowl and one for myself. We just ate cereal and talked.

I spotted the old black photograph album on the counter so I asked Dad, "Were you looking at the old pictures?" "Yes I was. Do you know if we have a picture of my brother in there?" My Dad had several brothers. I asked him which brother. When he told me, I began to look, discovering that he had torn out every photo of that particular brother and destroyed every one. I still cannot figure out what he did with the pictures. There were huge holes in the album, but not one picture of that brother, and not a trace of the leftovers. There had been hurt in Dad's heart by this one individual that he could not let go of. I had known that, but thought that it had all been dealt with and that Dad had either forgiven him or forgotten about the issue. You must remember that he had to have used the largest magnifier in the house as Dad was 85% blind.

I asked him why he was still so obsessed with the situation. He again explained the story vividly. Then I said, "Dad, he has been dead for well over twenty years". His reply was, "That's a damned good thing, because if he wasn't, I'd kill him". That was when I realized how deep the hurt still was.

We went back to bed in the wee hours of the morning and slept for a little while.

It was during this time with Dad that he told me he was sorry for the way things went with my brother. He said, "I was too young to have kids. I was a kid myself. I didn't know any better". I in turn told him, "Dad you need not feel badly about anything. You do not have to go to the grave feeling guilty. God has been good to me. I was able to work and arrange for my own retirement. I am fine and now I am able to help you". He would sometimes cry. Many mornings we had this conversation while he ate breakfast. It was soothing to hear him tell me that he felt badly for the difference he made between my brother and myself. It was also wonderful to not be resentful and be sincere when I told him how I felt.

I was able to arrange three separate weeks of respite for Dad in that year. He could be very difficult when he did not want to do something. I had to think of a way for him to go with an agreeable attitude, so that we could both get something out of this rest period. Not s simple assignment, but I knew that if I could get him there without a problem, it would be better for him and for me.

After much consideration, I told Dad that the government was willing to let him have an all expense paid holiday. The truth was we had to pay some money to make this week possible. There was no other way to get him there without a fuss. Hence, the first week of respite went well. I was able to go home for a week and catch up a little.

Dad seemed to have a good week and the change was great for us both. I totally had an enjoyable week of respite at home. Milt and the dogs were happy to have me back.

After this break, I was able to get a day for Dad in a facility that was called 'Come Share'. He enjoyed going there and it was good for me to have a few free hours. At Come Share they played games, had good music and lunch for the people. Sometimes they even had dancing. On such a day, I came in to find Dad dancing with a caregiver. One was dancing with him and another was holding him from behind so he wouldn't fall. Dad thoroughly enjoyed this, as he loved to dance. He enjoyed music and played the violin before he had a stroke. His fingers did not function well after the stroke. Anyhow, it was so good to see him enjoying himself.

As Dad got used to going to 'Come Share' they offered him another day, but he did not want to go there twice a week. He said one day was good.

Come Share was only about a twenty-minute drive, but Dad felt it was very far away. I knew that his dementia was worsening because he often would point to a road or a house telling me a story of when he lived there, which I knew never happened.

On our way to Come Share one Thursday morning Dad said, "You know Mom she did me a dirty trick". "Really Dad, what did she do?" "Well, she died". Oh my goodness. I had to come back with something to stop this thinking. After a few minutes I said, "You know Dad, she did me a dirtier trick". Now he was curious. "Ya, what?" "Well she died and left me with you." He hadn't laughed so hard in months. I wasn't sure what his response would be. Whew!!

He loved our dogs and often spoke of them to the folks at Come Share. When he told them of the tricks that Chiki could do, they wanted me to bring her to show the people. It was then agreed that I would bring her in for them to enjoy. I did that once in a while. The folks there really enjoyed seeing her perform and also loved to pet her. They told me stories of their own pets of the past and it was a good thing for them. As for me, I loved to do it, but I also missed the time to myself. Dad was pleased when I brought the dog, especially when she found him amongst all of the folks there. He was pleased to be special.

They had great entertainment for the people at Come Share. One such day they had old time music and were encouraged to dance. Dad loved music and he loved to dance. When I got there to pick Dad up one Thursday, one care aid was holding on to his belt and another was dancing with him. He looked so cute and so pleased with himself.

It was slowly getting harder to deal with Dad. It was difficult for both of us. As much as I wanted to be with him, I also wanted to be at home. I had many things that I wanted to do both at his home and mine. It got more and more difficult for us to get ready to leave his place. Some days Dad just wanted to stay at his place. I could understand that, but I also knew that I could not leave him alone. I would have had it on my heart forever, if something happened to him while I was not there. One day, Dad just refused to get ready to come home with me. After much coaxing, and persuading, we finally made it to our place. Dad was not in a great frame of mind and wanted to take a taxi back. He had never ridden in a taxi, so that was not a concern. As I cleaned up after supper, Dad sat on the stairs waiting to go home. Suddenly he just got up and started walking. He had a hard time walking, and used a cane. I convinced him to come back. I did not finish cleaning up. We just went to his place. There was no reasoning with him. That happened on several occasions. I could not let him go. He had lost all sense of direction, did not remember where he lived, and could not punch in the code for the alarm system.

After getting Dad into bed that night, I sobbed, and prayed for God to help me. I could not keep doing this. I got into bed and fell sound asleep. Dad slept well that night too. I guess the exercise helped. When I awoke in the morning, I had a man's name in my mind. I knew of him. I knew his wife Gladys a little, because we had been to a Ladies Retreat some time ago, and spent a little time together there. They also attended my church. When Mom was in the hospital, I saw her there. She told me her hubby had a heart attack and he needed to rest. She was just killing time. I brought her to our place and she had supper with us. I then took her back to be with her husband. That was all I knew of them. The name kept spinning around in my head. That evening, I called them. I explained to Gladys how I had prayed and how Gary's name was in my head. She told me, "Now two sets of prayers are answered". She had also been praying that her hubby would get some work. Gary began to come over once a week to stay with Dad. He played the keyboard and guitar. Dad loved music. This was a great arrangement. Gary would arrive. I would leave and go home. Dad and Gary would go out for lunch and then pick Gladys up at her job. They would then drop Dad off at our place. This worked for a while till he got tired of it and refused to go with Gary. Dad liked Gary and really liked Gladys. He kept telling me that Gary had a very good wife. That did not help when Dad had his mind made up that he would not do something.

My friend Krystyna had moved over to Vancouver Island before Mom died. I knew she could use some financial help as she had moved with very little. I gave her a call. She came over for two weeks. Dad liked her, so it was not a problem. She told me she would stay with him during the day, but I had to be there at night. Fair enough.

Krystyna stayed with Dad during the day and I would go home. Dad began to offer the house to her if she would move in with him. I was grateful that she told me this. He also asked her to read his bank statements. He told her it was all hers if she would move in. She was gracious and told him she was happy in her place. Several times during the time that Dad was in his home, Krystyna came and helped me. She and I got to know each other like family. To this day I am very comfortable with her and she with me, either in my place or hers.

Dad also began to tell people where he kept money in the house. It was necessary to change the address on this kind of information. Now all of his mail came to our place. I also had to remove his money because he was telling everyone about everything. He had money in his safe at the house. I took the money and put it in his safety deposit box. When I told him, he accepted it quite well. I explained that I was fearful for his safety and that this was better. He was fine with that.

He wanted me to stay with him permanently. He did not threaten suicide when I was with him. If he spoke of it, I would say something very casual like, "Well that would be a fine thing for me to experience. I don't think that would be very good". He would usually stop.

Not too long after this, he began offering the house to anyone and everyone. He wanted someone to stay with him at his place. He offered it to my neighbour, my cousin, and my friends, his friends and anyone that would listen. I wasn't sure how to deal with this situation. Eventually I got that sorted out.

One day when both the boys were here, Dad asked me to go to the safety box and bring him half the money. I asked him why and he told me he wanted to give it to the boys. Then he said, "You and I will split the rest". Fair enough. It was his money.

Summer came and the days were longer. That helped somewhat, however Dad was getting more and more restless and agitated. My friend Marge was on holidays and was able to help for two days a week. This was good for a while. However, slowly Dad began to complain that she was too bossy, or whatever else he could think of. He was never content for long. One evening when she brought him to our home for supper, he told me, "I don't want her looking after me any more". I asked, "Why not?" His reply was, "Well she is bossy and she hit me". I could understand what he meant by being bossy because she was very good with him and did not let him take advantage of her, but I knew she would never hit him. I told Dad, "I don't believe she hit you". "Well", he smiled, "She is bossy". Then proceeded to go sit on the deck. A few minutes later he was calling to her, "Come and sit with me".

It was sometimes difficult to distinguish the real from the imaginary. I was beginning to be pretty good at it. It was great to have day help for three days, two with Marge and one with Gary, and a few hours a day at Come Share. I got a few things done at home. The summer passed by too quickly and Marge had to return to her job, so those two days were for me to deal with again.

The days were shortening and Dad was getting more agitated. Tim was here and I went home. Tim was going to take Dad to his doctor appointment so that I could stay at home and do some things.

After lunch I got a phone call from Dad. He had my phone number in huge writing right beside his phone. He used a magnifying glass to make the call. His remark was, "So you are not taking me to the doctor today? I told him that Tim offered to take him. He said, "That's fine. I don't want to go to the doctor anyway". I told him that I would come and take him if that was better. "That's good", was his reply.

I got to the house around 3:30 in the afternoon. Tim was standing nearby and white as a ghost. Apparently he discovered Dad in the garage ready to hang himself. All that was missing was the stool. Dad could not find the stool to stand on. The rest of the apparatus was in place.

As we were taking care of this unpredictable man, I explained to the boys that he was not to be left alone for long periods. Tim had a project going in the yard and felt that Dad was fine. This was an eye opener and not a nice one. I took Dad to the doctor and told the doctor about the incident. He then prescribed some anti-psychotic medication to calm the suicidal tendencies.

When I got home and told Tim, his remark was, "We need a truck load of these". I was grateful that his sense of humour was still in tact.

At this point, Don also arrived to help out. Now they were both with Grandpa and I went home. The key for the storage area was hidden so that Dad did not have access to it. Dad had an assortment of ropes and other paraphernalia including garden tools in his storage shed. Of course Dad knew every corner of his home and the easiest ways to find things.

Don was with Grandpa and Tim was busy with something else. Grandpa had disappeared. Don called and he did not answer so he began to look, finding him in the storage shed. "Grandpa, how did you get in here?" "I have a key", was the reply. "What are you looking for?" "I need a piece of rope." He was obsessed with hanging himself. Don sidetracked him back into the house for a cup of tea. In spite of all the problems, we could not help but laugh about the key.

Dementia is a terrible thing to experience. I am sure it is just as bad to be demented as it is having a loved one suffering from it. I was getting concerned about how I would handle the things yet to come. Thank goodness I had learned to deal with things 'One Day at a Time'. It was a full time job just to keep him busy and off the thoughts of suicide. As long as someone was with him, or he was out somewhere, it was much better. However, it was pretty difficult to keep up with him.

It was somewhere in here that I found a young man in my church that needed to earn a little money, so I asked him if he would consider coming to stay with Dad on Mondays. He was ready to try. He had a grandfather living at his home and felt that he would be able to handle the situation. Thus I had Mondays to go home for a few hours. This young man came over on his bike and I gave him a ride home, on our way to our house for supper. This was a good arrangement for a few weeks, till Dad found fault with him and became difficult.

The Alzheimer Association sponsored a course on Monday nights, for two hours each week. I had heard about it and was told it was well worth attending. I knew that I needed to take this course, but I also had to find care for Dad.

I was fortunate that I had friends to help me, and some of Dad's friends too. He was not easy to deal with, but the people who knew the situation were willing to help out for a few hours a week. I took the course.

The Alzheimer's support course was a blessing for me. I learned so much. I recommend that anyone dealing with dementia in a loved one, which is the beginning of Alzheimer's, to take it. I realized that I needed to do some things. Once I took the lessons, I knew some changes were up coming. It helped give me the courage to do what I needed to do.

Dad asked me if I was paying the people who came to stay with him. I said, "Yes Dad, I am". He was visibly upset about the idea of paying someone to stay with him. "Why do you have to pay them? They don't have to do anything when they are here?" My response was, "Dad, I do not see people lined up waiting to stay with you, do you?" I explained that the people in the evening were just doing it to help out while I took the course. I made it clear that I needed to learn more about his illness. He was fine with that. I think he sometimes realized that he was difficult.

The problem was, Dad wanted me to be there at his place with him. In his thinking, this would have been the solution. Milt in the meantime was also deteriorating quietly, but he was not suicidal and was still able to help himself. I used to put his food into jars, so he could see it, and I was always home for a few hours a day, and made supper for us all at home. Milt was slowly becoming demented as well, however in a different way. Today I realize that there are many kinds of dementia. I feel that Milt's dementia was pill induced.

Milt became very reliant on me and trusted me to do what needed to be done. It was somewhat comforting to know this. He often asked, "I wonder if your Dad realizes what a good daughter he has?" I would have liked to hear how he was happy to have a good wife. This was Milt's way of paying me a compliment.

The habit was that while either one of the boys was with Dad, they would go out for supper and stay with him for the night. It was a time for me to sleep in my own bed. How grateful I learned to be for my own bed.

When one or both of the boys were here, they would take Dad out for supper and spend the night. It was one of those times. I had gone grocery shopping for us, getting to our place at around 3:15 in the afternoon. Milt was not home. He often went to the store for cigarettes or to the drug store for medications. I prepared supper and waited. I ate supper and waited. He came back about 6:30 in the evening. I was concerned and voiced it. He said, "I don't know what you're upset about, I was only gone twenty minutes". He may have fallen asleep in the truck after coming out of the drug store, and lost those hours. However he did not drive long after that. He did not say a word, just did not drive again. I took him everywhere he needed to go.

Time was a precious commodity with the situation with Milt and Dad. It was here that I changed doctors. I began to go to Milt's doctor so that I could take him and myself at the same time. His doctor was fine with that idea. This saved a little time.

I had been suspecting Milt had Parkinson's disease for a long time. During one doctor's visit with Milt, I asked the doctor, "Can I say something?" He said, "Of course". I told him I had done lots of research on Parkinson's and I felt that perhaps Milt was suffering from it as well as many other ailments. My thoughts and research of Milt having Parkinson's disease were validated, and he was referred to a specialist in that area. We had many visits with the new doctor regarding this illness. He was diagnosed and confirmed in a short period of time and was given twelve pills a day to help with the tremors.

During the drinking years and when he stopped drinking, I blamed the tremors on the alcohol, and the withdrawal from it. In hindsight, I now believe that he had Parkinson's disease for many years. I am sure the alcohol did not help the situation.

Milt became totally dependent on Tylenol Threes. He was addicted to them. It was amazing the tactics he went through to get more and more. I tried to help him through this, to no avail.

During a visit for a renewal of the Tylenol Three prescription, the doctor asked Milt, "Do you think you could be addicted to these pills?" "Nooo", was his reply. I had driven Milt there so I heard the whole conversation. I asked, "Is it ok if I say something?" The doctor told me, "Of course". I then looked at Milt and said, "You are addicted to them. You are addicted to cigarettes. You are addicted to alcohol and you are addicted to Tylenol Threes". Then to the doctor I said, "I do not want to fight about any of this any more". To which the doctor replied, "Neither do I".

I realize that as long as I was taking care of Dad and going to see him every day, Milt felt like he was not doing badly. His downward spiral came after Dad's death.

Dad's dementia was escalating. He was not happy no matter what or how much I did. It was difficult to have someone stay with him because he always found fault with each person. He complained about every one of them in a different way, always telling me that I should just stay with him. I suggested that he sell his house and we would sell ours and purchase a large rancher so that we could all live together. He told me, "That is a good idea, but let's wait for a while".

Milt in the meantime was slowly getting worse. His strength was pretty much gone. His tremors did not seem to get much better with the medication he was given. He was sleeping more than he was awake, and Dad just kept asking me, "What is the matter with him?" When I tried to explain that Milt was suffering from Parkinson's disease, he just did not get it. The truth was that Milt was suffering from many things. Polio as a child with three months in bed was not a good start. He drank for many years, which did not help. Diabetes was discovered several years back, for which he took medication. He had two brain aneurysms and many small strokes. Substance addiction was now very evident especially to Tylenol Threes. He threw these down like candy. Milt also suffered from Dementia, but he had a different personality from Dad and it did not affect him the same way. Milt also had an anxiety disorder. He was withdrawn and the dementia made that part more prevalent.

I spoke with Dad about Christmas. It was decided that he would stay at our house for a few days so I could prepare and we could enjoy the holiday. The first night was not bad but during the night Dad got very sick. He had the runs and was throwing up. Next day was fine but he wanted to go home. We managed to stay at our house till Christmas night and then I had to take him home. That proved to be a long day, as he never let up about going home, sitting on the stairs, and going outside to get a taxi that he did not have a clue about.

While Gary was with Dad one afternoon, there was a problem. Gary needed to pick his wife up after work and Dad refused to go. I had to go over and calm Dad down. He got angry with me and slapped my hand. I was holding a glass of water for him at the time. The glass broke. My hand hurt, and he was going to get up and walk. Suggesting that he sit down while I vacuumed up the glass, he got very angry. I had to force him to sit down. That was never an issue with my parents and myself. Respect was always there and I did not like what was happening. Things were getting more and more difficult. Eventually he calmed down and we went home to have supper.

After supper we went over to Dad's for the usual procedure. In the morning as I was getting him dressed for the day, he complained that he had a sore hand. "I'm sorry your hand hurts Dad. My hand hurts too." "How come your hand hurts?" he asked. "You slapped my hand yesterday. That is why we both have sore hands". Dad was so surprised, "I don't remember that", he said. I believed him and forgot about the incident, however I did know that I needed to be more serious about finding a placement for Dad.

During the month of November 2003, I began looking. There were not many nearby and I wanted to have him close to home. My friend came over from Vancouver Island once again, so that I would be free to look.

I found a nice, clean and warm feeling place about five minutes from my house, but there was a wait of approximately three years. I continued to look, finding a place about fifteen minutes away. It was clean and looked comfortable, but not as nice as the first one. I inquired about the care. I felt that this part was much the same in both places. Arrangements were made for me to come in with a deposit the following week for the one that was further away. The way things were going, I could not put it off for three years, or I would have to go there before Dad. I was concerned how I would break this news to Dad, deciding to wait till everything was in place.

The following Thursday, I was preparing to go in with the deposit for Dad's new home. Just as I was leaving the house the phone rang. When I answered it, it happened to be the lady I spoke with at the place I felt better about, and it was only a few minutes from my place. The coordinator said, I have good and bad news, which do you want to hear first? I told her, "the bad". She proceeded to tell me that someone had died. She said, "I remembered how tired you looked and how concerned you are about your father". There was a spot for Dad. Was this a coincidence? I do not believe so. God was once again intervening.

Everything was ready to be finalized and he could move in on January 3rd right after the New Year. Josh, my young friend came over to help me put some things in the car. I wanted to take as much as I could so that it would feel homey for Dad. It turned out to be easier than I thought to get him there. He asked, "What if I don't like it here". I said, "We will do whatever it takes, Dad. Let's just give it a try". The room available was on the main floor. The door to the foyer was right beside Dad's room, as was the keypad to punch for the door to open. He often asked for the combination. The staff gave him numbers and so did I. That seemed to satisfy him. After a few weeks he was able to go upstairs in the building to a more suitable environment for him. The people on the second floor were more social.

I have needed to make many life-changing decisions in life, but this was one of the toughest one I have ever had to make.

I made this decision to help everyone involved. It was difficult to leave Milt each day knowing his health was deteriorating. The boys had families of their own which made it hard for them to be here. I was grateful for every effort they made to lighten my load, and to be there for their Grandpa. I was very aware of the difficulties it caused them as well.

It was wonderful that I was able to get a placement for Dad so close to my home. I was able to visit him daily, and some days more than once. This was a pretty decent arrangement for all concerned, and the best that I could come up with.

There were many different ideas from various people, but I had to do what I felt was best for our family as a whole.

I have known people like this in the family, at work and in friendships. It is easier to deal with these folks if you can have some fun at the same time. It makes me think about the choices in life. Never is everyone happy. I could not keep up the pace I was going, so some big decisions had to be made.

A friend sent me the following article. It made me think about life and the people in it. Not everyone was content with the decision to have Dad cared for in a place other than his or mine. Not everyone was pleased with many things, but not everyone was involved in our lives either.

Tater People

Some people never seem motivated to participate, but are just content to watch while others do the work.

They are called 'Spec Taters'.

Some people never do anything to help, but are gifted at finding fault with the way the others do the work.

They are called 'Comment Taters'.

Some people are very bossy and like to tell other people what to do, but don't want to soil their own hands.

These are called 'Dick Taters'.

There are those who say they will help, but somehow
just never get around to do the actual work.

They are called 'Hezzie Taters'.

Some people can put up a front and pretend they are someone they are not.

They are called 'Emma Taters'.

Then there are those who love others and do what they say they will. They
are always ready to stop what they are doing and lend a helping hand.
They bring real sunshine into peoples lives.

They are called 'Sweet Taters'.

Author Unknown

Say what you mean, and mean what you say.

Chapter 9

SURRENDER

Come to me, all who are tired from carrying
heavy loads, and I will give you rest.
Matthew 11:28

When things got bad enough that I could not decide what to do, when I was so tired and unsure that I felt like just lying down and giving up, and when everything I tried failed, somehow this verse would come to mind.

Sometimes I could not remember the exact words, but I knew in my heart that if I let God take over, I could rest. The problem is that often I did not think about it, till all else failed.

Interesting how, as a human being, it takes so long to just 'Let Go'. Letting Go is not easy to do but if I remember the 'Letting Go' article, it really does help.

I love the hymn 'I Surrender All'. It makes a lot of sense. It all belongs to Him anyhow. No wonder it never works when I try to fix or control a situation.

"I surrender all. I surrender all.
All to Thee my blessed Saviour.
I surrender all".

This is the chorus to this precious song. I love the whole song, but this is all I really need to remember is the chorus.

Once again, I will flash back to December 1977. I am remembering these circumstances and the lessons learned. Sometimes it is hard to stay in chronological order, because many matters run into one another along the way. Some situations came up while others were still happening.

On December 17, 1977 at approximately 5:15 p.m. I did just that. I surrendered it all to the Lord. I had been sick for a week and off work. Milt left for another drinking spree and took the car that was working. I had to get to work. My little car was not in working order. I walked to the main road and my boss picked me up. Coming home, he dropped me off at the same corner. I was very tired and was slowly walking home when Milt pulled up and asked if I wanted a ride. He was smoking a cigar and had been drinking. He looked like a gangster or an actor with a poor attitude. We did not have far to go. It was difficult to see him like that again. He drove into the driveway of my home and asked, "What are we going to do about Christmas?" I told him, "I know what the kids and I are going to do. I don't know about you. If you are sober, you can join us. If not, I don't want to see you". With that, I got out of the car and said to the Lord, "I can't do this any more. Please help me". I felt like a ton of weight had been removed from my shoulders. I went into the house and fell on my bed sobbing for about two hours. The boys could not figure out what the problem was and I was not able to explain it. All I knew was that the dam had broken and I felt better.

Right now as I am writing this, there are several things happening in and around my family. As I think about each circumstance, I come up with lots of ideas that might help, however I also know that they are all individuals with their own thoughts and ideas. God is taking care of them too. My good intentions often cause conflict, or add more stress to an already stressful situation. So, I must 'Let Go and Let God' do His work. His plan works better than mine.

This does not mean that I have to stop caring. It just means I have to 'Let Go'!!!

It sounds so simple, but it is difficult to do until you practice it long enough. It is still difficult, but when I really need to use it, I know it works.

<u>Peace is not the absence of trouble it is the presence of God.</u>

My personal experience has shown me how to identify when I am not 'Minding my own Business'. A thermostat in my gut empties out when I am sticking my nose into someone else's business is how I can tell. I have this pit, actually more like a crater, in my stomach. It feels hollow and empty. Not a good feeling.

Every person has a thermostat. Some folks feel it in their heart, some get a dry throat, and some just get very tired. Others cannot eat. I have known people who get nauseous. My feeling is in my gut. That is my sign to give up and Let God take over. Just leave it alone. You will get to know when to back off. To trust your thermostat no matter what it might be. What a freeing choice.

A quote from the Kidney Foundation Newsletter also makes good sense: "We can't solve problems by using the same type of thinking we used when we created them".

Love is a great thing, but when it makes us crazy, it's not so great. It is awful to feel trapped. I have learned that no matter how impossible it seems at the moment, it does eventually get better, if I can 'Let Go' of whatever or whomever it is that is causing the problem.

By 1991, I had made many changes in my life. One of these changes was to try to travel a little.

Christmas Eve of December 1991, I decided to get baptized to let people know that I was serious about my love for God. Not one person from my family came to this event. Mom was concerned because it was not my church of origin. She asked, "Why are you not going to our church?" They had not been to church for many, many years. I asked, "What church is that Mom? You have not been in church in ages". She did not reply, but did not come either. Milt was not too happy either, so he did not come, and the boys were in the midst of making their own choices. I do not remember all the details. I invited four friends and I was content.

When I first started to attend my church Milt was not a happy camper, often saying, "If you are contributing money to the church, we sure could use some here". Or he would ask, "How much money are you giving to the church?" At this point, I said, "Milt, I am not giving near as much to the church as you are blowing up in cigarette smoke". No more questions or remarks about this.

I continued to attend church for another year, deciding to become a covenant member. Having been a member for over two and a half decades, I have not regretted the decision ever.

Eventually everyone accepted my church attendance, even Milt often would say, "You better hurry or you will be late for church". Those words were joy to my heart.

After my brother moved up country, he came back for a visit and also to pick up a boat that he left behind. It was an old boat and he did not have room for it when he moved. Upon arrival at our place, he was very upset and agitated. "The buggers said I could leave the boat and pick it up later. Now the damned boat is not there." On and on he went. Milt had gone to bed. Finally I suggested that David phone the people and ask about it. Well that started another tirade. What did I know about these people? Why would he call there when the boat should have been where he left it? The fact was that the original house had been destroyed and a new home was being built on the property. The boat was likely in the way. I asked if he would like me to call. He was too upset to think straight. After several minutes of dressing down, I just turned and went downstairs and did my ironing. He sat quietly. When my ironing was done, I came back up. He then handed me the paper with the phone number. Eventually he got his boat and left.

Another behaviour I changed made a huge difference in my life. I became very aware of what I shared with the alcoholic. When I shared something with him, he would often save it to use against me when he felt like it. I only told him what was safe and could not be used as a weapon. It was with great care that I shared my thoughts or feelings with him once I sorted that all out. At one point, I even told him I felt this way. I explained that I would be very careful what I shared with him. This kind of care saved me lots of trouble. This behaviour change was difficult for me to learn, because I am often spontaneous. I find it hard to hold back.

I have many good friends, so sometimes I would share with one of them, or just wait to see if I needed to share at all. My life was not in so much turmoil, once I figured this out. The fact of life is that alcoholism is an illness, and I needed to be aware of these things.

This lesson saved me a lot of heartache one Thursday morning. It was my day off and Milt often sat and talked with me while I prepared food, or did other chores. We were chatting when suddenly he said, "You must really feel guilty". I asked, "About what?" "About leaving like a thief in the night." I did not react, and I did not answer. There was no need to be defensive. I just waited. I knew him well enough to know that he would bring it up again another time. So I just became busy and did not hear for the moment.

A few weeks later, same day of the week, same spot, same circumstance, out of the clear blue he said, "You must feel pretty guilty". I asked, "About what?" "Leaving like a thief in the night." I replied this time, "Yes I do feel guilty". He then asked, "What about?" My reply, "That I didn't do it ten years sooner." That was the end of that subject forever.

After Milt retired, he would sometimes vacuum which was a big help for me. When I arrived home one evening, he had vacuumed and swept the carpet so that it was all even including the stairs. As I opened the door he said, "Can you walk on the sides of the stairs?" "Why", I asked. "Well I just swept them". I was tired and did not remember him ever walking on the sides of the stairs. "I do not ever remember you walking on the sides when I vacuumed, do you?" I came up normally and that was the end of that topic.

Without 'Surrender' those incidents could have caused huge fights, or I could have walked on the sides of the stairs and been resentful, or I could have tried defending myself. Defusing the situation eliminated many such incidents.

Without surrender I would not have had the pleasure of trips away from home.

During the Christmas period of 1987, my friend Rita was over for tea. We got talking about trips. Her hubby did not want to go away and neither did mine. After much discussion, we decided on a few days away. Both of us worked in education and had time off for Christmas holidays. After checking out flights, costs and accommodation, we decided to give Reno a try. The cost was reasonable, the flight short and we needed a change. It did not take long to fly to Reno, and neither of us had ever been there. Planning to take a trip to Lake Tahoe and other places while we were there was in the plan. When we arrived in Reno, it had snowed. We only had a few days, so decided to take in what we could right there and go on tours another time.

The life we were used to, compared with what we experienced in Reno, were two totally different worlds. Neither one of us were interested in gambling. We were mostly interested in seeing the difference between what we knew and what we were seeing. We tried the machines and decided to shop and eat instead. The few days we were there went very quickly. It was a good experience.

 This was a taste of the outside world, and I wanted more. My friend, Betty Lou and I were in similar situations where our husbands did not want to travel and we did. During the fall of 1990 we decided to take a trip in February after the Christmas season.

At work my busiest times were September, October and June. I was fortunate that I could bank some hours of time worked when we were super busy and take them later on when it was calmer. Betty Lou could plan her holidays ahead of time.

A decision was made that we would try a short trip to Palm Springs and see how compatible we were. Probably one of the wisest ideas we had was to tell one another when we needed a break. Then take it.

As soon as we decided to take this trip, I had to figure out a way to make some extra cash. I chose to try making some Christmas tree pins out of 'Friendly Plastic'. 'Friendly Plastic' was a new substance that could be heated and formed or cut into any shape you wanted. I began heating and cutting this material into tiny trees, sticking tiny pieces of different colours on for decorations. I put it in the oven for a minute or so. This is when the decorations blended into the tree. When this was completed, I glued a pin to the back, and lo and behold, a Christmas tree pin. I made one for each of the grandchildren, one for Mom and one for myself. After making several more, I took them to work, asking one of my friends there how much she would pay for such an item. She told me she wouldn't pay more than $8.00. This figure was reasonable for the buyer and for me. This little project became so popular that my mom would come over on Saturdays, and we cut and made these little trees all day. Eventually people began asking for earrings to match and I could hardly keep up. I sold enough to pay for my trip to Palm Springs.

We were looking forward to our trip to Palm Springs. Before we left, however, Milt took a spell of some kind. He had an anxiety disorder. Milt had never flown and was concerned about me flying. He was not keen on me going, so he likely worked himself up somewhat. I could not go without him being checked out and feeling better. After his doctor appointment and some medication, he was better and we were off.

Betty Lou and I held hands as the plane left the ground. How excited we were, and a bit scared too. When we landed, Betty Lou went over and hugged a palm tree. What fun we had there. We stayed in a reasonably priced motel. I did not feel safe, so each evening I moved the chest of drawers and put it so that the door could not easily be opened. We only slept there and it was clean, but we learned that for future escapades we needed to be more careful of our accommodations. To get the feel of how rich folks holiday, we went to The Marriott Hotel and checked it out just for fun. We toured the area where the affluent folks had homes. We saw Elvis Presley's, Bob Hope's, Liberace's homes as well as the Walter Annenberg estate. Desert Springs Hotel and Spa was wonderful. We had a massage there and experienced all seven pools, had supper and drove back to our quarters. Each time we drove somewhere we got lost. After driving around for a little while we always managed to find the corner we were familiar with, then we knew where we were. We picked fruit off orange trees, and went to the Date Gardens. I am very fond of dates and wanted to see how they grew. We even learned the romance and sex life of the date. We had a taste of many different kinds of dates which was really interesting because neither one of us knew there were so many varieties. My goal was to see the 'Date Gardens', and bring home as many varieties of dates as possible. Betty Lou was interested in the seeing the cactus at 'The Living Desert'. This too was fascinating. We saw many different desert animals and lots and lots of different cactus. The 'Wind Energy' windmills were something we had not observed before. The William Holden Collection at the Museum was unbelievable, and the tram experience was unforgettable. Palm Springs was quite hot, but once on top of the mountain, it smelled like home. We had a taste of how wonderful it is to experience something new, and we found we got along just fine. It was so much fun, we couldn't wait to plan another trip.

A dilemma arose at my job. A person was assigned to the school to work with me. We worked together for some time when I noticed that she was doing some strange things. She took an antique chair covering that was worn out and embroidered all night to fix it. The boss had purchased it for a chair he had bought. Flirting with the men and getting very excited when our boss would come in. One such day, she said to me, "Why does my heart flutter when he comes down the hall?" I had known this for a long time, but I could not say anything. Here was a good opening. I am very clear when I say something that is important. We were due to go on a break and so I said, "Let's talk while we have coffee".

While at coffee break, I told her, "If I were you, I would think about what you are doing. You have a husband and family. You have a lovely home. This man you are excited about has a history of women in his life. You have a lot to lose". This was all done to keep her from making what I felt would be a big mistake, however she did not take it that way.

Those were words I wished I had never spoken. After that she turned on me and made work life difficult.

My job was to delegate the duties to the people involved directly with the office. To be sure the office ran smoothly and that everything was completed as required was part of my duties. She was the other full time person so this made it very difficult, because now she was annoyed. The things that happened after that were unbelievable.

Rumours were spread around the school and the staff began to treat me differently. Notes were left by her "Do this or that, Diana's orders". Directions were imperative, given because the duties needed to be done. This went on for almost a year. She posted out of the school for a short time and then returned. We had three months to return to a job after taking a posting. Obviously, it was not that bad at this work site or she would not have returned. I made it clear that there would be no more shenanigans. Work was work and it needed to be done.

In the meantime, the staff began to notice the difference. Things became more bearable for me, and the boss we had was given notice of a transfer.

When our new principal arrived, this partner of mine began more trouble.

Firstly, we as a staff had made a book for our previous principal's retirement that was funny and very personal. She made copies of this book, and sent it to various people who were not involved. Word finally got around. The staff was not pleased. 'Thank you, Lord'. Then came the accusations that I was causing her an ulcer. Many such things happened. I was very tired of it all, but I did not know what to do.

Talking with my Mom, I told her I felt like quitting my position and finding another job. Mom's words were, "Don't you quit. Let her quit. She is the one who has a problem".

I did not enjoy being in this situation, so when our new boss arrived, I told him all about it. What an unusual way for a principal to begin a new term, in a new school. I did not like what needed to be done, but I also knew that I could not spend another term like the last one.

The new principal was great in dealing with the situation. He first asked me if I wanted to use his office to have a meeting with this woman. I told him that I wanted him there to hear what was said. It was important that all the issues be dealt with. I let her speak first. We discussed everything.

He suggested that we have a 'divorce'. This took some time, but eventually she did move on. Later I learned that there were problems in the other places she went. This did not make the previous year any easier, however it helped somewhat. This was a hurdle that I will never forget, but taught me a great deal.

After this person came another lady. This was a special individual. I knew that as soon as she came. She was comical and very gentle. In the beginning I did not know much about her except that in the school she came from, one of her duties was doing the bookkeeping. She had a problem with the accounting so she took it home and her husband did it. This was unacceptable, but no one knew. I was both pleased and concerned when she shared that with me. I was pleased that she was honest, and concerned about how the work situation would be. However I was determined that this arrangement was going to succeed. I paid close attention to what she was good at. One of her strong points was the telephone. Since we had three lines coming in, it was very important that we do it efficiently. That became one of her main duties, as well as attendance and typing. It soon became evident that phone numbers were mixed up in messages taken and other things as well. We talked about this and she shared with me that she suffered from Dyslexia and Depression. Well now it all made sense. I began to try to figure out what to do to make life bearable for us both. We eventually had a good system going that worked and we had eight good working years together. I still miss the fun times we had together, and appreciate having her as a friend.

It likely would not have been as easy to appreciate her if I had not had the previous experience. She retired shortly after I did.

To Surrender All to God is probably the most important lesson I have ever learned. To surrender and have freedom and serenity, I first had to face reality. I had to admit that life for me was unmanageable. I was powerless over alcohol, people, places and things. Once I sorted all of this out, it was easier to think.

After Milt's recovery from the Aneurysms, in July 1991, our lives settled down somewhat. I prepared plenty of meals for him. He was able to help himself. He was driving again, so he was able to pick up whatever he wanted. He did not wander far and our neighbours were wonderful about keeping an eye on things for me. Betty Lou and I planned another trip.

In February 1992, Betty Lou and I decided to go to Mexico. After a five-hour flight we landed in Porta Vollarta, where we were picked up by shuttle bus and driven to our hotel. A new experience for us being loaded into the bus like sardines: no seat belts, nothing to hang on to and away we went to beat heck. We stayed at a quaint hotel in the centre of the city, with bougainvilleas, hibiscus, banana, themacia and farmacia trees. There was so much to observe and so much to taste. Mexican people are very friendly, so the experience was warm. The first morning we experienced our first encounter with beach vending. As we walked a few blocks to the beach, we spotted a vendor selling jewellery shouting, "Good deal here, better than Kmart". We did get some good deals, and learned to bargain well. The next morning while going to the beach for breakfast at the hotel there, we saw a little bundle wrapped up under a palm tree, and discovered it was a little boy about four asleep. That was the only part I did not enjoy. There were many children begging everywhere.

One morning on the way to a restaurant in the hotel on the beach, a man much younger than I reached his hand out to me and said, "I'm very lonely". I just kept on walking. Betty Lou remarked, "That man just made a pass at you". We had a good laugh.

We walked the Boardwalk, known as The Malicon, where we shopped and saw many unusual things. The market place was fascinating, but the money was difficult to figure out sometimes. Many times Betty Lou would call me after buying something. "I can't understand this money thing. Did I get the right change?" At that time an American $10.00 bill was worth 3,000 pesos.

The Las Arcos Rocks were very interesting, as were the homes. The buildings were quaint and not painted. "No paint – no taxes", we were told, and there was no rhyme nor reason to additions on homes. Mismaloya Beach was fabulous, and the Mexican Fiesta was out of this world. The dancers were wonderful. I love Spanish music and dance. The fiesta was in a hotel on the other side of the city where things were much more costly. Getting there was something we could have done without. The cab driver stopped for nothing, went around everything, and got us to the fiesta early. There was time to take a walk, where we saw our beach vendor asking much higher prices. While talking with him we told him how we knew him and where we were staying. The silver necklaces and rings that we paid $10.00 U.S. for were starting at $30.00 on the beach near The Sheraton Hotel. After the vendor realized that we spent a lot at the other beach, Betty Lou bought several pieces of jewellery for her daughters at $10.00 American.

Our hotel was situated in the centre of the city and we could see a lot of area from our balcony where we often enjoyed fruit. The streets were made of cobblestone in that section of town. Daily there were men filling the deep potholes with a thin tar mix.

The room we were in was fine, but had a lot of things that needed to be repaired.

We even had a pet. One evening in our hotel room I spotted a salamander or maybe a gecko on the toilet tank. I called him 'Sal' for Salvatori. Each time I wanted Betty Lou to see it, it would disappear. She thought I was imagining things. Sal was there many times. I told her he was afraid of her. We had such a good laugh about that and the song I wrote about our room. The song is to be sung to the tune Maniana, and went like this:

Maniana, Maniana,
Maniana is soon enough for me.
The weather she is perfect.
The place is beautiful to see.
Without so much exhaust,
How lovely it would be!!

Maniana, Maniana,
Maniana is soon enough for me.
The toilet she is plugged up,
And the sink is plugged up too.
And if we have to take a poop,
We don't know what we'll do.

Maniana, Maniana,
Maniana is soon enough for me.
The curtain rod is stuck,
And lots of things is broken,
The window she is stuck again,
And a pop can holds it open.

Maniana, Maniana,
Maniana is soon enough for me."

It was at this point that we decided that on any trip after this one, we would have better accommodations. This one was better than the one at Palm Springs, but we would go finer yet.

There were many places to see and lots of places to eat. Often we had a late lunch after having fruit in the hotel for breakfast. We were told about one particular place, loved it and went there for supper every day. They had wonderful food and entertainment. Watching folks doing laundry in the Rio Cuale River intrigued us.

We spotted a street entertainer outside the market place. I sat on the stairs to listen to him play several times. He was a great guitar player and sang as well. As soon as he was done, he would take his teeth out, put them in his pocket and away he would go. Following him for a little while, we watched him do this several times. That was a different type of entertainment. He enjoyed seeing us and posed for some pictures.

The churches were very ornate, with beautiful stained glass windows. We went to spend our final few days with my cousin, Betty and her hubby, who lived in the next state of Nayarit a distance away, but she was able to come and pick us up.

With my cousin and her husband, we visited the village of Punta DeMita. It was a fishing village made up of palapa huts, including the church. These humble abodes were made of wooden structures with palapa leaves for the roofs. We took candy for the children. I took pictures of them as well, running out of film. They were so excited, I just kept clicking and they kept smiling. How I regret not having extra film. My cousin spoke Spanish and was able to communicate with the whole village. Betty took us to Paradiso Escondito, which means hidden paradise, where we had a wonderful lunch of shrimp and red snapper. After lunch I went to the washroom where a little girl about four was washing the floor with a mop dipped in the toilet that had not been flushed. I was happy we ate before I saw this. Betty and her hubby took us to several different places, but I was very fascinated with the Siera Madrais Mountains and the town of Valle De Banderas. The police drove around in a truck, some in the cab but mostly in the back with their guns very noticeable. I spoke with one and told him my son was a policeman in Canada. I became popular and they showed me all around the quarters. This area was quite small and you had to step down to get inside.

There was a wonderful church that we stopped to see in going through Valle De Banderas. This church was very old and very interesting. As we travelled through we found a shoemaker in San Jose De Valle, where Betty Lou purchased a pair of handmade shoes. We stopped to buy some fruit at a stand, noticing that the family lived behind the stand with curtains for walls of their home.

After this wonderful tour, we went to my cousin's home for a fabulous supper and a good rest. They had a pool and a beautiful view of the ocean. We viewed iguanas that lived in the brick blocks in the entranceway to their home. The next day they drove us to the airport and we were homeward bound. What a joyous time we had. On our flight home we talked, making a decision to go somewhere again the following year, maybe for a bit longer than this one.

Before leaving home for our Mexico trip, I had acquired a big duffle bag with zippers. When we purchased our treasures, we would put them into this bag. As the bag filled, I would unzip one closure and continue to fill it. Our bag was packed to the top. When we arrived at customs, we were asked what we purchased. Beginning to explain, I showed all my receipts and so did Betty Lou. We had nothing to hide. I told the man that I purchased items for seven grandchildren and Betty Lou for her daughters. He just smiled and said, "I am glad you had a good time". What a wonderful way to end a wonderful holiday!

A year went by so quickly and we were undecided about where we would go next. Finally choosing Hawaii in February 1993. We talked about where to go, when, how we would get around, and anything else we could think of. Eventually we arranged for our Honolulu Airport flight, and to stay at the Outrigger Surf Hotel. We also made reservations for a condominium in Kehei and a car rental there. The rest we would deal after we got there.

We arrived on February 4 and were greeted by our hosts who decorated us with leis that were pretty and smelled wonderful. Both Betty Lou's lei of carnations and freesias, and mine of orchids and carnations were beautiful and smelled awesome. What a surprise that was. We knew right away that we made the right choice.

We were transported to our hotel where we freshened up and went browsing to the Market Place that was just around the corner from our hotel. It was great to just get the feel of the place. We had an early supper and took a walk along the beach enjoying the air, sleeping well that night.

The next day we took a tour of Hillo Hattie's where they made moo moos, Hawaiian shirts and blouses and many other garments. The evening was spent on the Ali'i Kai Catamaran Sunset Dinner Sail that included dinner, music and cultural dancing. It was a great way to start our holiday.

After breakfast the next morning we were off for the Grand Circle Island Tour by bus. We saw most of the Island, then on to Hanauma Bay where the movie 'Blue Hawaii' with Elvis Presley was shot, then driving along the coastline where we took in the Island of Molokai and on to Halona Point. Makapuu Beach where we watched huge waves and surfing, on to Sandy Beach and Waimanalo, past Kailua and up the Pali Cliffs for a breath taking view of Kaheohe and Kailua from 1200 feet above sea level. We saw the rain forests of Nuuanu and past Pearl Harbour, on through small places, past the military base, and a plantation. We saw sugar cane farms and pineapple growing, learning that pineapple is from the cactus family. We saw the beautiful Mormon Temple and University, past the Polynesian Cultural

Centre where we attended the Imax Theatre, after which we headed back to the hotel. It was a great tour and the driver was very comical, so the day went quickly. In the evening we took the bus to a shopping centre and back to the hotel where we dropped exhausted and slept soundly, too tired to think about tomorrow and our tour to Pearl Harbour.

The bus took us to Pearl Harbour where we saw the movie of what happened on December 7, 1941. I got a bit upset and very sad, however it did happen and important for us to see where it took place. After leaving Pearl Harbour, the bus continued on with a small tour where we learned that tourism was their biggest trade, and that in twenty years the place grew from three hotels to one hundred forty. We went through China Town, on to see the Volcanic Crater where 30,000 men, women and families are buried. The statue there is of Lady of Columbia, which signifies peace. This is where the opening scene of 'Hawaii 50' takes place. We were so fortunate to see many different kinds of trees including the banyon, tangerine, hibiscus, plumeria, ulu, japong, banana, mulberry and many others. The flower of Hawaii is the yellow hibiscus. We went through the Rain Forest and on to Paradise Park. Something I never knew that I learned that day is if you were half Hawaiian blood, you could lease land for $1.00 a year for ninety-nine years and it could go on for generations. The bus driver was again very entertaining.

Since I could remember, I wanted to see Don Ho in person. I was there and he had a show on, it was important to see him. We went that evening arriving early. It was a fun as well as exciting evening. Betty Lou was in a goofy mood. We asked to use the washroom, and for whatever reason, we were allowed to use his private washroom. Betty Lou wanted a picture sitting on his toilet. Unfortunately the photo did not turn out, or maybe fortunately.

He was a wonderful entertainer at age sixty-five. He had his twelve-year-old daughter singing with him that night, so it was extra special. We had pictures taken with him, that I often enjoy reminiscing over, and am forever grateful that we saw this performance.

The Polynesian Cultural Centre was our goal for our fourth day.

I was very tired, and really wanted to have a snooze in the afternoon before going to the Polynesian Centre. I knew that if I told my friend this, she would be concerned about me, so I suggested that we split for a while that morning. I wanted to look at some things and so did Betty Lou. This is what we did. We walked over to the Market Place together and each went our own way when we got there. I ended up purchasing a ring for one of the children and a shorts and top outfit, after which I went to the hotel and crawled into bed and promptly fell asleep. I slept so soundly I did not hear her come in. We compared our purchases and found that we bought the exact same shorts and top outfits only in different colours. We had a chuckle and went out to eat before going out for the evening.

Wow!! What a show and what a Centre. The Polynesian Cultural Centre is like a 'Mini Expo', featuring Hawaii, Samoa, Tahiti, New Zealand, Fiji, and Tonga. I may have missed some. There were huts and cultural entertainment together with a terrific dinner and show of music and dancing. What an amazing day!!

The next day we went shopping in the morning, leaving for Maui on a two-engine eighteen-passenger plane at noon. Just prior to landing in Kahului, Betty Lou got airsick. She did not throw up, just felt like it. I had some nausea medication with me and gave it to her. We had done tons of shopping so she stayed with the luggage while I went to pick up our car. Our Metro was a little pee pot of a vehicle, but big enough to hold all our stuff. We headed out to Kehei, where our condominium was. By this time Betty Lou was feeling better.

From Kahului to Kehei was about a twenty-mile drive. We did have fun trying to find our living quarters for the next few days. What a lovely condominium we had when we found it. It took us a little time to find the beaches, get used to our directions and to find the grocery store. This all had to be done before we settled for the night so we could begin to explore the next morning. We learned that we had two pools to choose from in our condo as well. The place had an ocean view, with a blue sky and breath taking reddish-pink sunsets, with light one minute and pitch dark the next. Once the sun began to set, it only took minutes for it to change. Being so happy with our place made us decide that we should spend a morning or afternoon just enjoying our accommodations.

February 10th we were up with the birds, having a leisurely breakfast at home enjoying our surroundings. Around 9:00 a.m. we hopped in our car and were off to Lahaina, stopping off at a beach and getting some sun and a walk for about an hour and a half. Lahaina is a fishing village that displays sail boats, fishing vessels, and catamarans. They even had an old-fashioned sail ship with a pirate and the pirate flag. Museums and Art Galleries were plentiful and lots of shopping. The huge banyan tree that covered a whole rest area fascinated me, choosing to spend some time resting on a bench there while Betty Lou shopped. We had some ice cream and headed to another beach where we watched people swimming in the ocean, snorkelling, whale watching and boating, and returned to our lovely home. It was good to be back. Each of us had a shower, went for a walk and had supper out. It was a great day and we were ready to sleep.

It was a beautiful spot and we did not want to miss anything, so up early and off we went after a breakfast of cinnamon buns and coffee for me, tea for Betty Lou. The weather could not have been more magnificent. Another adventure was ahead of us

The sand was completely different at each beach we stopped at. Betty Lou collected a vial of sand at every beach. Some have pale sand, some reddish coloured. Other places had nearly black sand, and then there was pale, pale sand. A great variety of different kinds of sand, something we had not thought about before. It was wonderful to have our little pee pot to drive anywhere and everywhere. In the evening we drove to Wailuku just to look around. As we were driving I spotted a beautiful Poinsettia tree growing in a family's back yard. It was huge and beautiful. We backed up to have a better view. That was long time ago and I can still picture it. No longer nervous of where we were, it was very pleasant to feel at home. I spoke with a painter who was painting a church sight, learning a great deal from him. He seemed happy for the temporary distraction. We witnessed tomatoes growing wild, as well as cucumbers and hibiscus. What a day!!!!

It was sad when our last full day in this paradise came. It had rained in the night and by nine in the morning, the sun was out and it was hot. Spending the day 'Beach Bumming' was so incredible, we both got a little sun burned probably more from the wind than the sun, but made the most of our final lap.

Deciding to take it easy for the rest of the day, we stayed in and enjoyed our surroundings, going to bed early. Our flight home was early the next day.

When I awoke at 6:00 a.m., I could hardly imagine going to work the following morning.

The whole thing seemed like a dream when I got back. It was a dream come true and then some. What a great holiday, and what a friend to travel with.

After the trip my son, Tim said, "Mom, I remember when I was little you talked about going to Hawaii one day. Was it as good as you imagined?" My reply, "No son, it was much better". "So you'd go back?" "In a minute."

February 1994, wanting to have a change and a bit of a holiday, but spending quite a lot of money the previous year, we went on another expedition but not as extravagant. This time Las Vegas was our destination for only a few days. Flamingo Hilton was our home for the four days. This trip was like going into another world. The gambling strip was bright and busy. There was no night and day here. It seemed everyone had his or her own time schedule. I am sure that people who make their home in Las Vegas have a normal agenda, however this place seemed alive day and night. We made plans to see the Zeigfried and Roy show with the wild animals, and took in as many free shows as we could.

Gambling was a big attraction in Las Vegas. Neither of us was really interested, however one evening while Betty Lou was having a bath and was planning to watch some television, I decided to go downstairs and see what this gambling thing was all about.

I was very unsure of the whole thing and did not know what to do, so I just walked around and watched for a while. Getting braver as I took this all in, I decided to give gambling a try. As I was making this big decision, I watched two men come in with a huge wagon like contraption. They emptied the machines into this vehicle and pulled it away. This is when I decided thirty dollars was all I would gamble, losing it in a very short time period. That was the extent of our gambling career. Betty Lou did not even try.

We enjoyed our trip going from Casino to Casino to all the free shows we could find, shopping and savouring the good meals that were ever so reasonable and readily available. It was a great change and we enjoyed it, but it did not compare to our previous year's experience.

It was after this holiday that my friend Betty Lou and her husband got divorced. It had been a long marriage of disappointment for my friend. All she wanted was a good life.

A few years later, Betty Lou married a great guy named Jim. He is also a good friend of mine, but she now had a new travel buddy. I often teased him about that. I had new family commitments and not able to travel at this time anyhow. It was good to know that she found a good partner and that she was happy. We still have a good time reminiscing about our trips.

I thank God for putting this compatible friend into my life so that we could travel and have fun, at the right time. He also gave her a good husband. She was so ready for a better life.

Many times over the years, I felt that maybe if I had done something earlier in my marriage, my boys may have learned more about making changes before life got out of hand. Guilt even came into the thought process, before I finally 'Let it Go'. I did the best I knew how at the time. God knows that I did all I could, and hopefully my sons have figured it out too.

As it says in Romans 8:31 "What then, shall we say in response to this? If God is for us who can be against us?" I love this verse. Someone once sent me an article that confirmed this is my verse. It is a good one. What a freeing understanding!!

Sometimes events become a blur in my mind. I have a hard time putting them in the order that they happened. It just did not seem to stop. Many things began to happen after we moved back into the family home.

Don graduated from the RCMP and was posted to a small community in southern Alberta. What a joy it was to go to his graduation ceremonies. I was so happy to see him fulfilling his dream, and so proud to see him graduate.

I was disappointed that Milt did not want to come to the grad, but had already made peace in my heart about that. He didn't want to go, but I did. That is what happened. Milt missed a wonderful occasion, but that was not my choice, it was his. I had a fabulous time, and I felt proud and free when I danced with my son, after a delicious dinner. It was wonderful to enjoy myself with my whole being and not be obsessed with what Milt was doing.

Tim and I were there, as well as my parents. Milt's sister and her husband came as well. It was February and cold in Regina. I was so happy for my son the weather did not matter.

When Tim was in his teens, he decided to go to Don's. Already in a small community in southern Alberta, and just beginning his career, I am sure it would have been better for Don if Tim stayed home. However, he did go. Milt and I decided to go and visit the boys. Tim was always mistaken for being older than he was because he was a big guy for his age. We discovered that he had a job in a grocery store. He also had a driver's licence. I did not realize that in that province a person could get a driver's licence at age fourteen. We pondered all of this and talked with Don about it and he said, "It is a valid licence".

The boys seemed to be doing fine, but Tim was only fourteen and we would have liked to have him home. Tim wanted to be independent, and Don wanted to be a big brother. I think this was an issue. Once again, I had to 'Let Go'. He did come home, driver's licence and all.

Randy got sick before Don got married, and Tim was seeing a neighbour girl.

When it was time to go to Don's wedding, I was working in the Junior Secondary School and June was a very busy month for us. Don and Virginia's wedding took place at the end of June. I did not work in July and only part of the end of August. I was able to complete my work when I returned. Milt once again chose not to go. Randy was very sick and in the hospital. I wasn't sure whether I should go or not because of this. He told me, "Mom you go. If I were not in here, I sure would go". As it turned out, it was a good thing Milt did stay behind because it was a bad week for Randy.

It was probably about this time that he began having serious seizures. When he had a seizure, it would leave him speechless for a time and he would be very frightened. He had a bad one while we were at Don's wedding. I spoke with Randy on the phone after the attack, and he reassured me that I should stay and celebrate.

For the wedding I did stay, and I had a wonderful time. However there were some glitches before hand. I am so grateful that I had some Al-Anon program knowledge before this event, and that I learned to surrender.

It was Friday when we arrived and I planned to stay in Don's quarters while I was there. The wedding was on Saturday. I was supposed to take care of my new granddaughter after the wedding reception so the newlyweds could go away. My parents had their camper. Milt's sister and hubby had a motel room, and my two nieces' also had a room. I am not sure where Tim stayed. I cannot remember.

I'm sure that the arrival of us all must have been overwhelming, however, we were all there.

After a little while I was told that there was no room for me, and Virginia's sister would be taking care of Mandie. Great!! So what do I do now? I asked my nieces if I could bunk with them in the motel. That was no problem. We knew it was not for long, so we made do.

The next day we decorated the hall in the morning. The wedding was in the afternoon and the reception was in the evening. I decided to have a good time, and a great time I did have. The wedding was lovely, the food delicious and the dancing wonderful. About 11:00 o'clock Don came looking for me. "Mom, would you come back to the house and take care of Mandie?" "I thought your sister-in-law was doing that. My belongings are all at the motel". "Yes, well she has had too much to drink. Could you come?" "Of course, that was the original plan." We drove over to the motel and got my things.

In Romans 12:18 it tells us "If it is possible, as far as it depends on you, live at peace with everyone".

I had a wonderful weekend with my new granddaughter. My parents left the next day. The newlyweds returned, and now it was time to go home, see my son at the hospital, and go back to work. I had to be driven to Calgary Airport, which was a long drive from where we were. It turned out that I missed my plane by five minutes. There was another plane leaving shortly, with an extra charge of $60.00. Oh my! What a trip to remember.

In the Al-Anon Program, I learned that if there is nothing I can do about the situation, I must think about 'How Important is it?' When I thought about all of what had happened, I realized that in the big picture of life, I had to surrender. In a day or two, none of this will matter.

Milt picked me up at the airport and all was fine except that Randy was not.

His seizures were coming more often. There was more medication. Randy was taking 20 or more pills a day.

Another flashback:

Shortly after this, Randy was able to come home for a while. He did have to go to the hospital for dialysis, and it was so good that he had his car and could take himself there and back. I was home for the summer and enjoying him. One afternoon he began having chest pains. I thought he was having a heart attack and called for an ambulance. When they arrived, they told me he had a drug overdose and would take him to the nearest hospital. I said, "He did not have a drug overdose. Here are the pills he has to take. Please take him to the Vancouver General". "We will take him to the nearest hospital." "Fine", I said, "please help me put him in my car and I will take him to Vancouver General. They know his history there. Maybe they can help him". After some discussion, they took him to the General. I followed in my car. It turned out that he had fluid around the heart. They were able to help Randy and he was back home in no time. I will never forget how frightened I was, and how grateful that I had some Al-Anon behind me so that I did not cave in.

That same summer, our wonderful next-door neighbours had gone on a holiday and brought us a box of fresh pears. Randy had one and so did I. They were oh so delicious. Right after I ate my pear, I went to do some gardening. I came in and had a shower and we were off to visit Milt's sister and family. We were having a wonderful time when all of a sudden Randy became terribly ill. Tim had his car there so he took his brother and off they went to Vancouver General Hospital. It was a long drive from where we were. Milt and I followed. It turns out that Randy ate several more pears when I went outside. Because his kidneys were not working, his body had too much potassium. He was put on dialysis immediately. Randy told me later that he enjoyed the pears so much, he just did not think about anything else.

We had many emergencies with our Randy. How I wish that he did not have to suffer so terribly, however, I would not give up those precious times together where we discussed anything and everything.

While Randy was so sick, I transferred to a school closer to home. It was only a three-minute commute. This was a relief for me with Randy's seizure situation worsening.

Sometimes on a Friday Randy would call me at work. Mom, let's have a simple supper and then have a race. We would have a bag of sunflower seeds with the shells on. He would split the bag in half and we would see who finished first. While we were doing this, we would chat. And, chat we did. We shared a lot.

Milt had been sick. He had a bad cough as well, for which the doctor prescribed some cough medicine that really helped. He went back several times for more, and eventually was fine. Then I got the cough. I had to go to the doctor and when he prescribed the same cough medicine, he told me, "Hide it from the old man. He is addicted to it." I did hide it for a while and then the cough got a bit better and I forgot and left it out. One evening when I began to cough, I went to take some and it looked pale. I said to Randy, "Is this the right colour?" He replied, "I think Mom, it is anaemic. Dad added water to it". Then he asked me, "Mom, do you think you can live like this for another ten years?" I really could not answer him, so I said: "One day at a time, and we will see".

It was times like this that I was grateful that someone understood. Milt was not drinking, but he was taking tons of prescription medication plus anything he could get over the counter.

At one point I asked his doctor why he was prescribing all these pills. The doctor told me that if he stopped taking them now, Milt would have seizures. I did not understand how this could have happened. Why was he giving him all these prescriptions? I also knew that one person in the family having seizures was enough. I had to let this go.

Randy's girlfriend ended their relationship. It was more than she could take. She did not understand the seriousness of it all and told me that she felt Randy was putting on the seizures. I knew they were real. She needed freedom from it all. What could I do but 'Let Go' and be there for my son. He was very devastated by these circumstances. He loved her dearly, and hoped to be with her forever.

Life moved along in spite of everything else. Work continued and Randy had good days for short periods. One morning as I was preparing to go to work I said, "I should stay home with you today. We could play a game or go somewhere". He replied, "Mom, do you know how lucky you are to be able to go to work? How I wish I could. Just get ready and go, and have a good day". After that I once again realized how fortunate I was to be well and able to work.

Milt dealt with life with lots of medication, but he continued to work at this point. Eventually he started taking anti-depressants as well as the rest. The anti-depressants did help. He was better able to cope.

While everything was happening around me, I continued to go to work, but I missed my Al-Anon meetings when Randy was in the hospital. My friend who introduced me to the program started a group in her home beginning an hour later so that I could make it. She even wanted me to give it a name. I called it 'The Key to Serenity Al-Anon Family Group'. What a huge support that was for me. I am forever grateful to Audrey for this. That was the beginning of the group that I still continue to attend. After Randy died, we went back to the regular time, moving from her home into a church.

This wonderful program assisted me in getting through many upheavals. I know that it makes a difference in how I react to situations. While Randy was in the hospital, my sister-in-law came with me to visit him. She was telling him about something that was happening in her life and he said, "Go with Mom to Al-Anon. It will help you". This statement made me want to continue to get better and to help others. It has helped with the letting go process, with all the illnesses, with Milt's anxieties, with my family, and with my friends. It even helped me to deal with issues at work, and helped me plan for my retirement.

Going to church was a turning point in my life as well. I had given up on church after the death of my first husband. Then I made a decision to try again. God never left, I was the one who gave up. He never gave up on me. When I combine what I learn at church and in the Al-Anon Program, how can life be anything but good? At church I learn so much about Surrender, Peace, Joy, Commitment, Service, One Day at a Time and all the other things that make life worth living, especially Love. All that I learn at church, through Bible Study and Sunday school is reinforced in the Al-Anon Program.

I believe that self-help programs are wonderful things. We learn to share from the heart and to listen to each other. Some of my best friends come from self-help programs.

For many years now I have been sponsoring people from the Al-Anon Program, from the Freedom Session at my Church, and mentoring women as well. I also attend a Bible Study. All of these people have become very dear to me and we have become friends. For me this is all a 'Bonus'.

I found this little poem in a Kidney Foundation newsletter and gave it to Milt in an anniversary card:

"There is no joy in easy sailing,
When the skies are always blue.
There is no pride in merely doing,
Things that anyone can do, but
There is some satisfaction
And it's mighty sweet to take,
When you reach a destination
That you thought you'd never make."

These words felt right at the time. I never thought our marriage would make all the tests it had been through. I wasn't sure that Milt could stay away from alcohol. I was unsure of many things.

During a quiet period, Milt asked me an odd question. "When you get to heaven, which one of us will you choose to spend time with?" I was surprised by this, but by learning to wait a few minutes to answer, I was able to say: "I don't think that will be an issue there". He was satisfied with the answer.

My parents were aging, and my husband was sick. I was not getting any younger either. In November 1999 I wrote this poem while pondering how life would have been without God in it. Even when I make mistakes, or say something before thinking, life is good with God in it.

WITHOUT YOU LORD, WHAT WOULD I DO?

Today I feel worn, and kind of 'spent'.
I need to pray Lord, to be content!!

The joys are many, some troubles are new,
Without you Lord, what would I do??

There was a time when troubles were ample,
I learned to obey and live by your example.

The joys are many, some troubles are new,
Without you Lord, what would I do??

The years gone by have taken their toll.
Without you Lord, I'd never be whole.

The joys are many, some troubles are new,
Without you Lord, what would I do??

My gratitude is because of you.
You always show me what to do!

The joys are many, some troubles are new,
Without you Lord, what would I do??

When I call on you Lord, and do what you say,
My life just gets better, day after day!!

The joys are many, some troubles are new,
Without you Lord, what would I do?

After Mom died, I was devastated. She was a wonderful lady. She was ready to see me any time. I could bring my friends over to visit. Once in a while, she would say, "Just come by yourself". Now I can really understand what she meant. It is so great to visit with my children by themselves, as well as the grandchildren. Not often that happens when they become adults and have families of their own.

Then there was the issue of Dad, and his blindness and dementia. I loved my Dad and wanted to be there for him. The hardest thing I have ever had to do is find a home for his care. Going to the Alzheimer's course for care- givers' was another self-help program that made a huge difference. The Alzheimer support program is available to people by telephone now. What a great idea to help folks who live in rural areas.

Dad did not understand what could be wrong with my husband. Milt was younger than Dad, so Dad felt that he should be strong and healthy. Often Dad would ask, "What is the matter with him anyway?" My reply usually was "Lots of things, Dad", that seemed to quiet him till the next time.

I have developed into a firm believer that going to get help is not a weakness. It is a God given strength. It was difficult to admit that I needed help. I needed help when I became obsessed with my husband's drinking, and life fell apart. Help was required when my grandbaby girl was given up for adoption. I needed help when my son was very sick. Understanding was necessary. I needed help when he died. Help was needed when Mom got sick, and Dad needed heart surgery. It was important to be compassionate when my brother became ill and then died. I was lost without my Mom. I needed help when Dad became demented, and when Milt's Parkinson's disease became overwhelming. I have always needed God's help, to stay spiritually grounded and mentally safe.

In 2005 around Valentine's Day, the pastor at my church was giving a series of sermons on 'Love' and how important it is. He emphasized the fact that people should show their love for each other in different ways. He spoke of the difference between how men and women demonstrate love. I was very much intrigued with the messages except that in my experience and especially in the circumstances as they were at that time, most of it did nothing except make me sad.

I went to visit Dad right after church in the home he was in, and thought about this series of sermons. Without surrendering everything to the God of my understanding, I would not have been able to write the pastor a note about how I was feeling. Dad was very sick at the time. He had broken his hip and was too fragile to have surgery so he was in bed and could not move much. In the meantime, after visiting Dad I would go home to a husband sick in bed. While sitting with Dad as he dozed, I wrote my beloved pastor a letter. Here is a short description of what I wrote. I do not have a copy of the exact letter.

Dear Pastor,
Thank you for your very open sermons on love, communication and sex in marriage.

I very much appreciate that all of the things you suggest are helpful and could make a good marriage better or even great. Or better still open the door for a poor marriage to improve.

There is something that I would like to mention though, or ask about.

What does a person do in the event of illness in the marriage? In our home there has always been loyalty to one another, however, because of several different diseases afflicting my husband, we do not have a lot of the mentioned qualities that contribute to a normal marriage.

We have been married 47 years this year, and I cannot remember when we had an intimate moment.

I love him and I think he loves me. I carry on with my life while he watches TV and sleeps. He gets up long enough to have a smoke then back to bed. He takes a lot of medication for various ailments (Parkinson's Disease, two Brain Aneurysms, several Strokes, Diabetes, High Blood Pressure, Substance Addiction, Post Polio Syndrome and Depression). The original family doctor prescribed Tylenol Three for pain. Milt is addicted to them. They also make it easier for him to keep sleeping.

My Dad is in a Home. I don't feel much support from my husband. Once in a while he asks how Dad is.

Sometimes I feel like a walking tree.

Boy, a lot of emotion came to surface today. There are probably a few folks living like I do. What can we do?

It helps me a lot to know that when I die, I will have Joy, Peace and Happiness.

Please don't think I am unhappy. Life has wonderful people and my life is interesting, full, pleasant, busy and fulfilling. However, the special ingredients that you talked about are missing.

A service designed for these kinds of situations might be comforting.

I signed it and delivered it back to the church before I lost the courage to do it.

A few days later he called me at home and we chatted. A week or two later, he did a sermon that was helpful.

Thank you God for helping me!! Today I realize that not being spiritually grounded is the basis for all issues. However, hindsight is an interesting thing. I did not know all of this when it was happening. I do know, however, that throughout all of it, God has always been there. It was I who was not.

To go back a little bit here, Dad was having difficulties accepting the fact that he would never be able to walk without the help of a walker, and eventually he needed a wheelchair. I was able to find a nice light wheelchair for him, so we were able to sometimes take him out in the car.

During the supper hour, one evening in September, at the home where Dad was living, he decided that he would show everyone that he could walk. He got up and began to walk across the dining room where he fell. According to what I was told, he said he was fine and finished his supper. After he ate, he asked to be put to bed and promptly fell asleep. They put him to bed and then called to tell me what happened. When I received the phone call, I was told that he was fine and was asleep.

Right after I had breakfast the next morning, I decided to go over and see Dad. Upon arrival, I found him in bed and very quiet. He told me he was very tired. He did not remember falling the night before, however he did tell me that his hip hurt. I then lifted his leg gently and he winced. Immediately I went to the nurse's station and told them that I thought he had a broken hip. They called an ambulance and I accompanied him on the trip to the hospital.

After much discussion, it was decided that Dad was too fragile to operate. He was in shock and was not speaking at all. It was also now discovered that his Diabetes had escalated and he was receiving insulin injections. Up to this point Dad had taken medication in mild form for this problem, and it was mostly being controlled by diet. I begged them to do surgery after they told me that Dad would not be able to do much, and would have to stay in bed unless he was lifted out. I knew that this would be unbearable for Dad and the family.

Dad's dementia escalated after that accident. He never did remember falling, and it took him three weeks to speak again.

Each time I went to see Dad, he wanted me to help him up so he could go to the washroom or sit in a chair, or take a walk around the barn. Often in his mind, he was still on the farm. Sometimes it would be frustrating. I would tell him that he could not get out of bed. He would usually say something like, "I can get up. I went to the washroom this morning". "Ok Dad, let's go then." Of course he could not even sit up, never mind get up.

My Dad was a European man who did not have much contact with races other than Caucasian. When he was in the Rest Home, there were caretakers of all races. We had several embarrassing encounters with some of the workers being of different colour. Dad did not understand this at all, and made some rude remarks that made me want to disappear into the woodwork. After I explained to him that if he treated them with respect, they would do the same. Gradually he did accept that.

After the broken hip and being bedridden for months, Dad's strength was failing and the end was near. He shared with one of the girls who cared for him that he would like to see a Priest, having been raised Catholic. This happened to be on a Sunday. I was happy that he was reaching out. I tried to find someone in the Catholic Church but could not, so I tried again on Monday. Dad was slowly getting worse, so I wanted to be sure we could do this. Asking a friend who went to the Catholic Church, she gave me a number to call.

Another thing I have thought about is God's sense of humour. The priest I spoke with was very kind and offered to come that day. We made arrangements to meet at the front door of the Rest Home. I watched as a car pulled up and out came a black man. When he introduced himself, I wasn't sure how Dad would react, but I did not say anything. I had to 'Let this Go', God sent this man and I relaxed. We went upstairs to Dad's room and I asked the Priest to please wait while I went in to tell Dad that we were there. Dad did not open his eyes the whole time the Priest was there. He prayed for Dad, reassuring him that angels surrounded him, and he need not be afraid. I quietly thanked God and had a good cry. This man was wonderful, and I was grateful.

While I sat with him he often would think I was Mom. However one day he asked me, "Have you seen Mom lately?" "Dad, Mom died a long time ago."

"Oh that's right, I forgot."

Another time, he asked me to bring him the baby. I said, "Dad, there is no baby here". "Yes", he said, "He's asleep in the basket". This is when I began to just go along with his ideas, with a reply, "I don't want to wake him". These answers seemed to calm him more than trying to tell him what was really happening.

On May 17, 2005, my Dad died in the Retirement Home. I was grateful that he did not need to be hospitalized again.

Once again my Pastor came through for my family and me. He came to the funeral home and officiated at Dad's funeral. The Worship Pastor came and led the gathering in singing. Once more I was grateful for their presence.

Here is what I said about my Dad:

<u>Now about my Dad - September 8, 1915 to May 25, 2005</u>

My Dad, Nick Karenko, was born September 8, 1915. His mother died when he was six years old and his father when he was sixteen. Dad and his younger brother were left on the farm together.

In 1934, Dad and Mom were married and stayed married till Mom died 68 years later. They had two children, my brother and myself. My brother, David, died a few years ago. Dad and Mom had three grandsons, seven grandchildren and two great grandchildren.

Dad had a knack for making things work. It was a huge change from farm life when we moved to the British Columbia Coast, but Dad's ability to make things work were evident. He always found employment and provided for us. Dad was a self-made entrepreneur. He never wasted anything and he taught us the same. If he couldn't use it, and no one else could either, he would burn it or bury it. They very seldom had garbage for pick up. If it could be composted, it was.

Dad repaired cars, trucks and equipment for himself as well as other people. He taught himself from books and practice. You must keep in mind that Dad only had a grade four education. How hard that must have been for him. In those days, if he was needed on the farm he could not attend school.

To help put food on the table, Dad repaired anything from lawn mowers and bicycles to women's shoes.

Dad did many things when we first came to B. C., but his last position was with Park and Tilford Distilleries as their maintenance man. He worked there for many years. Their discarded barrels became planters.

We still have one of the many cabbage slicers that Dad made from used planer blades. Whenever someone needed help, they called Dad. He could do plumbing, carpentry, electrical work, yard work, painting and whatever needed to be done.

Things were tough for my parents in their early years. They never went to a movie or out to dinner. After they retired, Dad loved to go out and eat and they became regulars at Ricki's Restaurant. Ricky's even gave Dad a watch. I think they went there for lunch for ten or more years. He was so proud of that watch.

Dad was a hard worker and he passed this on to us. I can remember him coming home from work and having supper, then falling asleep with his head on his arms on the table. After a snooze, he'd go out and repair something for us or someone else. Dad never went to bed until the project was completed. He always finished what he started and nothing could wait to be fixed. It had to be done right now!! Sometimes that made life very interesting.

Dad taught us all a lot of things. Some good, some not so good!!

Family, friends, work, card and board games and planning were Dad's passions. He planned for all of us. Not everyone appreciated it, but he did it anyway. He planned for all of us and worried about everything and everybody. So you see, Dad was a very busy man.

When Dad was 86, he did not pass his driver's test. I was with him that day and it was so sad to see him disappointed. That was a big blow to him. When I think of it now – this is how Mom and Dad got around in the car. Mom could see, and Dad could hear!! That is how Dad drove the last few months. Anyhow, he had this idea that he could get his licence back because he got a letter from the Superintendent of Motor Vehicles. The letter stated that he could try again. It was hard to convince him that the Superintendent of Motor Vehicles was not waiting for him to be back on the road. The truth was that he could not see.

Dad always had the idea that if you were able to have a bowel movement, you'd be fine. When Mom was in the hospital, Dad decided she needed a laxative, and he got one ready.

At one point during the last period that Dad was still at home, Tim and Don were there with him. They found him in the storage area looking for a rope to hang himself. They calmed him down after which Tim decided to help keep him safe, so he hid the key. Not too long after, Don discovered Dad back in the storage area. Don asked "Grandpa, how did you get in here?" "Oh," he said, "I have a key".

After Mom died, Dad was a lost sheep. After being together for so many years, he was totally disconnected. His Dementia became worse and since he was blind and his hearing was going, all that was left was what he ate. Once he could not eat, I knew he would not last long.

The staff at Guildford Seniors Village was kind to him, and we are grateful to them. They were so patient when the Dementia surfaced, and so good to him since he broke his hip. Thank you to all of you.

There are two people we cannot leave out. They are Glen and Gabrielle. Glen has been so kind to Dad through thick and thin. He enjoyed the good days and was there for all of us through the bad ones. He came to see Dad every day two or three times. He just talked to him and was his friend, even when Dad did not respond.

Gabrielle was there always. To visit Dad, to chat a while – but she was 'oh so there for me'. God put you there for me Gabrielle. I know this for sure.

O yes, and to my friend Jenny, for the note of inspiration in my letterbox at church every week. So sweet and so helpful.

There is one more very important thing I'd like to say, and that is that in Dad's final days, he made peace with our Lord God, and accepted him into his heart. Thank you to Ed, the visiting pastor from my church, for helping Dad in this area. If ever I doubted that there is a God, the peace Dad had at his death is proof again that He is our Keeper and our Peace, and He is definitely in Charge!! Some of us may not have a chance like Dad did. I am also at peace, because Dad is now in a much better place.

Thank you all for coming. Please join us upstairs for refreshments and a chat.

Milt was too sick to come to Dad's funeral service.

During the goings on, Milt just continued to deteriorate. The man suffered from so many different things. He had Polio as an adolescent and spent three months in bed. This disease affected the left side of his body. He had a jerk in his arm that was very annoying for him. It was always important that his cup or glass was only three quarters full. He was an alcoholic and smoked heavily. Milt had many small strokes. Diabetes also developed over the years. Depression was overpowering for Milt as well. Parkinson's disease was another thing he suffered from. Parkinson's was not detected till later on in his life, although I feel he had it between 20 to 25 years, or maybe longer. He was addicted to prescription drugs and over the counter ones as well. All of these ailments were hard for him to deal with, but they were not easy to live with either. Learning about all the different issues was a big help.

In the last three years that he lived, he began to show his affection for me in different ways. Sundays before I would leave for Church, I always went in to the bedroom and told him I was leaving and approximately what time I would return. He often told me, "You look really nice today". Or "You smell good". Those little things meant so much to me, I only wished they had come sooner, however I learned to be grateful for them.

This time was challenging because Milt did not want to be cleaned up. I am sure it hurt when I tried to wash his body, but it had to be done. It was difficult when I would go to clean him up and he would beg me not to. This was the case the last week of his life. On Monday I went in to clean him up and he said, "Just do the necessary, and leave the rest. I am not up to it." I did that. On Tuesday it was the same. On Wednesday, I just had to wash him and change the bed, so I came in with two small buckets filled with water, a wash cloth, towel, and some soap. "Now, what are you going to do?" He asked. "Honey, you need a wash and the bed needs changing." "Not today. I am not up to it, please do it tomorrow." "Monday, and yesterday, you were not up to it. Today you are not up to it, and I think tomorrow will be the same. I think you will feel better cleaned up, bed changed and fresh underwear." I placed the water on a chair near him and started with his head. There wasn't much hair any more, which made it easier to do. Moving downward I just kept washing, rinsing and talking. He was upset and said, "God you are rough". You must remember that this man was six foot two. Even though he had lost weight, he was not tiny. To move him around took all the strength I had. I just kept washing and said to him, "Next time around, you will have to find a gentler one. For now, you are stuck with me, and you will be clean." He just smiled. As I got nearer the mid section, I could tell it hurt him. I tried to be gentler, but determined to complete the job. I then proceeded to cut his fingernails and toenails, and change the bed. "You must feel better?" He smiled and thanked me. I was exhausted and had a rest.

On the following Sunday morning after Milt was asleep, I went to do my volunteer time with the Sunday school children. He was still asleep when I got home, but he was on the floor. I was able to get him back into bed. He immediately fell out of bed again. Not able to lift him up the second time, I called Tim who was not far away. He came and put his Dad back to bed.

No sooner had he left the premises, Milt fell again. This time Milt was too exhausted to help me. I gave him a pillow and covered him, then told him I was going to give our dogs a run, after which we would try again.

That evening, January the 15th, I had to call the ambulance even though he begged me not to. He had a seizure as they were taking him out. There was surgery the next day. After much suffering and several seizures, Milt lost his battle with life. On January 17, 2006, Milt died after only two days in hospital.

When Milt died, we were best friends. I am so grateful that I can say that, because we definitely were not always.

Here is my tribute to my husband at his funeral:

<u>Milt Holt</u>
September 29, 1930 to January 17, 2006

I would like to thank everyone for coming here today to say good-bye to Milt. Also, Thank you to the people who have come over to spend time with us at our home.

Many of you brought food, some brought flowers and lots of memories. We have cried and laughed and that all helps. It has been great not having to cook. I really have not felt like cooking. So, Thank you.

Thank you to the folks who have travelled a long way to be here. I know the roads are not great at this time of year and you came any way. It is so much appreciated.

Milt was born in Minnedosa, Manitoba on September 29, 1930, to John and Vera Holt.

When he was a teenager, the family moved to B. C., where they lived in Burquitlam, which meant between Burnaby and Coquitlam. (Now called Coquitlam) There were 5 children, 3 girls and two boys, Milt being the youngest. Milt's sister Myrt, who has been like a sister to me, is the only remaining sibling. Over the years, we have shared a lot. Myrt and Stan were there through thick and thin.

Milt worked on a chicken farm when he was a young man going to school. He then moved on to work with a dog trainer who trained dogs for the RCMP. He quite enjoyed this job and spoke of it often. From this job he did many different kinds of work, one being a crane operator for Dominion Bridge. During this period of time, Milt and I met. I was a widow with a young son. Milt legally adopted Don and together we had two more sons, Randy and Tim. It wasn't easy sailing and the skies were not always blue, but Milt and I would have celebrated our 48th Anniversary this summer. Seven grandchildren and 2 great grandchildren were added to our family during this period of time.

Milt made a decision to take another kind of employment, due to frequent layoffs at Dominion Bridge. He was hired by Weldwood of Canada and went to work at Flavelle Cedar Mill in Port Moody. It turned out that there were also layoffs at the Mill. In this time frame, Milt took another job with Timberland Sawmill in Surrey. Milt worked his way up from a millworker to tallyman to lumber grader and then was a mill supervisor for many years till his retirement in 1985.

After Milt's retirement, Tim brought a German Shepherd pup to keep him company. Prince and Milt were inseparable for many years. They spent every day together. Prince was Milt's dog unless you had a leash. We had many good laughs about that. He was Milt's dog, till he thought he was going for a walk.

Milt was a private person with a dry sense of humour. In a serious conversation, he would sometimes come out with something totally unexpected that would make you crack up in laughter. He was a very knowledgeable person who read the paper from end to end. Not many people knew of his knowledge because he was very private and seldom showed or shared what he knew, unless he felt it was necessary for one reason or another. Milt was a gentle man, and very few people were aware that he had trained and competed and won boxing events.

Our middle son, Randy, was sick for nearly three years, and died in 1982. That was a difficult time for the family. We were all affected in different ways, and Milt had a hard time accepting Randy's death.

Milt enjoyed woodworking in his workshop. This gave him an outlet for his creativity and privacy. He also finished the basement of the family home where he made many original creations and loved doing it. We are still enjoying the effects he created there. In the late 1970's Milt added a large deck to the house using the deck as the roof to his workshop. He also added an overhang to the front of the house giving it a porch effect. He loved to work on things around home, and spending his time creating. He spent hours creating picture frames, mirrors with frames, plate holders and many other things.

Milt suffered from various different illnesses. He had polio as a child and spent many months convalescing from that. When Tim was two years old, Milt was on his way to his shop while the boys were playing soccer. He went to kick the ball and slipped. Thinking that Dad was playing with them, Tim jumped on him. No one knew that he had a broken hip. He then crawled from the spot where he was hurt to the back door, then called me and told me he was hurt. I then called the doctor and described what Milt had told me. The doctor said, "He has a broken hip. Call an ambulance and take him to Royal Columbian". At that time, we had no spare cash and three children. Surrey was quite different then. Milt thought this through and told me to go next door and get Guenther. He said to load him in our old pick up truck, which was a '56 Dodge Fargo, and take him to the hospital, that way we would avoid the cost of the ambulance. So, Guenther brings over a camp cot and between us we loaded this large guy into the back of the truck. This was no easy task, since he had a bad break. You must remember our roads were mostly gravel, and our truck was old and rickety. Riding in the back was not exactly smooth. It wasn't even smooth in the front. Well Guenther is with Milt, the kids were taken care of by another neighbour and we are off to Royal Columbian Hospital. The pain must have been something else. We made it and they operated and pinned the hip. He had that pin till now. Milt had Osteo Arthritis that gave him trouble for many years. In 1991, Milt had two Brain Aneurysms. Shortly thereafter he had a stroke, which left him recovering for several weeks. He also was suffering from 'small strokes' at different times caused by arterial problems. Milt also endured the symptoms of Parkinson's disease, which gave him tremors and other things associated with the illness, including depression.

As a young man, Milt spent lots of his holidays and spare time on the ranch with his sister and brother-in-law. He loved the ranch life and helped with branding, herding and other ranch duties. He was content to watch his favourite western movies. These were a comfort to him. During the last few years of his life with Parkinson's, he stopped reading the newspaper altogether. Milt was not a complainer and was content to watch his shows in the quiet of his home. He kept telling me not to worry. That he was fine. He did not want to leave our home. He loved to be at home.

During this last while, it was difficult for Milt to accept that he needed help and sometimes it was challenging. I prayed for God to give us Peace throughout all of this, and for strength and knowledge about how and what to do. God did what we needed. I had notes throughout the house reminding me that, "God will make a way". I trusted in what I believe and we made it.

God took Milt home on January 17th, 2006, after only two days in hospital.

After 48 years of marriage, and the years we shared were not always easy, I felt very much alone. This was magnified by the fact that most of the rest of my family had also died.

Once again Pastor Kevin came to my rescue, officiating at my husband's funeral service. The worship pastor was there as well to lead the singing. I always choose 'How Great Thou Art' because I can never get over how awesome God's creations are. It was comforting having them there during this sad time in my life. Many of my church family attended Milt's funeral, along with family and friends. Several people who had worked with Milt also came.

After Milt's death, his sister Myrt and I planned to spend more time together. There were conversations on the phone and the occasional visit while everyone was sick, but not much time to really be together like we enjoyed. We began to enjoy each other's company once again. In June that same year Myrt called. We chatted for a few minutes, then she said: "I have something to tell you. You must not be upset by this because I have been fortunate". "I feel that I am not going to like what you are going to say." Myrt proceeded, "I went to my doctor yesterday and I have been diagnosed with liver cancer". "Oh my goodness, so what happens now?" I was shocked and completely devastated. She was my friend as well as my sister-in-law. My head was spinning. I thought now I would have time to spend with her. Myrt was a courageous woman. She told me, "Don't be sad Di. The doctor told me that I would get more and more tired". She told me that she chose not to take treatment, as the disease had progressed and the treatment would only prolong the agony. She also said, "I have had many good years since my breast cancer surgery". I was already grieving and she was still here. I had to change my attitude, and fast.

Myrt's youngest son was getting married on July 1st of that year and she really wanted to be there. Mona, her daughter asked me if I would consider flying to the wedding with her mom. Of course I did that. We left on a Friday afternoon. She was able to walk to the gate of the airport from the cart that took us there. Myrt was then wheeled onto the plane in a wheelchair. Upon arriving at our destination, she walked down the stairs of the plane to the waiting wheelchair. Her future daughter-in-law picked us up.

The wedding was wonderful. It was an outdoor garden wedding, and the weather was beautiful. She left the wedding early and I followed a short time later. When I got to her son's home, my sister-in-law was already in bed and asked me to come in and chat.

We talked, we laughed and cried and reminisced. It was during this joyful visit that she asked me if I minded her nickname for me. She always called me 'Di'. I loved it and felt warm when she said it. I said, "Of course I don't mind it. I love it, but why are you thinking about this now?" "I just want to go knowing that you didn't mind." We laughed some more.

We stayed over that night and the following night, leaving for home on the Monday. By the time we were departing, she was not able to walk and had to be lifted into the plane.

By August she was very weak, and by mid-month she was gone. It was with sorrow that I said good-bye to this lady, at the Celebration of her Life.

August 2006.
Re: Myrtle Anglin
My Sister-in-law
Sister
Friend
Confidant

Myrt's brother and I were dating at the time I met Myrt and Stan. Being a young widow with a two-year old son, meeting these people for the first time, I was nervous.

They welcomed us, and immediately we became friends. Milt and I married and had two more sons. Myrt and I have shared many joys and sorrows over the years. I didn't have a sister and Myrt became my sister. Accepting my son was no problem. He became one of the family and that was that. That probably drew me closer to them than anything.

I remember when we all had very little money. Myrt and I both could have used some new underwear and shoes. Well at that time Army & Navy had an annual shoe sale. There were tables of shoes. $1.00 Table, $2.00 Table, $3.00 Table and so forth. Myrt & I got wind of this sale and decided to check it out. We only had one car in each family so we had a plan. Stan dropped her off at our house on his way to work. I drove my husband to work, and came home again. We had coffee and off we went. I can still see her in that store. We sure did have fun. Can't remember how many pairs of shoes we got, I just know we had a great day.

Another memory is: One Sunday, after dinner, we decided that we should have our ears pierced. Again, Myrt got dropped off at our house. I drove my hubby to work and now we are mobile again. I was nervous. Not sure if she was, but she was being brave. We were trying to decide who would go first. She said, "It's ok, I'll go first". She was being the big sister.

I will never forget when one of Myrt's children was having a difficult time. When Myrt called me regarding this particular incident, I knew we were sisters and friends. We talked at length about this and a lot of other things as they arose after that.

During the years that we raised our families, we used to have the New Year's party at our house and we had great fun. They often stayed the night and we celebrated New Year's Day too. We spent many Christmases together until our families grew. Then we each had our own.

School holidays, or sometimes during a long weekend, our boys used to spend time at the farm. They loved that part of holiday time. Lori used to stay with us in the city and I think she enjoyed that too. Our boys liked the idea of having a sister for a while.

Myrt and Stan's eldest son, Gerry was preparing to be married. Before Gerry and Sharon's wedding, Myrt and I were together and she said, "I think I'd like to buy a new dress for the wedding". Now you must remember that buying a new dress at that time was a big decision. She wanted a nice dress, but not too expensive. It had to be something you could wear after the wedding. It was decided that we would go to New Westminster to purchase this dress. At that time Columbia Street was very active with several good stores. She told me what to look for and we both looked. She also said, "Don't pick green, because it looks hideous on me". Well we looked and we looked. Finally we found several and she went in to try them on and I still looked. I did find a beautiful dress and it wasn't really green but kind of. I took it into the dressing room and she says, "That will look awful". I said, "Try it on and let's see". "OK", she says. Well let me tell you we laughed till tears came down. She really did not do green well.

When one of our boys was very sick and in hospital off and on for almost three years, Myrt & Stan were wonderful. They came to visit him often and made sure I had a walk and some food before they would leave. That was so good of them since he was always at Vancouver General Hospital and they lived in Aldergrove. Myrt used to bring him fresh peas from the garden, because she knew he loved them.

There were other times of difficulties and they were always there for support, and a good laugh. Surprising how a good laugh can fix a lot of things.

Ron, Myrt and Stan's youngest son was getting married a fair distance from here. I had the privilege of going by plane with Myrt to Ron and Sandy's wedding. We spent a great deal of time talking and sharing, crying and laughing. She used to always call me 'Di'. That weekend, she wanted to know if I ever minded. I told her I loved it, and I asked her "why are you thinking about that now". "I just need to know", she said. We had lots of tears and laughs that weekend. I am so happy I went.

I could go on forever because we have been family for nearly 50 years, however I will close by telling you that I will miss her terribly and wish we could have had more time together. God had other plans.

My thoughts were many and not always good. I knew that God had something for me to do because I was still here.

The Serenity Prayer is always a great help to me:

The Serenity Prayer

God Grant me the Serenity

To Accept the things I cannot change,

The Courage to change the things I can,

And the Wisdom to know the difference.

There are so many ways and so many areas in life where this prayer can help. The most important thing is not to misinterpret what it is trying to say.

To accept the things I cannot change does not mean that I have to put up with cruelty or abuse or any such thing. That is where the courage part comes in. We know what needs changing. Sometimes we do not want to do what it takes to change it.

Then came another blow. My dear friend Gabrielle had asthma and suddenly became very sick in December 2006. Her husband had just died in November. In January 2007 Gabrielle also died. What a shock! What a loss. It was always wonderful to have her to talk with and share what was in our minds and hearts. Here is what I said about my dear friend.

GABRIELLE

Gabrielle and I have known one another for over 35 years. We met during the years our boys were in Scouts. She and Glen used to have meetings at their house. During this time one of my boys was in Scouts and later was in The Drum and Bugle Band. This is when we got to know each other. After that ended, we went our separate ways and then we met again when Glen was in the seniors' Village, as was my Dad.

Once in a lifetime, if we are fortunate enough to find someone we can relate to with similar values, goals and dreams, we can consider that to be a desire fulfilled. That is how I felt about my friend Gabrielle. We both liked to do similar things, and I always felt like she understood where I was coming from. I never needed to explain why I felt one way or another. If she felt differently about something, we would talk about it and come to some agreement suitable to both of us. This did not often happen. Sometimes it was good to hear a different point of view, to help me through a situation. Mostly we just accepted things as they were and enjoyed our friendship.

I never knew that life could be so much fun doing really simple things until I met Gabrielle. We spent many hours together. Sometimes we just went for a drive, sometimes out for lunch, sometimes just sat at home and talked, either at her place or mine. We played cards too. Often we just had tea and talked. Every morning, for at least three years we talked on the phone. We could talk forever, every day. Always there was something one or the other had to share. After sharing whatever, we would discuss if we did the right or wrong thing. Many times we would get on to some subject and laugh ourselves silly. We discussed our lives, our supper, her children and grandchildren, our breakfast, my children and grandchildren. Talking and sharing our lives gave us the strength to carry on. Gabrielle had Glen and I had my husband. Both men were sick and we had lots in common. On the spur of the moment we would decide to go somewhere or do something. Go to see someone and we even went to a movie together. The plan was to go and see the latest movie with Wil Smith called 'Pursuit of Happiness'. Right after the Christmas Holidays we planned to see that show. Arrangements to go to a 'Spa' and have our feet pampered gave us yet another laugh. We made this appointment and left early that morning because of the weather. Since neither one of us ever had this done, we were a little excited and apprehensive. The Spa was in Port Moody and many of the lights were out on our way there. It took an hour or more to get there. When we arrived, we discovered their power was out. We had to postpone our appointment. The place called us but we had already left. Well what do we do now? All the power was out in Port Moody, so we headed to Coquitlam Centre. We thought we would have a coffee at least, but then got side tracked there. Gabrielle was in the mood to shop, and it doesn't take much to get me going, so we shopped. She actually bought two things I think. Then we went to Surrey, had lunch and came home. We seemed to be able to enjoy anything together in spite of the circumstances. Even a sandwich at McDonald's was great.

One of our very most pleasures was shopping for shoes. She loved shoes and so do I. For my birthday last year she gave me a card that said, "When we're 88, we'll still be friends. And we'll be complimenting each other on our cute orthopedic shoes". On the blank side she wrote "Diana, Dear Friend. Thanks for our on-the-go fun times together.

After Church on Sundays, I would pick my friend up and we'd spend the afternoon doing some silly thing. Like we sometimes went to Wendy's and shared a baked potato, some chicken strips and a salad. Nothing fancy, just fun. Sometimes we went more serious. We'd have a smorgasbord brunch, or go to a nice place for a change.

We understood each other. There was no pressure and no musts. We just went with the flow.

She enjoyed the simplest things. When I bought a new car, she was so excited for us. Us meant her and me. We did a lot of driving together. When I got the car I did not tell her. She knew I was thinking about it and looking. We were going to Burnaby to work on 'Angels for Aids', something that we had been doing a few times. We went to a friend's home to dress these Angels. We had lunch there, dressed the Angels, had fun and it was a simple way to enjoy the winter weather. She made things like this fun and exciting. It was good to see her enjoying this venture and getting out a little. The work was simple but it took time, and Gabrielle enjoyed artsy stuff. We had many laughs during these ventures, and earned $1,500.00 for the 'Angels for Aids' project. Anyhow, I picked her up in the truck. I brought my dogs along to look like I was taking them for a ride. I told her that my car was parked in the neighbour's driveway for whatever reason, I cannot remember now. She accepted that. Now we are leaving to go to Burnaby, so I told her we had to go next door to get the car and took her to my new one. She was so excited and enjoyed the car as much as I do. When we got home she told Glen, "Guess what? We got a new car". I will never forget that. She knew we would go for some adventures in this vehicle. I am just so sorry that it had to end so soon.

Talking about enjoying crafts and simple things, Gabrielle was a wonderful knitter. She could knit in her sleep. That was her most enjoyable activity. I told her that in my Church we had a morning where the street people were given a warm place to go, with coffee, breakfast and clothing. She immediately began knitting toques for these people. She was able to make a toque in an evening. I did not ask her to do this she just did. She had compassion for people. As soon as she had two or three done, she would give them to me and I passed them on. There are several people whose heads are warm because of Gabrielle.

Gabrielle loved her family more than anything in the world. She was so proud of all of you. She had her concerns and her dreams like all of us, but she was full of contentment knowing that each one of her six children was living a good, full life. She never boasted but always was grateful that each of you turned out so well. Gabrielle was happy to know that her grandchildren were growing up the same way. She loved you kids so much. She always spoke of you with Love, Gratitude and Admiration, so remember this as you continue on your life's journey. She would love to be remembered for the rest of your lives.

The Friday before Gabrielle went into the hospital, I had called her in the morning and asked if she wanted to go for a ride. I needed to go to Cloverdale and she loved to go for a ride. She told me that maybe she should go to the Doctor's first, so I said fine. Just get ready and we will go. We did that and she seemed quite anxious while waiting for the Doctor. Sort of paced the floor, which I had never seen her do before. The Doctor gave her three prescriptions. We went to the pharmacy to get these filled, and while we waited we went into Value Village to look around. Gabrielle's breathing was always heavy, but this day it was really bad. When we got the prescriptions, I told her we would go to Cloverdale another day and that maybe she should just go home and rest. Which is what she did. That afternoon or evening, she went to the hospital.

When we got to the parking lot that afternoon, we talked for a moment before she got out of the car. It was that afternoon that we planned to exchange our children's telephone numbers. We always knew what was going on with each other, and thought it would be a good idea to have each other's kids phone numbers in case something happened to one of us and we could let our kids know.

When Glen and my Dad were living in Guildford Seniors' Village, Gabrielle and I got to know each other really well. We could have a good time in spite of the situation, and we used to have a good chuckle sometimes over the silliest things. I think that helped to lighten the load we were carrying. We knew each other 30 years before and with life and children we lost touch with each other. This was a reconnection of something that we could have enjoyed for those years, however this is how it was meant to be.

After my Dad died, Glen was able to come home to be with Gabrielle again. They were so content with each other and he was so happy to be home. Gabrielle was happy not having to go out every day. I think that was a good year for them. These two people were meant to be together. They understood each other. They were happy just to be close to one another. They were meant to spend their life together. That is how it seemed to me.

In a lifetime, a person has many acquaintances, and some good friends. I feel like I was blessed to have been able to spend these last few years with my friend, Gabrielle. We had many fabulous talks, wonderful laughs and spent much quality time together. I will miss her like crazy. I do already. There will probably not be another friend in my life that can compare to this friendship. There will not be another Gabrielle. Goodbye my Friend. I will miss you!!

I was missing my friend terribly and probably even more so because so many others who were close and dear to my heart had already died.

I had to 'Surrender' all of these feelings of loss. I needed thoughts of my purpose here. I asked God to give me peace within my soul.

Someone told me this and it has stuck in my mind: "If you keep on doing what you're doing, you'll keep on getting what you're getting. If you don't like what you're getting, change what you are doing". This is so simple, yet so difficult.

Albert Einstein once said: "Peace cannot be achieved through violence, it can only be attained through understanding". God knows I try to do this, but honestly it is a lifetime process. Sometimes it takes a while to understand some things.

I especially find it a struggle to understand some of the areas in the lives of my young grandchildren. However we love each other deeply. This saying really helps me here: "The dead might as well try to speak to the living as the old to the young". If I can hang on to some saying and get a chuckle, it really helps to move on.

Very often I have to read my 'Letting Go' article and talk to God seriously. This usually helps me to see where and how much if any of it is my business. I pray for their safety. I pray for their health and well-being. I pray that they will be happy, and most of all I pray that they will turn their lives over to God and be spiritually grounded.

As you can tell, I love quotes and biblical verses that help make life easier to deal with. Sometimes they do not come to me easily. I must have a million of them, or close to it, so I just need to draw one when I need it.

I want to remember what Roy Goodman said; "Remember that happiness is a way of travel, not a destination".

Is it better to be right, or to be happy? I use this one a good deal, and I also know as Josh Billings said: "Life consists not in holding good cards, but in playing those you do hold well".

Even when I am in pain, I do not want to be one. Maya Angelou said this and I can relate to it. We are fairly close in age. I guess we have experienced similar circumstances.

To see a young couple loving each other is no wonder; but to see an old couple loving each other is the best sight of all.

Do not ask the Lord to guide your footsteps, if you are not willing to move your feet.

Love is being myself and liking it. What others think of me is none of my business. This helps me to 'Surrender'.

Chapter 10

SERENITY

Before you can break out of prison, you must
first realize that you are locked up.

WHAT IS SERENITY

SERENITY Is not freedom from the storms of life.
It is 'Peace' within the storm.

SERENITY Is not something that protects me from hard times.
It is a special kind of strength that helps me to face
my problems and work through them.

SERENITY Is at hand when I learn to 'Let Go and Let God'.
Then I will have time to count my blessings, work
on my shortcomings, and enjoy one day at a time.

SERENITY Helps me ACCEPT the fact that I cannot change
another human being.

SERENITY Gives me COURAGE TO CHANGE THE
THINGS I CAN.

I can't change anyone else, but I can change my attitudes and myself.

HOW TO ACHIEVE SERENITY

I will separate in my mind, the sickness or problem
from the person who suffers from it.

I must transform good resolutions into good habits.

I will not let my inner peace be disturbed by confusion around me.
(I say, "I will not let anyone or anything Muddle my Puddle".)

I will be gentle and tolerant, while maintaining my right to individuality.

I will listen and appreciate and not judge the source of what I hear.

I will stop reacting to everything that occurs. When I react, I
put control of my 'Peace of Mind' into the hands of others.

These articles came from Al-Anon literature. When I read them I realized
that it is so. After much thought, I decided to put what I read into practice,
and use them to live by and enjoy.

I was very conscious of the fact that I was a widow again, and now also
an orphan. My parents, my brother, my in-laws and my best friend had all
died. My children were living their lives. The grandchildren were growing and
do not need a depressed grandmother. They are making some big decisions
in their lives.

What am I going to do now? I wallowed in this for about a month. This is
what I decided; they are all gone and I am still here, so I better do something
other than feel sorry for myself.

Continuing on with my sponsorships, mentoring and working with the
children at my church, and attending the program for people over age fifty,
was enough to keep me busy, but I felt like I needed to do something more.

I made the decision to write some children's books. Life was just buzzing
along. I was so busy, making the decision, should I write fiction or true? I
had tons of ideas from things that happened with my own grandchildren,
plus the fact that I worked with children most of my life. I decided on true
happenings. I wrote the stories. Finding a publisher was another challenge.
After about a year, I had seven published children's stories. My goal was to
write the 'Grandma's Silver Series', so that I could leave something of a legacy
for my children, grandchildren, and great grandchildren.

Was I thrilled with the outcome? You bet!! When my eldest grandson
asked me, "Why are you doing this now?" "So that you can read them to your

children, and so that you will remember that no matter how old you are, you can do what you put your mind to do." "Cool", was his reply.

After the fact, you can always find something that could have been different. I was wishing that I had called the little books Grandma's Treasures, and wished that I had not put certain things there a certain way, etc. etc. After hoping and wishing for a few days, I decided this is the way it is. What to do with these little books was the next decision.

I have two sons, one daughter-in-law, seven grandchildren, one granddaughter-in-law and two great grandchildren. I wanted to do something they could keep and add to.

Looking for the right way to do this was as much pleasure as actually getting it done. While out shopping a while later, I came upon these beautiful boxes. Just the right size for everything I wanted to put into them. I purchased two that were brown and looked like leather. These were for my sons. There were silver ones with hearts on them for the boys, and ones with purple and red hearts for my daughter-in-law and the girls. Some of the boys are men and the girls are women. In my eyes the boxes were perfect.

I began this mission with joy in my heart. In the beginning I started by lining the boxes in a row and putting things in them. This became an impossible mission, so I did two at a time, starting with my sons' boxes. At this point I was realizing that I was enjoying this probably more than they would. Non-the-less, I kept going. I made folders for 'Fun Stuff', 'Helpful', 'Useful' and an envelope for 'Personal'. Into each of these boxes went a set of 'Grandma's Silver Series.

A personal letter went into an envelope for each one. That was wonderful therapy for me. Into my sons' envelopes went much of my personal thoughts for their future use, and hopefully will be of help to them. I had written poems for my sons, so they got a copy of them. Everyone got a copy of my poetry that was published and any other that I had written. You get the idea. This whole process took the best part of a year.

It was a relief when this was all done. I sent two boxes by courier. It turned out that Don and Charles came for a surprise visit and I was able to fill their car with their boxes. They seemed happy to take them, and saved me a lot of work and money. The rest were given personally. Whew!! Another 'Mission Accomplished'! It felt good to have completed this ambitious project.

Doing these things may seem silly to some people, but for me it meant serenity. My sons know the love I have for them and my wishes. The rest of the family know this too. Writing the personal letters was such a wonderful experience for me, and hopefully for them as well. The great grandchildren will have the opportunity to remember that they had a great grandmother who cared about them and loved them.

I am very fortunate that I have many good friends, great kids, and wonderful grandchildren and great grandchildren. Everyone was pleased that I did what I wanted to do.

One of my granddaughters lived with me several times. I got to know her well. Another one came often to stay for a few weeks at a time. It was fun getting to know her better. They are all free to come and go as they wish, knowing they are always welcome.

I do not always agree with some of their decisions, however I have learned that they are all adults now and are free to make their own choices. We all grow as we learn from our options.

If you have a family, especially with teenagers, then this little poem will make a lot of sense to you. It may even help. Many years ago I found this written on the bathroom door in a restaurant in a small town, in the country, where I had taken my parents for a drive and to lunch. When I read it, I wrote it down on a piece of paper and put it in my purse. I have kept it all these years. It sounded like something I was feeling.

It's not my place to run the train.
It's not my place to see how far the train's allowed to go.
It's not my place to shoot off steam, not even clang the bell,
But, let the damn thing jump the track and see who catches Hell!!

That little poem helped me through many a time with my family. I just read it and remember that somewhere there is someone else going through similar things. I would love to meet the person who wrote this.

When the boys and I lived in the rented house, there were many times when I asked, "Where are you going?" The answer was, "Out". Or, "Who are you going with?" The reaction was usually, "I don't know yet".

After many times of the usual interaction, I decided to use a different approach. As I was leaving the house, I would say, "Bye Boys". Their reply was usually, "Where are you going?" My reply, "I don't know yet". "Who is going with you?" After a while, they got the idea. The thing was that they wanted to know the details of my life, but were not keen on me knowing theirs.

It is very rewarding for me to have boys that are caring, kind and good. Working in a Junior High School really reinforced this. Even though we had our teen stuff, the boys were always respectful. We had our moments, but generally they were great kids.

I remember the time I got home from an Al-Anon meeting and found a safety pin on the bathroom counter and one of my stud earrings missing. I knew instantly which son had pierced his ear. Well it was his ear, another incident to 'Let Go'.

There was a time when one of my boys constantly wore a heavy, flannel shirt. Spring, summer, fall and winter this kid was in a red flannel shirt. After a while, I went to see the counsellor at his school. What a neat man this fellow was. He told me to buy another shirt exactly the same and wash it a few times. Give it to the boy so he can wear one while the other is washed. Washing it was not a problem. He did that before he went to bed.

What a simple solution. He also told me that he could guarantee that this phase would not last for long. It was not what I wanted to hear, but having someone reinforce what I was thinking really did help. Interesting how we all look at things differently. The counsellor said, "I guarantee that he will only do this for a year or two". Once again going for help was a freeing experience. So simple, yet living with it daily did not seem easy. Just knowing someone understood and had a simple solution was fabulous. He was right. The phase did pass.

There were so many serious, really serious things in life, yet these little ones can be a thorn in your side.

At one point when Randy was going through all of his difficulties with the dialysis, he had a pimple on his forehead. He picked at that thing and complained about it, and put stuff on it. I said, "Randy it is just a pimple, leave it alone. You are bitching more about this pimple than any of the surgeries you've had". He replied, "Mom, it is the zits that kill you not the surgeries". We laughed hard.

There were times when Randy was at home on the couch, and I would be doing something in the kitchen. He called me one such time and told me, "Mom, there is no better sound in the world than you puttering in the kitchen". Another time, I was hanging a picture and hammering. This time, he shouted, "Whatcha' buildin' Ma?"

These memories are wonderful and give me peace.

A few more flashbacks come to me as I am writing.

Somewhere I read, "No matter how you feel, get up, dress up and show up". This has helped me hundreds of times. When Randy was sick, there were times when I did not want to go to work, but always felt better when I did.

After Mom died, I spent a lot of time with Dad. Milt was sick too. Some Sundays I felt like just staying home. I got up, dressed up and showed up for church and my volunteer coaching position. I always felt better because I went.

When the lumber mill where Milt worked moved, he chose to take the retirement package instead of moving to the new premises. At his next birthday he would have been 55.

When this was announced, Milt was terribly upset. He called me at work, and sounded like he was sick. I asked him, "Where are you?" "At work". "Are you sick?" "Kind of." "What do you mean?" "Well I just got a layoff notice, or a choice to work in Squamish."

Squamish is quite a distance to travel and Milt did not like being away from home, so I knew instantly that he would choose retirement. The problem was that he was noticeably upset. My reply to him was something like this: "You have often talked about how you wish you could have some time away from work. Well now you will". He told me, "I did not want it this way, and not now". "You could stay with someone who will live there during the week and come home on the weekend." "Thanks, hon", he said, "I feel better already. I don't have to decide today, so we'll talk about it later."

Eventually he needed to make a decision about the retirement package. As we talked about the options, he wanted to know what I thought would be wise to do. The suggestion I made was: "If this was my retirement package, I would take the pension for life". His reply was, "I need the money now. I will never make 65". I told him, "You do not know how long you are going to live. You could live to be 100".

The next day while I was at work, he went in to make the retirement arrangements. Upon arriving home, I found that he took the plan to age 65.

I was disappointed in his choice, but it was his decision. He asked me what I thought the night before. I made a suggestion and he did not use my idea. I had to 'Let it Go'. It was a done deal. That does not mean I was happy about his choice. It just meant that it was done, and I could not do anything about it.

I had learned to 'Let Go'.

A few years before Milt turned 65, I suggested that we purchase a new truck for him. "How are we going to do that?" he asked. "I have been thinking that we can do this before your pension stops." I said. "How?" Was his question. "Let's go to the bank and see if we can get a loan." "What? A loan now?" "Sure. When is a better time?" "You think we can pay it off before I am 65?" "Yup!! I will repay whatever you do". "You will?" "I will, but the truck has to have a seat in the back". "What for?" "For someone to sit in if necessary." He was trying to be responsible and said, "There are only two of us we do not need a back seat." He just did not understand why we needed a back seat. I felt that we would probably need it for several reasons. I felt it would be handy to just put things there if we were both in the truck, and if there was another person involved, someone could sit in the back. We discussed this several times. He could not see the purpose of having a back seat. Eventually Milt met a man at a gas station that had a little truck. He asked the fellow how he liked it. This person told him he loved it but wished it had a back seat and told him why. Finally he could understand the sense in this. I was ticked that it took a stranger to confirm what we talked about. I was pleased that he had been tossing it around in his mind.

My next day off, we went to the bank. No problem there. Off we went to find a truck. We found one but the colour was not right. After several calls, it was discovered that there was one in another city that was turquoise. We waited till it came. Another day off, and now we were ready to purchase the vehicle. I felt that we should have a liner in the box and a canopy. Milt was not interested in that. He felt we could not afford it. My thought was that we could not afford to wait. This would most likely be the last truck for us. After much to-do, we got the truck with a seat in the back, a liner for the box and a canopy.

Milt was so happy with his new truck. We paid for it within a year and a half. What can be done, if the will is there? Wow!!

As it turned out, he often drove our elderly neighbours to their appointments. The extra seat in the back of the cab was very useful. Purchased items were put into the back where there was a canopy to keep thing dry or just out of the way. The canopy is very handy when the dogs need to go for their veterinary appointments.

On the day of Milt's 65th Birthday, he asked me; "What am I going to do now?" "What do you mean, what are you going to do?" "Well my pension is finished. I will have to live on my government pension". Thank you Lord for showing me how to let go. I was able to reply, "I really don't know what you are going to do. You do have that bit of money you were paid out when you retired. At least you did what I suggested with it". Milt said, "I am not sure how to do that. Will you come with me?" I told him, "Sure".

Everything was arranged for him to draw on the little bit of money that was invested. I am grateful that I learned to accept what I could not change. He lived another 10 years. That would have been a long time if I had hung on to the fact that he did not pay attention. Here is another article on 'Serenity' that was very helpful to me.

SERENITY

Serenity is the ability to tolerate an injustice without wanting to get even.

Serenity is patience. It is the willingness to postpone immediate gratification in favour of the long-term gain.

Serenity is perseverance, sweating out a project in the face of heavy opposition and discouraging setbacks.

Serenity is the capacity to face unpleasantness and frustration, discomfort and defeat without complaint, collapse or attempting to find someone to blame.

Serenity is humility. It is being big enough to say, "I was wrong". And, when right, the serene person is able to forego the satisfaction of saying "I told you so".

Serenity is the ability to evaluate a situation, make a decision and stick with it. The immature spend their lives exploring possibilities, changing their minds and in the end they do nothing.

Serenity means dependability, keeping ones word, coming through in a crisis. The less serene are masters of the alibi. They are confused and disorganized. Their lives are a maze of broken promises, former friends, unfinished business and good intentions that never materialized.

Serenity is the art of living in peace with that which we cannot change, the courage to change that what can be changed, the wisdom to know the difference.

This is very similar to the Serenity Prayer, but with much more explanation.

I need all the help I can get, and am grateful for it.

Getting help when I needed it has made my life great. Milt and I were best friends when he died. If nothing else, this is enough for me to be grateful, but there is much more. Make peace with your past, so it won't mess up the present, is a very important concept.

A few years before Milt died, he had lost a lot of weight. One morning he was very upset and I did not know why. He teary eyed told me, "I lost my wedding ring". I began to search for it. He spent a lot of time in bed, so I stripped the bed and sure enough I found the ring. Milt was so pleased. I was pleased as well, not so much because I found the ring, but more because he was so distressed that he had lost it. I remembered when he had thrown it against something, and delivered it to me together with a very confused letter, during a drinking bout. I did not say it, just thought about it. I was happy that I used the part about serenity that said, "Serenity is the ability to tolerate an injustice without wanting to get even".

A few months later, Milt once again confessed to losing his wedding ring. I searched everywhere I could think of to no avail. Several days later, I was vacuuming the bedroom where he spent so much time. There was an unusual sound. I stopped vacuuming and asked him to get up for a minute explaining why. He helped me to move the bed and sure enough, there was his ring. Milt was one happy camper. He cried again. It touched my heart that the ring was that precious to him.

A year or so later, Milt was very upset when he told me, "I lost my wedding ring again". I looked and looked everywhere possible, but could not find it, thinking that this time it was gone for good. He often wore a heavy jacket even when it was warm. I was still pondering about the lost ring a few days later, and decided to check the deep pockets in the jacket and guess what? Yes, I found the ring for the third time. We were both pleased. I said, "I guess you are meant to be wearing this ring". "I love my ring", he said. This time he put it on a thicker finger.

Milt continued to lose weight, and once again was visibly upset. When I asked what the problem was, he confessed, "I can't believe I lost my ring". This time we could not find it.

As I worked in the garden near the big cedar tree many months later, I happened to notice something glistening in the sun. I moved toward the cedar tree where it was coming from and there was Milt's wedding ring hanging on the end of a tiny dead branch. When I brought it in, I said, "I found something today that you will be surprised to see". Not thinking about the ring, he could not guess. When I gave it to him. He wept.

I was happy that the ring meant so much to him, but even more pleased that I did not bring up the time he threw it, and later delivered it to me in an envelope together with the letter that made the counsellor realize we were dealing with Alcoholism.

I realized that I was definitely enjoying 'Serenity'.

When Milt died, I wore his wedding ring. It was a bit big. I planned to have it sized, when one afternoon I noticed it was missing. Oh my, now I lost it. I searched the normal places but could not find it. The next day, I went to take the garbage out and there it was right beside the garbage can. Wow, five times I found it. I then put it on the chain around my neck, and later had it attached to my ring and hopefully it will not be lost again. It still amazes me that I was able to find it five times.

I love this saying, "Life is not fair, but it is still good". How true is that?

Many friends have come and gone, and I treasure the lessons I have learned from each and every one. One thing I have learned is to put a premium on the few who appreciate me for who I am. Over the years there have been many family decisions and choices that did not sit well with me, but I learned to separate my mind from the problems, and still love the people. My family is like any other family. We have our differences, but we love each other dearly.

I try very hard to not "Let anyone or anything 'muddle my puddle'. I found this little treasure in the Alateen daily reader 'One Day at a Time'.

My friends are always ready to talk, if I want to talk. If they need an ear, I am there for them.

In the Al-Anon Program there are people who need sponsors. I have sponsored many people, who have become good friends. The people from the

Freedom Session, also a self-help program at my church, have asked me to sponsor people taking the program. My best friend is a lady that was sent for me to sponsor. Mentoring women has been very rewarding. I have done this for many years and have made wonderful friends from there as well. Two have moved away and I hear from them very often. These two women have young families and it is wonderful to keep in touch and be part of their lives, and they a part of mine. There are several women that I mentor, and many that I sponsor. What a privilege for me.

It is great to listen to a person in need of an ear, maybe share some of my own experiences or maybe not, depending on the person and the circumstances. I listen and do what I feel God is leading me to do, give them a hug and turn it all over. God knows what we need.

I have discovered that God has given me the ability to listen to people and be there when they need a shoulder to lean on. Many have told me that it helps when they talk with me. I feel great when I am helping someone through tough spots in life. It was wonderful to make this discovery. We had a series of sermons on God given abilities, and this was one of my discoveries. It has always felt good doing the mentoring, sponsoring and other opportunities. Now I understand why.

Surrender is a wonderfully freeing experience that allows me to enjoy my life as well as help others. Through surrender, I have learned to enjoy many things that I would have otherwise missed. Without surrender, I would not have serenity. A sense of reality is absolutely essential to having serenity.

I knew I had serenity when Milt and I had this strange discussion. He was having a smoke in the chair that he shared with our dog Pepper. When he would go to have a cigarette, he would say, "It's my turn Pepper". She would get off and he would sit down. He was smoking and I was cooking in the kitchen with the back door open. Out of the clear blue he came up with, "Will you miss me when I am gone?" I asked, "Were you planning on going somewhere?" "You know, when I die." "Well", I replied, "I miss the cat, so I am sure I will miss you". We had a good chuckle, and he never asked me that again. Sometimes I wondered where those thoughts came from.

To withdraw from an argument may not make you the winner, but what you have saved is your own dignity and grace. As I said before, it is important to pick your arguments. They must be worth the effort and whatever else it takes.

Our background and circumstances may have influenced who we are, but we are responsible for whom we become.

The serenity prayer follows. It will give you something to hang on to when it is needed. This is one prayer that has been very instrumental in my life.

THE SERENITY PRAYER

God, Grant me the Serenity to accept the things
I cannot change, Courage to change
The things I can, and the Wisdom to know the difference.

What really helps me to keep my serenity is to always pray to the God of my understanding, and to be ready to carry the message to others.

About a year after Milt's death my young friend, who lives in another province now, wanted her grandpa and me to meet. She told me, "I think you and grandpa could have a lot of fun together. You understand farming and he loves his farm. He likes to have fun and you do to. Here is his number. He would love for you to call him". I replied, "Honey, I have never called a strange man in my life, and do not plan to start now. If he wants to talk, please give him my number and have him call me". Several weeks went by. I had forgotten all about the conversation, when one evening he called. We chatted for over an hour. He had a farm and I grew up on one, so there we had lots to talk about. After that call we spoke at least once a week for about three months. He told me his wife had died and he had remarried and that marriage did not work. He also told me that he wanted to get married again. As we were talking one evening, he asked, "I want to go on a cruise. Would you like to come?" I told him, "I'm not ready to anything right now, but if I did we would each have a room and meet for breakfast". He laughed.

Two or three weeks later he called to tell me he was going on a cruise, and when he returned he would come here so that we could meet and go out to dinner or do something. I told him that was fine.

It seemed like the day before that he told me he was going on the cruise, but the two weeks on the ship went quickly. It was Friday and he was in fact in town and not that far away from where I live. "Can we meet somewhere for dinner tomorrow? My treat", he said. I replied, "Sure we can do that". He suggested that I choose a restaurant since he did not know the area. I chose a convenient restaurant that was sort of in the centre for him and me and that was on a main drag. His daughter was bringing him there and I was going to drive him back to her place.

He was waiting for me when I arrived. He came over to the car, took my hand and away we went like we had known each other forever. I got a big kick out of his outfit, which included a cowboy hat and cowboy boots. Dinner was great, and the evening went well. Two hours passed quickly. When we were ready to leave he asked, "What will we do now?" "What would you like to do?" I questioned.

He hesitated for a moment and then said, "I do not know much about this place, so you decide". I suggested, "It is rather late and getting dark. How about we go for a drive and then I will take you to your daughter's". He told me he would like to see where I lived. In turn I explained that it was in the other direction and it would be to dark to take him back since I was not to familiar with his daughter's area. I could tell he was annoyed, but that was fine with me.

On the way back to his daughter's home, he made an inappropriate gesture toward me. I told him I did not know him and did not want to have an accident, then continued to drive. When we arrived at his daughter's, I admired the area and commented on a lovely home on top of a hill with a well-kept yard. I love beautiful flowers and well-kept yards. He then said, "That is a lot like my place on the lake at home. You would like it there." I replied, "Maybe one day I will see it". There was a car like my old one sitting a few feet away, so I went over and looked at it, explaining why I was interested. Just then his daughter came out, telling us that she had baked a cake and had tea ready. We went in and I enjoyed the visit and the tea and cake as well.

It was time for me to leave, as I had to be up early the next morning. He followed me to my car and wanted a kiss. That was fine. He then said, "What about tomorrow? Can we get together tomorrow?" I told him, "Sunday is a big day for me. I go to church, then to spend time with the children. I did not know you were coming and I have planned to go out to lunch with friends. That will be enough for me for one day. Can we do something on Monday? Give me a call and we can spend the day. I will show you around." He was visibly annoyed, and I left.

I did not hear from him again, and found out later that he took the first flight he could get and went home. About three months later I heard that he married someone from his area.

Oh well, that was an experience to remember. Once again, I was grateful to have learned to let go and be at peace. Serenity was wonderful.

The three most difficult things to say are: "I Love You" "I am sorry" and "Help Me". These most difficult things to say are the best when you say them.

How right James M. Barrie was when he said, "Always be a little kinder than necessary."

Be who you are and say what you feel…
Because those that matter, don't mind,
And those that mind don't matter.

Chapter 11
Joy

Don't compare your life with others, and 'Be Grateful'.

The best vitamin for making friends is B-1.

Don't be afraid that your life will end, be afraid that it will never begin.

Life for me did not begin until I reached out to God and other people.

Comparing my life with someone else's is setting myself up for hurt. Everyone has a journey that I know nothing about. It is like expecting something and when it doesn't turn out the way I want it, I am disappointed. One of the things that I have learned is to not expect. I am seldom disappointed. If I get a disappointment, it is because I have had an expectation that was not met. It is even hard to take when an expectation of myself does not turn out the way I want. When my children were young, it was important to have some expectations. They are now adults.

I heard about a student in a university who had trouble completing a paper on the 'Wonders of the World'. When she did finish it, she received an honourable mark. Many wrote about the Panama Canal, The Grand Canyon, The Great Wall, etc. She contemplated a long time and then wrote: "I think the Wonders of the World are: to see, hear, touch, feel, laugh, and love!"

After re-learning how to do this again, what a joy life is!!

Once again, burn the candles, and use the nice sheets. Wear the new outfit. Don't save it for a special occasion. Today is special. The things that mean most cannot be bought or built. Like the birth of a baby, the smell of fresh bread, holding your baby and knowing that this is a miracle, to laugh till tears run down your cheeks, and to love all of it.

When we were youngsters living on the farm in Alberta, we went on field trips and sports competitions to other schools like the kids do now. The only difference was that we were loaded into a cattle truck and driven to the destination that way. This was so normal we never gave it a thought. We were excited just being able to go.

As I was remembering, I thought about the time I was about eleven and living on the farm, going to the two-room school. I was asked to take part in a 'Poetry Contest'. I was so nervous. Students from other schools participated in this contest as well. We had to drive about fifteen miles to get to the school that held the event. I won first prize for reciting this poem:

I think that I shall never see
A poem lovely as a tree.
A tree whose hungry mouth is prest
Against the earth's sweet flowing breast.
A tree that looks at God all day,
And lifts her leafy arms to pray;
A tree that may in Summer wear
A nest of robins in her hair;
Upon whose bosom snow has lain;
Who intimately lives with rain.
Poems are made by fools like me,
But only God can make a tree.

By Joyce Kilmer

Even as a youngster, I loved poetry and writing. As I matured, I asked Mom for my exercise book full of poems. She said, "I threw it out. I didn't know you wanted it". My parents were very practical. Writing and poetry were not financial derivatives, so were never viewed as important. The poems were thrown out because they were not considered useful. I was disappointed when I learned this. My parents did not understand the value of such things. It was hurtful at the time. I still would love to see what I had written. That was then and this is now.

I am grateful that in spite of all of life's challenges, Milt and I were able to encourage good work ethics for our children. There is one particular memory of our son Randy. When the boys were youngsters, they had chores to do. One of the chores was to sweep the driveway. They took turns sweeping the driveway. It was Randy's turn. Each time he would say, "Mom, you have to show me again. I don't know how to sweep". So I did show him many times. Finally, I said, "Randy, you know how. Just go and do it". In the meantime, his friends had come calling on him to go out to play. When I looked out, the boys were sweeping and Randy was supervising. I did not say anything hoping it was supervisory skills at work.

Several years later, Randy worked for Loomis Couriers. When the shipping and receiving department was not busy, they had to sweep the area. During supper one evening, Randy told me, "Mom, you would not believe how many men do not know how to sweep". I asked, "Do you think you would know how, if you hadn't swept the driveway a few times?" We had a good chuckle.

This is a nice reminder that makes me happy to know that the boys learned some living skills while they were growing up.

Aware of being grateful has changed many situations into positive areas like the time that I spoke up while visiting with my parents before my 43rd birthday. Mom, Dad and I were having tea and we began to talk about when my brother and I were youngsters. I brought up wanting a bicycle, "Dad you have no idea how badly I wanted a bike. I felt so misunderstood that you did not think I needed one. You told me girls don't need a bicycle. Do you remember the Sunday morning I got up real early, before anyone else, and took David's bike for the day? I rode all day, and was so sore that evening. Mom remembered that day. Dad did not remember but he actually listened and tried to justify the reason I did not get a bike. I merely told him that I felt it was unfair that my brother had several bikes and I did not even have one. The following Saturday, Dad was at my door with a three speed bicycle. I was touched and enjoyed the bicycle for many years. It was not just the bicycle. He listened to me. It made him happy too.

There are so many precious moments that I treasure. When two of my grandchildren were with us one summer, we were playing the word game 'Boggle'. Victoria and I were playing and her brother, Randy was just watching. I came up with the word 'dork'. They both laughed. "There is no such word". "Oh yes there is", I said. "We used to say that when I was a teenager. He is such a dork." "That is not a word." I got the dictionary and said, "Ok, let's look it up." I found the word 'dorking' which is a bird. Then we got the giggles and laughed till tears were running down our faces. I'm not sure why we laughed so hard. It was one of those rascally moments. To this day I don't know why we laughed so hard. In the morning I found little flags in my plants saying things like: "Grandma's cool" and "Grandma's fun". I did nothing but laugh with my precious grandchildren.

Over the years I have enjoyed being grateful. Picking my arguments has been instrumental in making life more joyful. Forgiveness for everyone and everything has made me free. That doesn't mean that I don't get hurt, or that nothing bothers me. Of course not! The difference is I no longer hang on to this stuff forever and ever. I used to get hurt easily and hung on to it till the next one fell in my lap. This did not give me time to enjoy anything. I argue about things that are important to me, and let the rest go. Most things are not worth thinking about. One of the Al-Anon slogans is 'How Important is it'. It is one of my favourite. 'Keep it simple' is another that I use often.

I am so grateful that I had a friend who guided me to Al-Anon. In an Al-Anon/Alateen booklet 'A Pebble in the Pond', it says, "You can make a difference". "A pebble thrown into a pond can change its whole surface.

You can make a difference." I like to think that changing myself made a difference in my loved ones lives. It sure has made a huge impact on mine.

If you wait, all that happens is that you get older. I am so thrilled that I went for help, and have been able to enjoy what I learned.

How precious it is to remember when I decided to purchase a computer. Tim was excited for me, and made some good choices for me in regards to the computer. When the computer arrived he programmed it. I have enjoyed every moment of that decision. To make it even better he surprised me with a proper chair and a pad to go under it.

Another time, it was Mother's Day. Tim and his children were here. They love homemade lasagne so that's what I made. Supper was ready, but they decided they needed to go somewhere first. It was a long time before they got back. I was disturbed because supper was drying out. Upon their return, they presented me with a lovely gold chain. I was totally overwhelmed. I was annoyed because supper was not as good as it could have been, however, I did not let that spoil my surprise. The chain went so well with the other one they had given me several years before. These are all bonus times that I am so able to appreciate and enjoy.

Remember the young woman to whom I had written the letter when her husband drowned? Her mom wrote me a note every week that my Dad was in the home during his final months. It turns out that her father suffered from Alzheimer's disease a few years earlier. She understood what I was going through. Isn't God great? Jenny and I have become good friends.

The children I spend time with in my church are between four and six years old. They have given me some wonderful chuckles, and tell me some interesting stories as well. We were having crackers and cheese together one Sunday. One little girl put cheese between two crackers and said, "See, now I have cheesecake". My white hair sparks many questions. One little guy asked, "How old are you, about 50?" In my head I am thinking, I wish, then replied, "How old?" "Well" he said, "You have old hair". My hair is completely white and has been for many years.

During one season we had a little guy who often came to Sunday school with holes in his socks. The children decided to tease him. He was upset. I wasn't sure how to deal with this situation and thought about it for a few minutes, then asked, "What day is it today, and where are we?" The children answered, "We are at church and it is Sunday". I replied, "Well, he is wearing his 'Holy' socks". No more problems.

A little girl came to class really happy one Sunday. She stretched and said, "Oh it feels good to be a five year old". Another Sunday I asked the children "Why do you think God made the dark?" One of the boys replied, "So I can use my flashlight".

One little girl loves to run. She would just run and run. It did not matter if anyone else ran, she just did. As I arrived on Sunday morning, she handed me a little doll that resembled a baby girl. She said, "Can you hold my baby for me. I took the doll and said, "Sure, I'd love to hold your baby." In return she told me, "Please be careful with her, she was just born yesterday". How sweet is that??

One little guy used to love to pretend he was someone else and liked to be called that name. It went something like this, "Today I am Sonic". Later on I noticed he had two straws taped around his ankle. "What is this, I asked?"

"This gives me power over the Universe." I was thinking I'd do that as soon as I got home.

Reading the story of Joseph and the coat of many colours with the seven good years and the seven bad years, playing with a little car while listening, one little boy said, "I know the tires on my car are Good Year".

While practicing for our concert during Christmas season, I wanted to show the children how great they could sing. I showed them that when they sang loud and clear, it gave me goose bumps. I said, "I sure hope you sing like that the day of the concert". On the special day they sang really well. When we got back to our classroom, they asked, "Well did you get goose bumps?"

If I hadn't tried working with these youngsters, I would have missed a great deal. I have enjoyed every moment with them, and have learned a lot from and because of them. All I had to do is open up my heart and try.

How wonderful when they come to see me now as adults, to visit and share their lives. While they are youngsters, watching them grow is so rewarding. It is powerful when they come to talk as adults. You never know which child's heart you will touch. They all touch my heart in their special and various ways.

I decided to sponsor a child through World Vision. That has been a wonderful experience, and a great feeling. It is good to know that a child is having a better life because of something I am able to do.

'Choices' was not something I thought about, but I sure do now. I enjoy having choices. The things I choose to do are ones that cheer me up, like publishing my 'Grandma's Silver Series'. Getting the boxes for the family and filling them with special things. I hope they will enjoy all of that went into these containers for many years. Writing letters for each one was heart warming for me.

As I was filling the boxes, my mind was everywhere remembering things that happened as they were all growing up. I think the most enjoyable part for me is knowing that the grandchildren trust me enough to say what is on their minds.

Mandie came to visit with Don when she was a youngster. As I was resting on the floor cozied up in a blanket she said, "It's chilly in here Grandma". I opened up the covers and said, "Come in here". We were chatting when she commented, "Grandma, I hope you live for a long time. If you die, I have nothing to come here for". We discussed that we would do as much fun stuff for memories as possible.

One summer when Mandie was about nine and spending some time here, she was outside playing. Suddenly she came running into the house crying. I wondered if she was homesick, or had been hurt. "Why are you crying?" I asked. She sobbed, "I don't want you to die grandma". I said, "Honey one day I will die, but we will make lots of memories before that happens". "Okay", she said and went off to play.

The one and only Mother's Day I spent with Don and family in their home on the prairies, they hung signs all over the house, " Happy Mother's Day Mom". My daughter-in-law, Virginia, made two ceramic ducks for my garden, and my granddaughter, Mandie, made a ceramic gnome. It is as fresh in my memory today as it was the day it happened. It was a time for my daughter-in-law and I to enjoy being mothers.

Another summer, I picked Mandie up from Cadet Camp and brought her home. As she came in the front door, she took a deep breath and said, "Yes, this is Grandma's house. No one else's house smells like Grandma's".

I went to surprise Charles for his 12th Birthday. Charles and I went out to celebrate. First we went out for supper. I asked him to choose a movie. He pondered and then said, "What if you don't like the one I pick?" I told him it was his birthday and his choice. I could live through anything he chose for two hours". He picked 'Dragon'. It is a marvellous movie in which I cried. When we came out he went, "Whew, I sure am glad you enjoyed that show". After the movie, he suggested that we go to Bower Ponds for a walk. It was a beautiful evening. The lights were reflecting on the Pond as we strolled. While we were walking I said, "Charles, I have had a great day", to which he responded, "I've had an awesome day".

During this trip, I also spent time with the other children. It was then that Anthony said, "Grandma, I wish you didn't have to leave on Tuesday". How precious is that? How blessed I am!

Charles was here with Don for a visit when he and I went for a drive in the country. We had fun looking for mansions and castles, chatting all the while. Talking with Charles is fun because he is a man of few words. We admired cars he would like to buy. He told me he would like to buy a 'Lamborghini'. I asked if I could drive it. He answered, "No, I don't think so". I did not say anything for a little while. Then I told him, "Well I guess that means that I will not let you drive my car". After a moment of silence he replied, "I guess you could drive it". Since that time, he has driven my vehicle many times. So far there is no Lamborghini. I am waiting.

One enjoyable part of Charles is that whenever he does not like something, he says "Oh, ma-an". I enjoy hearing him say that. "So much better than cursing", I told him. This is also the time when he told me he was not having children till he is a 'billionaire'.

Anthony was here with Don for a few days. He and I were on an expedition on the Skytrain. Anthony spotted a long road and asked, "Grandma, is this the road to Avonlea?"

Another time as I was making pancakes for everyone, Anthony and I were talking. He said, I am going to be a pilot and I will take you to the Museum in an 'SR71 Blackbird'. There will be dinosaur bones there. Anthony suffers from a developmental disability, and he has a vivid imagination.

Randy and Victoria were with us for the weekend. Vicki kept saying she couldn't remember this, and forgot that. Randy said, "Vicki, you'd better have surgery and remove the eraser from your brain".

Victoria and Randy spent many weekends with us, and holidays too. One such visit they decided to make 'Solar Weiner Cookers'. They lined a small box with foil, with wieners on a wire through the box. The wieners were cooked in the sun on the wire. What an experiment that was. For several weeks we had solar cooked wieners.

As Randy and I picked blackberries one summer evening, he asked, "Are you going to make a pie, grandma?" "Sure am". "Well when I grow up, I'll make you a pie. You can pick the berries." "Great, Randy I'd love that."

Randy and I were driving along, when he said, "Grandma when you are old, I will buy a big piece of land and I will have a big house. In the back of my property, I will build you a little house and you can have a bit of my garden". "Oh, that will be great. I can give you some veggies too." "Well in that case, you can have half the garden".

I enjoyed Victoria's love of pretending. While we were outside one day I jokingly asked Victoria, "What is your name anyway?" "Ria" she said. "Dad calls me Tori, and Randy calls me Vic, but I am 'Ria'. I feel like a movie star or someone very important like a princess or prime minister, or even a nurse or a teacher. Hence came my little book 'Victoria', in the Grandma's Silver Series.

I was reading. Vicki was trying to do the same thing. I licked my finger to turn the page. She licked her finger and turned the page with the other hand. Another day I was singing in the bathroom while I was doing her hair. I was singing, "Yes sir, that's my Baby". Then she sang, "Yes sir, that's my Grandma".

The day Victoria turned five, I baked her a cake and frosted it, sprinkling coconut on the top. We were on a picnic and I was going to cut the cake. I could see the disappointment in her face, so I asked, "What's the matter?" With tears in her eyes, "Grandma", she said, "I don't like coconut". We scraped off the coconut, ate the cake and carried on with the day.

After Tim and his family moved, the children were here during the summer. I asked Randy, "Would you like me to send your birthday gift by bus, or would you like to have it now. He replied, "Grandma, wouldn't you like to see the expression on my face?" What could I do but give it to him then.

Keshia, Randy and I went to White Rock for fish and chips and a walk on the beach. There were seagulls everywhere, so we fed them too. Keshia gathered seashells and was having a great time. "This is my favourite place I ever went to. This is the best day of my whole life", was her description of the day. She was about four at the time.

Keshia was here with her Dad for a few days, they were getting ready to leave, when she said, "I'd like to stay just one more night".

Both families were here one summer. I took Virginia and all seven grandchildren to the Imax Theatre. Keshia and Nicki were holding hands. The lights went out and one whispered, "Are you scared?" "Yes. Are you?"

When Keshia was about five, we were going somewhere in the car, Randy, Victoria and Keshia were with me. I was humming as I often do when the children are around. Keshia asked, "Do you always hum when you drive?" I said, "I guess I do when you kids are with me. Do you like it?" She replied, "Actually it is quite annoying". I quietly chuckled.

My eldest son was a police officer. He had come to visit bringing his youngest son Nick who was about four. Nick and I had gone for a walk to the park near us. On our way to the park we heard a siren and Nick asked, "Grandma, do you know what that is?" I said, "What is it?" "It's the cops." I asked kidding, "Do you know any cops?" "No", he says. I asked again, "Are you sure you don't know any cops?" He replied, "No". I left it at that, but when we were home again, I said, "Don, will you introduce Nick to a cop? He tells me he doesn't know any." So Don asked Nick, "What do I do when I get ready for work?" Nick replied, "You get changed and go to work". Don, "What do I wear?" Nick, "A uniform". "So what do I do?" "You go to work", says Nick. "What's on my head when I go to work?" "A hat", replied Nick.

One more time, Don asks, "So what do I do?" "You go to work". "What's on my hip?" Nick, "A gun and holster". "So what do I do?" "You go to work." "Ok, Nick, what do I drive?" "A car", says Nick. "What's on top of the car I drive at work?" Nick answers, "A light". "So Nick, what do I do?" "You go to work, Dad!!" "Well", says Don, "I am a cop". That was quite a discussion. I guess it never occurred to this little guy that his dad was a policeman. We did have a chuckle over that one.

Taking some of the grandchildren on the Sky Train and the Sea Bus, Keshia and Nick were very busy looking for 'Free Willie'. Keshia said, "I saw Free Willie, and he is not afraid of boats".

I knew the grandchildren were growing up. We had a sheet of paper in the glove compartment of the car to jot down who sat in the front last. After some time they came back for a visit. This trip Randy sat in the back. I remembered that it was Randy's turn to sit in the front so I said, "The sheet of paper is still in the glove compartment". Randy answered with, "It's ok I'll sit in the back".

Another time, both families were here and I had four of the grandchildren with me in the car. As we drove along, I said "When I am old, I hope someone will take me with them in the car". Randy replied, "I am sorry to tell you this Gram, but you are old". That was some years ago, I wonder what he thinks now.

My 'Grandma's Journal' is full. I could write a whole book about what my precious grandchildren, as well as other children, have said and done. I will save that for another time.

Every day I am grateful for my friends. I have people in my life that range from birth to old age. My neighbour and friend died at age 102. When we celebrated her 100th birthday, she took a knife and mucked up the icing where it said 'Happy 100th Birthday'. She was very funny and said, "Everyone doesn't need to know how old I am". We all had a good laugh.

When I told her about the situation my brother's estate was in, she just said, "I always knew you could not put an old horse and a young one together".

Around age 99, I asked her what she attributed her longevity to, and she told me, "I think oatmeal porridge and humour". At her age she could be very funny. She told me many stories of her life that helped me to be grateful.

Sometimes she would call me and ask me to come over to find her 'stick'. That is what she called her cane. I would go over and find it on a door handle or propped up somewhere. Now I realize that she just wanted someone to talk to. When she needed to go grocery shopping, I asked her to make list and I would get it for her. She would say, "No you won't. I want to go". So we would go.

Being a sponsor for people in various programs is a joy for me. Knowing that most of these lives will improve makes me happy.

Attending the program at my church for people fifty and over is precious time spent with folks my age. I love these people and enjoy sharing time with them. The Bible Study we have before lunch is a great time for learning as well as sharing.

My Thursday night Life Group has turned out to be more than a Bible Study. These women have become so dear to me it is not possible to explain, and they spoil me which is great.

The Al-Anon group I belong to is special. These people, both men and women, are broken when they arrive. After three or four months, it is an amazing transformation. They begin to have hope, and are happier people. I have sponsored many people, and will continue to do so. It feels good to take phone calls forwarded from the central office that leads people here. For as long as I am able, I will attend this magical place.

Freedom Session at my church is also a twelve-step program with the same twelve steps as the Al-Anon program with biblical increments. It is an in depth study that has helped hundreds. I am a dedicated sponsor to some of these people.

Enjoying being a children's ministry coach at my church has been rewarding over the past two and a half decades. These little ones bring energy to my soul. To be able to pass along to them what I have learned is a good feeling. Their stories and their interpretations are the best.

Someone recently sent me this via e-mail. There was once a little boy who told his dad that he knew what the word 'BIBLE' stands for. The dad was surprised and asked, "Ok son, what does it mean?" "Well it stands for Basic Instruction Before Life Ends". This certainly makes sense to me.

It is a joy for me to help people when I can. The most enjoyable part is getting to know them. Once they have shared their innermost secrets, how can we not be friends? When they turn out to be cheerful, happy people, wow!!!

I have developed lifelong friendships from the various groups and I play cards every week with some of them. What fun we have, and what we share is priceless.

Another friend I have loves to play the Scrabble game. We play and talk and we laugh till we cry – what a joy in life. A simple pleasure!!

Attending Al-Anon has helped in all areas of life. I was able to begin my journey into retirement when I began to realize that I had choices. If I had not realized that I could make some wise decisions, retirement would not have been possible.

The staff from the school made a party as a celebration of my retirement.

There were about a hundred thirty people there or more. The card has this many signatures, but some may not have signed the card. This card was painted by one of the teachers and a mom from the school. Milt made a frame for it that took him a long time to do. This frame was the last thing Milt ever made, so that makes the whole thing even more precious. The painting still hangs in my kitchen, nested in the beautiful frame. It is lovely. There were many family members there and Don surprised me by coming. What a day that was!

Retirement was so exciting for me and what memories I have. The last and wonderful was the assembly for me with the whole student body in the gymnasium. There was a song made up that they practiced. The whole school sang it to me that day. I can still hear them. During the assembly they presented me with a framed copy of the song. As I mentioned earlier, they also gave me a huge bag of pull-tabs from cans in memory of my deceased son. It was so heavy it took four strong young men to carry it to my car. This went to the Kidney Foundation to raise funds to send children on dialysis to a special camp. What a memorable day that was!

A few years after retirement came my 65th Birthday. One of the teachers I had worked with asked me out to lunch. She came to pick me up and had to go back home because she said she had forgotten something. When we got to her place, she suggested that I come in because she needed to go to the washroom. Inside her home was a good number of the staff from work. They had hidden their cars and I was totally surprised. That is another wonderful day to remember.

I feel great when I recall the simple things in life. I love to think about my boys and their activities in the early years. The eldest son enjoyed Scouts, Marching Band and those kinds of activities. There were many fund raising functions and rallies. One such time the boys had to build a covered wagon. Milt and Don built one. This was so much fun to watch. I enjoy thinking about it now, just as much as I did when it was happening.

Tim and Randy, our two younger boys loved the sports scene. They played baseball, soccer and hockey. We had early morning hockey practice twice a week, one each. Then there was a game each. I drove them to practices and went to the games, often going from one rink to another. One Saturday they had a game about 70 miles from home and then another 50 miles in the other direction. We began around 2:30 a.m. and finished late in the evening. I was so tired that I told the boys I would rest in the car while they got ready to play. The next thing I heard someone knocking on the window of the car. I told them I was coming and they yelled, "We finished and are ready to go home now". I slept through that game. Many of my lunch hours I spent resting or sleeping after early practice mornings. The girls I worked with were great at calling me when my lunch break was over.

Don, our eldest son played baseball as well, but he was often disillusioned with the coach of the team. This man would shout angrily at the boys, sometimes bad enough that he would have to leave the game. It took the fun out of it for Don. After the season was over Don asked, "Do I have to play baseball?" Of course the answer was, "No you do not have to play baseball". He was involved in a Drum and Bugle Chore and absolutely enjoyed that, playing the bugle in that group and the trumpet in another.

All three of my sons were avid swimmers. I never did learn how to swim, so I made sure they all did. It was important to me. It was so much fun to watch them learn. I would suggest certain changes in what they did. They would have a good laugh because I could not even float. Randy eventually became a great diver, being asked to take part in a competition in Japan. He told me, "Mom I want to dive for the fun of it. I don't want to be in competition". That was ok too.

My dear friend, Berta and I were always involved in the fundraisers, in the banquets and whatever else was happening with all of our children's activities. After many years of doing almost every volunteer job that was involved, we decided that we should sit across from each other at the meetings. If one or the other even looked like volunteering again, we had to give each other a good kick. It helped, but often we still ended up doing the work. I am happy today that we did these things. Our kids were busy, and so were we.

My 70th birthday was so special. Only one granddaughter could not be there, all the rest were. There was so much food left over that we did not need to cook the whole time the family was here. There were about 150 in attendance and we raised $600.00 for the Food Bank, plus a double layer of food, in the back of our truck, collected for the Food Bank. What a fun time we all had, and what a joy it was that there was no alcohol. The grandchildren did not notice or miss it, and I hope it was a lesson that alcohol is not necessary to have a good time.

The two eldest grandsons took pictures and put it on a disc so I can enjoy it whenever I want to.

Buying our last truck is such a joy to remember. It was a lot of effort at the time, but oh how Milt cherished his truck. He polished it every day. No kidding, he did. Just ask the boys. He was not well and could not do much, but he polished his truck. It makes me smile still. There was not a crumb, no dust, and no garbage bag in this truck, and it was shiny.

That truck is still in our carport. I use it to transport the dogs to the vet. When the children or grandchildren come by plane, they have a vehicle at their disposal. Besides all of that, it gives me great pleasure to remember how and when we purchased it. It is an old vehicle that is like new.

Making photo albums for my sons, Don and Tim, was so much fun. I looked at each photo to decide which were worth putting into the book. I cried and I laughed and I shared with my friends the memories that these pictures brought. That was a rewarding gift for me to do for them. I am sure they are enjoying them too as well.

I am so grateful that I asked for and got help. I can hardly believe that I was able to reach out in so many ways, and receive help when I was ready to accept it.

Going to Al-Anon was huge in changing my life. I did not ask my friend to take me there. She made the suggestion. However, the responsibility is mine to keep going.

Audrey was also instrumental in taking me to church, which I have continued to do for the past three or so decades. Going to church and being part of the Children's Ministry has been a pleasure for me, and a huge help in changing my life. As a coach in the Sunday school program, I love being with the kids and especially enjoy hearing their stories. The things they say are priceless.

I was willing and able to go to a Christian counsellor for a good period of time, which gave me another perspective, and more tools for life. I reached out to the counsellor at my son's school as well. He helped.

Sponsoring Alateen for ten years was a learning process for me as well as for the teens. This program is for teenagers living with the disease of Alcoholism, or ones who have lived with this disease. Learning from their point of view is quite different. They taught me things: like we as adults have a choice to leave or to stay in a situation, they do not. They sometimes feel like the parent who is not drinking is worse than the one who is, and I know this is so from my own experience. They feel that the adults in the family don't always hear or acknowledge them, and many more such dilemmas. This was very helpful to me. Knowing that many of the teens made better decisions after attending was enough for me to continue. I know that some were able to finish school and move on to better lives. For a period of time, one of the boys attending Alateen and I went into schools trying to help other teens with alcoholic or addicted parents. That was a wonderful experience for both of us. We were reaching out to the students looking for help.

I have been asked to speak at Al-Anon rallies, anniversaries, birthdays, and other activities. This helps me to realize how far I have come in my years of attending meetings. It makes me think back to the time when I first started and how my life has changed. I have attended many rallies, anniversaries and birthday meetings, and have spoke at some. Here is an outline of one such talk I gave in the year 2007:

My Al-ANON Story

It is coming up for my 30th year in Al-Anon. This does not seem possible.

Before I got into the Program, I did everything that made our lives worse. I worked like a fool, paid bills, taxied the kids around, made sure that everyone had clean clothes and work boots, did the gardening, made sure the cars were in order, etc. etc.

The alcoholic in my life was a very mild, kind, and gentle person, but when he consumed alcohol, he would become a complete opposite. The atmosphere totally changed. We would be frightened. He threatened to drown me in the bathtub. One night he was going to throw one of the boys and his friend through the living room window. Luckily he was drunk enough that the boys were able to defend themselves. Many such things happened. I do not need to describe each situation. You know what happens.

When things just kept getting worse, I went through a time where I became numb. The worst things did not penetrate my emotions. I was like a walking tree, and I thought this was detachment. During this period of time, my boys and I moved out of our home. It did not matter what happened with the alcoholic, I was numb.

After several months of being on my own, I had lots of time to think and learn about Alcoholism. That was after 18 years of living with the problem. I had time to learn that Alcoholism was an illness - I did not cause it, could not cure it, and for sure could not control it. That helped me to sort some things out.

Later on the Alcoholic found out where we lived and came back into our lives. He promised me that our world would change, and all would be well. You all know the rest of this story. However, now I had some knowledge of the Disease. It was more than two years before things began to slowly change. We eventually went back home.

We were only home for three months when our middle son got very sick. He was sick for nearly three years. This was a definite test of our relationship and the disease of Alcoholism. It was during this time that I realized how much healthier I was getting.

Both my husband and I worked and our son was in hospital about two years out of two and a half. Sometimes on a Saturday I thought that we would do some things around home and then go to Vancouver General Hospital together, only to find that Milt had already gone without me. Without

Program, this would have caused a War. I had learned to accept the fact that he was having a difficult time, because often later in the day other people went to see Randy and he did not want to deal with that. So, I learned to be grateful for little things. Like the fact that I had a car, I had my own money and I could drive. I just did what needed to be done and when I was ready, just went.

During the last stages of our son's life, my husband could not get out of bed. One such day, it had begun to snow. I went to the bedroom and said, it is snowing out and I am worried about driving. Our snow tires were not on. He said nothing, but got out of bed and went outside and put on the snow tires. I went about my business and went to the hospital, grateful for what he had done. One more time, saved by the Al-Anon Program. The truth was that Milt was now addicted to pills, prescription drugs as well as over the counter pills and cough medicine, anything that did the job.

When our son died, I was prepared for the drinking to begin again. IT DID NOT. Once again, I was grateful. We had experienced so much pain. He was very upset, but he did not drink.

I have learned in this program that the more I tried to control others, the more I was controlled. Emotions became reactions. I had never been aware of choices. Once I realized that I had a choice of what my day would be like – my life changed. No more did my day depend on the moods of others. 'My Day' was my day and still is. I didn't know I could choose to be happy. I did not know that I did not have to control every situation, that every outcome was not my responsibility.

In Al-Anon I learned that if I have an expectation – I am setting myself up for resentment. I do not have expectations, and consequently do not have much anger or resentments. I have learned that I can be happy even if everyone and everything is not going my way. I choose to accept the things I am not able to change or control, and use my energy on changing me. Changing me is enough work for me.

Learning that if I share a problem, it is only half as big afterwards. If I share a joy, it is double the pleasure.

When I become obsessed with someone or something, I miss everything else. So, I try to "Go Slow and Let Go" "One Day at a Time".

I am grateful to have learned to be 'Grateful'.

I got my 'Freedom' back and 'Happiness' is what I strive for every day.

I have learned that even when I have pain, I don't have to be one.

It is very evident that Al-Anon is instrumental in helping people to understand that we do not have the necessary attributes that it takes to change people, places and things. They begin to realize that there is a Power Greater than we are.

The Alcoholic in my life died in January 2006. We were able to talk and enjoy each other's company to the very end. I was able to take care of him at home – Thanks to Program. We were together for 48 and half years, and when he died we were good friends who had respect for each other.

Thank you for coming, sharing and helping my life to be great. Because I learned to 'Forgive', and 'To Let Go', I have Serenity in my life.

I would like to leave you with this little poem that has helped me hundreds of times.

DECIDE TO FORGIVE

Decide to forgive
For resentment is negative.
Resentment is poisonous.
Resentment diminishes and devours the self.
Be the first to forgive,
To smile and to take the first step,
And you will see the happiness bloom
On the face of your human brother or sister.
Be always the first.
Do not wait for others to forgive.
For by forgiving,
You become the master of fate.
The fashioner of life,
The doer of miracles.
To forgive is the highest,
Most beautiful form of love.
In return you will receive
Untold Peace and Happiness.
"Only the brave know how to forgive. A coward never forgives."

Printed in a Kidney Foundation Newsletter

Volunteering at Health Fairs, and being on call for people who are living with alcoholism has also been exciting. Knowing that I could be responsible for someone getting much needed help is a good feeling. The rest is up to them and God.

My four legged friends have given me pleasure beyond description. Over the years we have had a total of ten dogs. I enjoyed each and every one of them, however I did not have as much time to devote to them as I have with the last two. We have had several cats, a chipmunk, an iguana, and a rabbit. At one point we also had fish. I am grateful that my children had an opportunity to learn how living creatures should be treated.

An enjoyable memory is when our son, Randy, had an iguana. He made a leash for it and often took it for a walk just after the supper hour. Walking down the street with his pet was such fun for him. Many of the neighbourhood women were outside gardening or just enjoying the fresh air. When they saw him coming down the road, many ran inside till he passed. He thought that was hilarious.

My little 'Chiki' was able to entertain many youngsters who were in the hospital. I enjoyed this program that gave so much satisfaction to the children and to Chiki and me as well. She is a natural for this job. My regret is that I had to stop when many of the people around me were ill. Now she is getting older as am I. It takes a good two hours to get her ready to go, and after that I am too tired to do it and so is she. So, we will enjoy the memories.

Another wonderful part of the hospital visitation was going to my parents afterwards. They loved to hold and cuddle her. She does not like to sit for long periods, so no one gets tired of her. I have taken her to seniors' homes and schools for their enjoyment as well. Chiki and I were a team for a reading program at a school. The children read to her and she performed for them as a reward. The children loved it and so did Chiki. I have taken her to my church for special times, so the children have enjoyed her there as well.

Pepper learned all the tricks that Chiki could do, but I could not take her to the places Chiki went. She would knock the children over. She is just a different natured dog, and quite big. It has been a pleasure to teach these two animals and then watch them perform. They really work together as a team in their own yard. I am excited to know that I was able to teach my dogs to perform like they do.

I know for sure that what Josh Billings said is true: "A dog is the only thing on earth that loves you more than he loves himself". Or something a friend said to me, "Money can buy a good dog, but not a waggly tail". Our dogs all had wagging tails, each one of them. We treated our animals like part of the family.

Being part of the fundraising dinners for the street kids of Brazil has been a rewarding experience, especially when I see the photos of what we have accomplished. My friend Beata is instrumental in this fundraiser. I met her when I worked in the Junior High School and we have remained good friends for nearly 40 years. She was as happy as I was when my little books were published.

Presently I am able to go to visit a few people who are not able to get out. Sometimes we play cards, and sometimes we just talk. I know that the time I spent with our Randy has taught me a little about visiting these folks.

One thing Randy said to me once during his illness was: "Mom, what I like best is that you do not treat me like I am sick". I knew that I was doing something right.

At church we have a ladies' brunch with a variety of themes. There is a table set up at the head, with four women on the panel called the 'Take 4 Panel'. These women represent four generations. I am the eldest. Sometimes my job is to pray, sometimes to answer questions. The last brunch we had, I made juice from my own berries for everyone to taste, giving the people in attendance the recipe. Other times I just represent my age group. Before the event we have a meeting, sometimes at my home. This is where we really get to know our guests. At first I wondered about my part here. I am old. They don't need me here. I am not able to contribute much. There are many smarter than I am that can be more useful. However, I am enjoying the opportunity, and am learning a lot. We have had some very interesting guests at these functions. We have interviewed a Chinese Medicine Doctor. A wonderful Polish violinist was another special guest that told her incredible story of how she came to Canada. One of our guests was an interesting lady who lived in Canada and was moving back to a predominately Muslim country where people are still living very dangerously. She felt she had to go back there to be supportive to her family and also to bring good news to the people there. During the Olympics period in Vancouver, we were privileged to have a torchbearer as one of our guests, and we got to hold the torch. We got to hear some interesting stories about the Olympics from one of the volunteers who attend our Church. Rejoicing in the love these young women show for me is so warming. I am privileged to have them in my life. I feel the love they have for me, and share my love for them. I am passionate about representing the women of my age category, and relish every moment of the people we interview. We always learn something and have loads of fun. If God wants me to do something, I know he will show me the way.

'Don't take yourself so seriously. No one else does'. The world will go on even when I am not here. I wrote this one down so that I will never forget it. Enjoying a good fun story and laughing out loud lifts my spirit.

This is one of my favourite stories. There were two enthusiastic hospital interns walking down the street. They spotted an old man with an unusual walk. One said to the other, "What disease do you think he has?" "It looks like Parkinson's disease to me." "I think it's M. S." "Well, why don't we just ask him?" So they walked up to the man. One of the interns spoke, "Sir, we are interns from the hospital, and we are wondering what disease you are dealing with." "No problem", said the old fellow. "Tell me what you are thinking". "I think you may have Parkinson's". "Sir, I thought you might have M.S." The old gentleman replied, "I thought I had gas".

I try very hard to feed my mind with thoughts that cause me to be peaceful and happy. I think about the memories that are cheerful and wonderful. There are many others that are not. They need to be put to rest.

Milt and I went on a marriage retreat many years ago and the leader came up with this story:

Celibacy can be a choice in life, or: a condition imposed by circumstances.

While attending a marriage encounter weekend, Joe and his wife Sue, listened to the instructor say, "It is essential that husbands and wives know the things that are important to each other". Then asked the men: "Can you name and describe your wife's favourite flower?" Joe leaned over and whispered, "Robin Hood all purpose, isn't it?"

Thus began Joe's life of celibacy.

I could relate to this one and never did forget it. I have since received different versions of it, but the idea is still the same.

God cannot give me great blessings if I do not believe that he will, and I believe he has blessings for me.

Learning to reach out for help was the best thing I ever did for myself. There is a lot of help available for us, but we must be willing to do the footwork. We have to get into the basket. Thinking about doing something is not enough. I had to make the effort and I had to do what I needed to do.

Learning the realities of each situation coming in my direction really does help. I am learning how to manage my own life, and be supportive to whoever needs it.

"Do not ask the Lord to guide your footsteps, if you are not willing to move your feet". This sentence has been a huge help to me, as well as "God wants to give you great things, but even He cannot give you any greater blessings than you can believe in". I knew I needed to move my feet, and believe in blessings.

Happiness comes through doors you didn't even know you left open. So many wonderful things come my way now that I am open to them.

Many summers were spent with the grandchildren when they were young. They would come and stay for a while. My best memories of them are during those times.

A few years ago the two eldest grandchildren, Mandie and Charles, were with us. I had planned a surprise for them, telling them that I had something planned for Friday and they would love it. Friday we did not have the greatest weather, but not bad. On our way out, I had to stop for gas. As I got into the car I said, "Sure do hope there is a place for me to sit down at Playland". Did they laugh and laugh? I had to laugh too. For two weeks I kept it a secret and spilled the beans on the way there. I think they enjoyed that part as much as the rest of the day. They chuckled all the way there and we had a great day.

My grandchildren write me wonderful letters, leave me special messages on my answering machine, and send special cards. They bring me chocolate, beauty cream, perfume, kitchen gadgets, and flowers. I have received nuts, pudding, clothing, pictures, garden ornaments and many other precious gifts. One of my granddaughters doesn't believe in buying cards so she writes things on a piece of paper. On Valentine's Day she wrote me a lovely note on a grocery list.

The grandchildren are all busy making their own lives worthwhile, so it is fabulous for me just to know that they think about me in their busy schedules. They themselves are the greatest gifts, greater than anything they could give me.

When my grandson, Randy, was about two and a half, he brought me a gift. "Grandma, I brought you a present", he said, handing me this little parcel wrapped in a piece of toilet paper. I responded with, "Randy, how come I get a present today?" He told me, "You always give me presents I wanted to give you one". It was a little coin that he wrapped. I was so touched I still have this little gift and treasure it. Randy now chooses perfume, or other special things.

When Randy was about two, he was with us for the weekend. A big black fly buzzed around the room. I got the fly swatter and said, "I am going to schmuk him", which I did and the fly fell dead on the floor. These schmuking situations arose periodically with different bugs. One day he was misbehaving. I warned him a few times and then I said, "If you don't behave, I will have to schmuk you". He instantly begged, "Please grandma, don't schmuk me, I will be good". I realized he was really afraid, so I asked him why he was so scared. "Well I see what happens to the bugs when you schmuk them." I had some explaining to do that day.

A great memory is when Victoria was about four and loved to perform. She would take a teaspoon to serve as a microphone, stand on the fireplace and say, "Ladies and gentlemen, now I will sing for you". The ladies and gentlemen were usually my Mom and I. This is a sweet memory.

Keshia, another granddaughter took singing lessons. Keshia lived away from here, but when I was involved in the fundraiser for the street kids of Brazil, Keshia came four or five hours by bus to entertain the guests. How proud I was to have her sing. Often we could not hear her as it was a small place and noisy, but I heard her fine. For those moments, that was all I heard.

It is fascinating to see all of these grandchildren's lives blossom. I just love to watch them bloom. These young people do not realize how special they are to me, and how I love to hear about their dreams and hopes.

Randy and his girlfriend came out for a holiday a year or so ago. I was very tired so I went to bed. There was a knock on my door. Randy came in and asked, "Can we talk for a minute?" "Of course." "Well Grandma, I thought you'd like to know what I am doing and my plans for the future". We had a half hour talk and he told me about his plans and what is happening in his life. I will cherish that night forever.

My heart breaks for the grandson, Anthony, whom we call A.J., with the developmental disability. He is a loving and kind young man, and it is sad for me to realize that it will always be a struggle for him and everyone involved. The one thing that helps is that he too is a 'Child of God', and he will be looked after. This situation is difficult for his parents. I also know that they will grow from all of the circumstances involved here. The gift we receive at the end of a struggle is growth, if we choose to accept it.

My sons, Don and Tim have never ever forgotten my birthday, Christmas, Thanksgiving, Easter or any other important occasion. If they are not here, they call, but they never forget. How special is that? The grandchildren have had good influence. I am forever grateful for this.

As I am remembering these very special events in my life, I can't help but think about the time I went to visit Don and his family in the winter of 1997. Retirement was great; now I could see my granddaughter, Mandie, take part in The Hunch Back of Notre Dame. It was so wonderful to be free and able to do so. Immediately I called several airlines and was able to get a reasonable flight. The weather was cold but lovely. It was so exciting to see my granddaughter perform.

I knew she was a good little actress, but was never privileged to actually see it in person. This was a retirement bonus.

The next day I stayed home with the children while my daughter-in-law, Virginia, took a little time for herself. I made supper for us all and after we ate I suggested that we go for a walk. It was a beautiful clear night with the moon shining brightly, a perfect evening for a walk with the grandchildren. All four grandchildren were happy to do that. Nick and A.J. were ready to go so I said, "Let's just go. Charles and Mandie can catch up with us. It had been lovely out that March day and the road thawed a bit. The evening got colder and it froze again, and snowed just enough to cover. I stepped forward. My foot slipped and down I went rupturing the quadriceps tendon. I heard the cracking sound, thinking I had broken a bone.

Virginia had been watching us through the window. As soon as I fell, the two older grandchildren came running over. "Grandma, can you get up?" "I don't know, just give me a chance to get my head together", I answered. I was feeling nauseous and shaky. Virginia came out. I could not get up. "I think I broke something", I said. "I heard a cracking sound when I fell."

Don and Virginia had a van that had a broken part, which they had ordered and were waiting for, so the large sliding door could not be opened. With a lot of help, I was put in the passenger side of the van and Virginia drove me about seven miles to the hospital. The pain was terrible except when I held my leg up with the other foot. When we got there, she found a wheelchair and took me in to emergency. X-rays were taken and the doctor was beginning to tell me what my options were when Don came in. He had been at work. Feeling badly that he had taken time to come, "How did you know to come? I don't think I am going to die from this". He laughed and asked, "So you don't want me to come unless you are going to die?" We all had a chuckle. The doctor then began talking with Don, "Tell me a little bit about your mom". Don asked, "What would you like to know?" The doctor asked, "What does your mom do?" What is her lifestyle?" I was waiting to hear Don's reply, "Well, my mom is a busy person. She does everything. She has a beautiful garden, teaches Sunday school, has tons of friends, walks a lot with the dog (we had a German shepherd at the time), she just retired in June. What else do you need to know?" The doctor was still talking to Don, "That's all I need to know. There are a lot of miles in this lady yet, but she needs surgery right away". The surgeon then turned to me and said, "You have ruptured the quadriceps tendon in your leg. This tendon controls every movement including your toes. I need to reconnect the tendon". I was in shock but I said, "What you are telling me is that I really have only one choice". He replied, "No, you have two. You can leave it as is and for the rest of your life you will drag that leg. That will cause you no end of problems. However, if I operate and you do what I tell you to do, you will be able to walk again". I was thinking about Milt at home. I was thinking about being with the kids for a long period of time. How would I get to the washroom at their place? Where would I sleep, as their bedrooms were all upstairs? I wondered how I would get my garden in order in the spring. Eventually I said, "When can you operate?" "Tomorrow morning early", was the surgeon's reply.

The surgeon was very kind to me after the surgery. He told me to try to move my toes every time I thought about it. His advice was this: "You have to stay in the hospital until you are able to use crutches. You cannot fly home for at least three weeks, and when you get home you must not take the brace off except to shower. Take it off in the shower and put it back on after the shower before you get out.

When you get home, you must see another specialist. You will stay on crutches for a year with physiotherapy throughout. Do what I say and you will be fine".

When the doctor came in the first morning, he asked, "Well are you moving your toes and lifting your foot?" "You've got to be kidding", I said. "Yes I am kidding, but I want you to start trying right now. Move your toes and lift your foot every time you think of it". "Ok, I will. Thank you". He came to see me every morning for the seven days I was in the hospital.

I was in the hospital for seven days, and was discharged to stay with the kids for another three weeks. I was there for over a month instead of the original planned five days. On the way home we picked up a walker, crutches and pain medication. When we got to their house I saw that they had set up a hospital bed in the centre of their living room, I asked, "Why not put me over in the corner, out of the way?" Virginia told me, "Where the bed is now, you can see out the window, see the goings on in the hallway, be part of the dining area and if you get tired, the doors can be closed". They had really thought this through. It was different for me to need help. I did not want to be a pest. For the first few hours, I just planned strategies on how I would get around. Virginia was so kind to me, but I did not want her to spend all her time taking care of me, she had four children and a husband. We talked about the help I would need, "I don't want you to worry about me. I will be fine and will figure things out. As long as I am quiet, please just carry on, but if I call you please come because I will need you". That worked well for us and we learned to enjoy each other for who we are. I decided to enjoy whatever I could. It was great to be able to get to know my daughter-in-law while Don was at work and the children at school. What could I say except be grateful? Even though I was in pain, I had a lot to be thankful for. When my hair became so unbearably oily, I asked Virginia, "Please would you wash my hair when you have time? I can hardly stand it". "Sure", she said, "After Don goes to work and the kids go to school, I will do that for you". When the time came, she did indeed wash my hair and gave me a sponge bath as well. I slept like a log after that. When I left to come home, both my daughter-in-law and I cried. We had become good friends. Romans 8:28 in my Bible says: "And we know that in all things, God works for the good of those who love Him". I was on crutches for a year like the doctor told me to be, after which I used one crutch for a while. The doctor was right. I am walking.

I wrote the doctor a letter of thanks when I was finally able to get around again. I thanked him for saying the positive words to Don while I was listening. It would have been easy to give up. For an active person with many projects, it sometimes was difficult to sit with my leg outstretched in the brace. I did a lot of reading and visiting with friends who were kind and came over, but mostly I could hear the doctor saying, "There is a lot of miles in this lady yet".

Linda and Eric, my neighbours have lived next door to me for approximately forty years. We have never had a crossword. I know that we can count on each other in an emergency and enjoy celebrations as well. They feel like family. When their children and ours were maturing, their son and daughter often came over if they were upset about something. I would talk with them like I did my own children, getting to know them well. When their daughter, Carol Ann, was in her teens she was dreaming of becoming a doctor. Our four oldest grandchildren were visiting one summer. Suddenly it became very quiet. I went searching for the reason. They were deeply absorbed in a medical book she was reading to them on a blanket under our huge cedar tree. I quietly left them with their reader. She did become a doctor. When she got married she asked me to give the Toast to the Bride. I was able to share some special moments. Len, their son had dreams of his own, often coming over when he was little, telling me, "I am with the Fire Department and I need to check your furnace". Sometimes it would be the wiring", or whatever it happened to be that day. He became a plumber and has enjoyed his dream. More fantastic memories in my life!!

On the other side of me lives Lorretta, an 89-year-old lady, who is like a second mother to me. We have shared stories, garden clippings, grandchildren, recipes and most of all a friendship to remember. The house she lives in was our first home. She was so helpful to me when my Dad was ill. I could take him over to her place for tea and a visit. Lorretta and I have shared secrets, and dreams. One of my boys introduces her as, "Our neighbour, counsellor, banker, other grandma, aunt, and friend". When he was young and needed to talk, she was there. She used to lend him a dollar or two once in a while. I did not know this till later.

I have wonderful neighbours all around me. The folks that live behind me have been there for over fifty years. We do not live in each other's pocket, but always we are there for one another. How wonderful is that?

My Al-Anon sponsors slowly changed. One went into another self-help program due to changed circumstances in her life. One started to travel and is never around, and two died. I needed a good sponsor. I sponsor many people, so it is good to share what I have learned and to watch them mature and become hopeful and happy. However, I personally need someone to share with. Such a person came into my life. God knows what I need. I just need to remember that.

My friend, Nettie and I do lots of simple, fun things together. We seem to be able to spend hours and hours together and never run out of things to do or talk about. She has also been helping me in my garden for a few hours every week. After her husband died, her home was sold and she misses the yard. Now her longing for a yard is fulfilled and I have some help. Once again, all I needed to do is reach out and ask. Humility and inner peace go hand-in-hand. The less you try to prove yourself to others, the easier it is to feel peace. I found it difficult to admit that I could not do something. Now it is much simpler. "Keep it Simple" is once again the Al-Anon slogan that I must remember.

How many people are willing to go to visit folks they did not even know in the cemetery? Well my friend, Nettie, and I have put the two dogs into the truck and headed off to visit my family in their respective resting spots in the graveyard. We let the dogs go for a run down the hill after a ball, and come back up. The animals have exercise; we have fresh air, and visit the memorial sites. We may go to lunch afterward or come home and play cards. A simple thing to do, but not all friends are willing. We have wonderful talks and always feel recharged afterward. I am grateful for this friendship. Though we are older women, we are young at heart and great gardeners.

My nieces, Mona and Lori often bring me flowers when they come to visit. They tell me that I once said, "If you are going to bring flowers, bring them now". They have not forgotten things I have said over the years. I remember one Christmas, Lori and her husband had an open house. When I arrived, they had many guests and Lori was busy. I said, "Lori, I hardly know anyone, so how about I keep the kitchen tidy so you can enjoy your guests?" She was pleased about that idea, but surprised me by what happened next. I had a tea towel in my hands when she said, "And, don't wipe your nose with the tea towel". I asked, "Why would you say that?" She then reminded me about the times she stayed with us as a youngster and I had said that to her and my boys as they dried dishes. I had a good chuckle and was pleased that she still remembered little things that happened. It is wonderful to know that my nieces love and respect me. They have now decided that we need to do something special at least once every two months. I love that. It is especially wonderful as they are the daughters of my beloved sister-in-law Myrt.

So often I have taken things for granted. There are so many things to be happy about. It is so spectacular when I realize how much I have to be grateful for.

It is fun to receive neat surprises coming my way from Don and Virginia, such as updated pictures of the grandchildren and great grandchildren, or something ornamental for my garden. While getting ready to leave from a visit, my daughter-in-law told me to go pick up something that was being made for me. When I went to pick it up, I discovered a crystal with a picture of the great grandchildren and myself. What a lovely thing to do for me before leaving.

This week I had a beautiful hand made card in my letterbox at Church. It is so beautiful, as is the hand made envelope. The words are lovely. Now I am on a search to find this person. I cannot for the love of life figure out who this is. Another adventure.

A young man who was a neighbour comes to chat when he needs someone to talk to. Some of the young people who were in my Sunday school classes come to visit or discuss issues that they have. They tell me that they can trust me not to say anything to anyone. How wonderful it is that a young person would find it helpful to talk with me.

All my family come when they can, calling on special days and even on ordinary days. I have so many friends around me that make my heart sing. Young people come to visit. I have a car to drive and a home to live in. My health is not perfect, but could be much worse.

I must have moved my feet after asking God for help, believing that there were blessings for me. Old age is like flying through a storm. Once you're aboard there's nothing you can do. From the little book 'Old Age is Always 15 years Older than I am'. How true this is: I will fly, or maybe walk or limp, through each storm. I am aboard and I am going to do all I can to stay afloat.

**I am grateful that I did not grow into a bitter
old lady. God is so good to me!!**

May your life be like a roll of toilet paper, long and useful!!

**"A cheerful heart is good medicine. It is slow death
to be gloomy all the time." Proverbs 17:22**

Chapter 12
THE BLESSINGS OF A CHEERFUL HEART

An arrogant man stirs up strife, but he who trusts in the Lord will prosper.
Proverbs 28:25

All I have and all that I am is by the Grace of God.

Here I go again with the quotes, Bible verses, and sayings that continue to assist me in my daily life. I have so many favourites that I have been thinking of writing a book about them.

Having cheer in my heart has brought so much meaning to life that I want to share it with the world.

Before I began this book writing adventure, there were many questions that I asked myself. Maybe no one will ever read what I write? If I write down what happened, will I look stupid? If I open my heart, will I make myself vulnerable? What if my children don't like it when I share parts of our lives?

My main objective is to help someone along the way. The rest does not matter.

Exposing my soul to the world is not something I ever thought I would do. Revealing some of the hidden parts of my life may help others to enjoy theirs, and realize that hidden secrets are often part of the problem.

I prayed about the whole idea, asking God to make it possible. Soon the questions were put aside, and I began to move forward.

In my favourite book 'Basic Information Before Leaving Earth', my Bible, I find so much comfort, and so many tools to make life worth living.

Psalms 139 is my very favourite psalm. "O Lord, you have examined my heart and know everything about me. You know when I sit or stand. When far away you know my every thought. You chart the path ahead of me, and tell me where to stop and rest. Every moment, you know where I am. You know what I am going to say before I even say it. You both precede and follow me, and place your hand and blessing on my head.

I can never get away from my God! If I go up to heaven, you are there; if I go down to the place of the dead, you are there. If I ride the morning winds to the farthest oceans, even there, your hand will guide me, your strength will support me. If I try to hide in the darkness, the night becomes light around me. For even darkness cannot hide from God, to you the night shines as bright as day. Darkness and light are both alike to you.

You made all the delicate, inner parts of my body, and knit them together in my mother's womb. Thank you for making me so wonderfully complex! It is amazing to think about. Your workmanship is marvellous – and how well I know it. You were there while I was being formed in utter seclusion! You saw me before I was born and scheduled each day of my life before I began to breathe. Every day was recorded in your Book!

How precious it is, Lord, to realize that you are thinking about me constantly! I can't even count how many times a day your thoughts turn towards me. And when I waken in the morning, you are still thinking of me!

Surely you will slay the wicked, Lord! Away, bloodthirsty men! Begone! They blaspheme your name and stand in arrogance against you – how silly can they be? O Lord, shouldn't I hate those who hate you? Shouldn't I be grieved with them? Yes, I hate them, for your enemies are my enemies too.

Search me, O God, and know my heart; test my thoughts. Point out anything you find in me that makes you sad, and lead me along the path of everlasting life." Psalm 139

When my world is spinning out of control, I find Philippians 4: 6 to 8: so comforting. "Don't worry about anything; instead, pray about everything; tell God your needs and don't forget to thank him for his answers. If you do this you will experience God's peace, which is far more wonderful than the human mind can understand. His peace will keep your thoughts and your hearts quiet and at rest as you trust in Christ Jesus." It keeps me calm.

There are so many other helpful verses and sections, that it would take another book to tell you the blessings of it all. So my suggestion is that you read as much of the 'Bible', Basic Information Before Leaving Earth. It took me many years to read it and read it again and again, till I began to get it. I am still reading it and learning more each time.

Of course not everyone requires the same kind of help that I have needed. What I am trying to portray here is that we need not be afraid to ask for help in whatever area it happens to be.

Seeking help was one of the big factors in showing me the blessings in my life. Not only did it make me look at things more clearly, it made me learn about each individual issue and see where my part is in each situation. It may be a huge part, or it may be nothing at all.

Within the immediate family, two husbands, three children, and seven grandchildren, we have dealt with so many illnesses that have made me feel like a nurse without the credentials. There was Cancer. My first husband was the first. My brother had Leukemia. One of my granddaughters has had to deal with Scoliosis, having two rods put down each side of her spine to repair the situation. Diabetes runs rampant within the family, as well as Depression and Dementia. There is a history of Strokes. Mom had Internal Bleeding. Several family members had Osteoporosis. Arthritis and Arthritic Spurs are common in our family. Allergies have affected several, with the youngest granddaughter being most prominent. We also have been endowed with Diverticulitis, Thyroid Problems, and Sherman's Disease. Degeneration of Vertebrae and Discs is another common family trait. Brain Aneurysms and Hemolytic Uremic Syndrome are ours too, with Haemolytic Uremic Syndrome leaving Randy with Kidney failure. Bi-Polar tendencies are in the brood as is Autism and Schizophrenia. Asthma, High Blood Pressure and Heart Disease are a common problem in these kinfolk. Vericous Veins including Hemorrhoids have been a problem. We have dealt with Alcoholism and Substance Addiction. Alcoholism, Polio and Substance Addiction had a large impact on Milt's life, as did Parkinson's disease. Dad had Macular Degeneration and was 85 percent blind. I may have missed some.

Wow, there has been a lot to deal with. I am so blessed to have been able to determine where my responsibilities lie in all of this, and do what I can to the best of my ability.

Of all of the afflictions mentioned, Milt suffered from at least nine of them. Throughout all of his afflictions, he never lost his sense of humour. I am grateful that our marriage ended with death and not divorce. That in the end we were best friends leaves me feeling cheerful and grateful. What a feeling of satisfaction to have made it through. We had many hurdles and lots of laughs along the way. One time is very vivid in my memory. When Milt was diagnosed with Diabetes, I proceeded to learn more about it. My cousin had it and I asked her a lot of questions. Deciding that he should have a blood-monitoring machine, I went out and purchased the necessary strips. The machine came free when you bought the strips. Excited that now we could keep an eye on this scenario, I came home ready for action.

Milt was pleased and everything ready, we began. I poked his finger, drew the blood and put it on the strip that was in the monitor. Nothing happened. "Never mind", Milt said. "Try again." Again we did the same procedure. Still nothing. I re-read the instructions. I watched my cousin do it. What is the matter? "Ok", he says, "Let's do it again". After the fourth try, I sat down frustrated and read the instructions again carefully. This time I found out that I had the strip in upside down. Each machine is different. "Are you ready?" I asked. "I think I know what the problem is". "Oh good". Milt replied. "I think I need a transfusion." My goodness did we laugh.

How wonderful it is to enjoy humour today and not feel guilty about having a little fun. There was a time when I could not enjoy anything without wondering what was coming next to spoil it. I can hilariously laugh without thinking about anything else and I want more.

One of my granddaughters, Victoria, was working on getting her driver's licence. I gave Victoria the car keys and told her to practice in the driveway. She was nervous because she had never driven my car. She asked, "Grandma, could you just show me where everything is and how it works?" I got into the car with her beside me and I said, "You can practice turning around right here in the driveway, and parking and backing up too". I decided to show her how to turn around right there, then gingerly backed into a tree. "See how easy that was." Did we have a good laugh? Yes we did, and not only did we laugh, it broke the ice and she practiced calmly. I went into the house feeling rather silly, but free to see the humour in this situation.

It is wonderful to be able to laugh at life situations that I can do nothing about, and not feel guilty.

I am grateful. I know that God works everything for the good of every one who loves Him. Once again I remember reading in Romans 8:31: "If God is on our side, who can be against us?" So many times this comes to me, especially if things are not going well.

When I let myself dwell on the estate of my brother, it upsets me because it would have been great to have the money to assist my grandchildren or whatever else, but today I know that this may not have been a good thing. God will take care of our needs as He has up to now. He has His hand in the lives of the others, so I need not think about this. It tells us in Psalm 37:10 that the wicked will disappear, and it is so.

Having people to share life with, the good times, the hard times, and the tough times, is so special. These visits may be about their lives, their family's lives or my family. Whatever happens as we go along the 'Train of Life'.

To have a variety of friends to share with is amazing. When a young man brings movies over for me to watch, I am so excited that he would even think about that. He had already seen the movies, but watched them again with me. These movies were funny, and he said that I was funnier to watch than the movies.

One young man came over and wanted me to explain the difference between wisdom and education. I told him I had to think about that for a bit.

Then said, "I think wisdom comes from living, and education comes from a book". He was happy with that.

Sometimes young people come over to just play a game, have a chat, a cup of tea, share a problem, go to the park, show them what my dogs can do, or share what I have learned. It is all so special and such a pleasure, and what a blessing!

Treasuring and sharing experiences that are positive, gladdens my heart. Barb, one of the young women in my church asked me one Sunday, "Will you be home on Saturday morning". I told her I thought I would be. She suggested that we have breakfast together. Of course that was a great idea, but what came next was a surprise and a joy. Barb said, "I am going to come over early and make you breakfast". "Great!" It is habit for me to get up early, but when the doorbell rang at 7:00 a.m., I was surprised. There she was with all the makings for breakfast. What a great morning we had. Did I feel special? You bet!!

My young friend, Helen got me a gift of special tea and a teapot. This tea is supposed to have healthy qualities. When she gave it to me she said, "Now drink this tea. I want you to live for a long time". This young woman shares a lot of her life with me, the good, the not so good and the in between. What a treasure she is to me.

When I was not well on the day of our group meeting and could not go, it was so warming to hear Alison tell me, "It just isn't the same when you 're not there".

I met a young woman, Tina, who is an avid Al-Anon member. She asked me to be her sponsor and we have since become wonderful friends. Her birthday is the same day as my granddaughter's that was given up for adoption, which was special as soon as I found that out. My Mom and I exchanged an Easter egg during the Easter Season. After my Mom died, I asked Tina if she would like to do this. She was pleased. It is a ceramic egg painted blue and it is fun to find something to put into the egg and exchange it every other year. I did it first. The following year she gave it to me, and so on. It feels like a special bond between us to me. We have shared so much, Tina and I. It was especially important during the time of her husbands progressed Alcoholism and eventual death, and after the death of my husband. Once again, we are not in each other's pocket, but always there when the need arises, or we want to do something special or just chat.

Another great memory is: For my birthday, Tim and his family got me a digital camera. While I was outside one afternoon, he was taking pictures. When he took one of my dogs and myself, I did not think much about it. After completing my project I decided to relax and play a game on my computer only to discover that picture on my screen. What a nice thing to do.

Don and Virginia find it difficult to know what to send me for special occasions, so quite often, they wait till they are visiting and see what I need or want and get me something special. The last time they were here they purchased a VCR and DVD player all in one. I needed that item and was very happy when I received it.

Another time I got a new kettle, so you get the picture. It is so neat to know that they think about me.

The little books in the 'Grandma's Silver Series' have brought me so much delight. How heart warming it is to know that my little books have already brought pleasure to children in many countries: Africa, Peru, England, United States, and Scotland that I am aware of. Not to mention across Canada. My love for children is so deep. This warms my heart.

Another friend I met through a neighbour. Iris lives a long way from here, and when she found out about my little books being published, she was so thrilled for me. She purchased a set for various people in her life, and sent me pictures of the children reading them, as well as positive input notes from the adults. This is another 'Cheerful' time for me to celebrate.

To enhance children's reading skills, a friend of mine, who is a tutor, purchased a set of my 'Grandma's Silver Series'. She gave me some letters the children have written about the books, giving me details of what they loved about their favourite ones. What delightful moments those are.

A gentleman friend asked me if I still had some of my little books for sale. I told him I did and had some in the car. He purchased a whole set. The following week, he told me that the grandchild he gave the set to, enjoyed it so much that he wanted to buy another set. Next week, he purchased another for a third child. I was so pleased.

My plan for this book was to insert all the special notes and letters plus other things the family has written me, but one of my grandchildren did not want me to share this with the whole world. She felt that it was personal and private. I have to respect that. I have decided to just generally share what they have done. Please keep in mind that these are only a few that I am mentioning. There are two big boxes of notes and cards that I have saved. Sometimes when I get lonely for my family, I take them out and read them.

There is a third box of special notes and things that friends have given me that serve the same purpose. Sometimes just reading something positive lifts me up.

Victoria, my granddaughter, knows how much I love flowers and often brings them to me as a surprise, many times with a note on a piece of paper or a grocery list. She doesn't believe in cards. I just love the fact that she thinks about me.

Mandie, my eldest granddaughter, left me a surprise note after my 70th

215

birthday party that I found long after they left. She left me some money to go out for lunch. It was not easy for her to do as she has small children and is a single mom. I treasure that note. She often sends surprises with her parents when they come to visit.

Alexandra, my great granddaughter is now old enough to write and has written me some wonderful words to treasure. I am so grateful to be around to enjoy all of what is still to come. When Alexandra told me that she had the letter I wrote her several years ago, my heart sang. I can hardly wait to read what Austin, her brother, will write. He is still little.

What I really enjoy and cherish, are the notes and things my children, grandchildren, great grandchildren and other people think to give me. Sometimes the simplest things are the most treasured. Not to mention the special times and things that we have shared.

Charles, my eldest grandson and his girlfriend, Dalice, came for a trip and spent time with me. That was precious. Dalice left me a lovely note with some special tea they had purchased. I loved that. At Christmas time they sent me a card with both of them speaking personally in the message. That was so cool.

Randy, the second eldest grandson and his girlfriend, Kim, send neat gifts with lots of thought behind them. One Christmas I got beautiful perfume that they were excited about, and when I use it, I think of them. This past Christmas they sent me gifts that had a lot of thought behind them. He was remembering times that he spent with us as a youngster. He decided I needed these items. Randy is the one who knocked on my bedroom door to come in and share his dreams and ambitions. How special is that!!

Nick and Keshia, the two youngest grandchildren have been blessing me with copies of their report cards, honour certificates and many other special things, some accompanied by letters. These young people are just beginning their futures.

There have been so many interesting times with the grandchildren. Their futures are often on my mind. Just before Christmas I was preparing cards to mail out when my mail arrived. There was a handwritten letter from Keshia, one of my granddaughters. It is such a special letter that made me happy and sad all at the same time, but so full of love.

Nick, the youngest grandson has always been conscious of the coming future and has lots of plans. I am hoping to be around to see what he does, but for now just hearing his ideas is exciting.

A few years ago Nick was visiting. He was helping me take down some shelving and cleaning out a corner. All of a sudden I heard him calling me. "Grandma, there's a huge spider in here." I asked, "Are you afraid of spiders?" "I am. I hate them." "Well you don't have to love them but you needn't be afraid of them. You are a big man and stronger than they are". "Grandma, what's your definition of a man?" "I'm not sure, I have to think about that. What's yours?" He got down off the ladder and came over and gave me a big hug. Then he said, "I think a man is someone who can hug his grandma and tell her he loves her". We continued our project and we were both happy.

Two more great memories for me: When I decided to purchase a computer. Tim was patient, making a lot of the purchasing selections for me, since I did not know enough to do it myself. When I wanted to buy a new vehicle, he was with me every other day while I sat and drove about a hundred fifty vehicles before finally purchasing one.

After the delivery of the computer was made, he programmed it as simply as possible so that I could make it work. He bought me a proper chair and a mat to go under it. I would probably still be thinking about this purchase, if Tim was not able to help. I am grateful for his help.

Randy and Victoria were spending some time with us during their spring vacation; we decided to make Easter bread Ukrainian style. We had flour, pans and a big mess everywhere, but we sure did have fun, and we baked up a huge amount of wonderful bread. This is a priceless memory for me, and I hope for them too.

My grandson, Anthony, who is developmentally disabled, continues to have a special spot in my heart. I have had fun and interesting times with him. Arriving here by plane on one visit, I took him for a scenic drive after picking him up at the airport. He had his camera and would shout, "Stop the car Grandma. I want to take a picture. It is so green here". I was touched, when he was going home he left me some of his music. I think of him when I hear this music.

Another time as the family was leaving for the flight back home, Anthony wanted the radio turned up in my car. His mother told him we could not hear each other when the music was on, to which he said, "The question is what does Grandma think?" I had to think fast and replied, "I like to hear you when you talk". He accepted that.

I have a book with memories of what the grandchildren said and did. This book also contains stories of the Sunday school children and other neat occasions spent with children. I cannot write them all in here, but they are so precious to me.

How exciting it is when the grandchildren share their accomplishments. Randy recently completed the first phase of an apprenticeship. When he called to tell me how well he did, my heart sang.

These past few months, Don, his wife and Anthony came for a visit bringing with them Alexandra and Austin, the two great grandchildren.

Alexandra told me that she still had the letter I sent her when she was little; I was thrilled that it was special to her. We all had a fabulous time together.

During one visit my daughter-in-law, Virginia looked at the curtain in my computer room. She asked, "Can I wash that curtain and re-hang it for you?" I replied, "You don't have much time, but if you want to, that would be nice". Virginia has a flair for decorating. When she finished with it, it was beautiful. It was such a treat to have her use her creative talent on my window.

My sons have always been supportive. I so much appreciate this. It is hard to describe. Calling or coming is something they have always done, and they never forget special days like my Birthday, Mother's Day, or Christmas. I love that. They come up with the most unbelievable ideas that surprise me, but their support, caring, and always being there is the most precious.

Dreams for my sons and their families are so grandiose that it is hard to explain. My heart bursts with love, and it is such an honour to be able to enjoy all these people, knowing that God has a plan for each and every one of them. God allowed me to have them to love, even our son Randy who was only with us for a short time. Some people are not able to have children at all. My job is to 'Love' them and learn from them. I can do this easily – as they are the treasures in my life.

I have learned to 'Let Go and Let God' work in their lives. To be there to listen, to share and love them is contentment for me. If I had not learned what I did along life's road, I may have missed out on what God had to bless me.

Eleanor Roosevelt once said, "No one can make you feel inferior without your consent".

My Dad always told me "Old age is not for Sissies". Now I know this is true.

Giving to those in need is an area I like to be active. To be able to have the strength to give 'Hope' where it is necessary is another area I strive for. Giving love and encouragement whenever and wherever I can gives me great enjoyment. My job is to be kind and good to everyone, but not a doormat.

Would life have been so good to me if I hadn't reached out for help? I doubt it. I am forever grateful to Al-Anon, Church, Alateen, Drug and Alcohol Abuse Counselling, Christian Counselling, school Counsellors and wherever else I needed to search for answers.

God gave me a home to live in and enjoy, and a beautiful yard to take care of. I love to do both, and am happy to share whatever I can, with whoever wants to spend time with me.

If I try and fail, I have temporary disappointment. If I don't try, I have permanent regret. In my story, my goal is not to hurt anyone, but to help someone. I try my best to share God with my friends and family. I pray every day that each of my family and friends will ask Jesus into their hearts. He is ready to come in when we are ready to accept Him. It is also my deepest desire that people reading my story will make that decision. This is my greatest dream.

I am looking forward to what God has in store for my tomorrows. I have written the following words for all of you with Love.

> When your life is full of sorrow,
> And there's no hope for tomorrow.
> When your soul is aching,
> And your heart is breaking.
> If I can ease your pain,
> Then I will not have lived in vain.

Thank you Lord for helping me to fulfill my dream. 'Utter Cheer' comes into my heart as I am completing this book.

"Remember, if God is for us, who can be against us". Romans 8:31

We have two lives: One we are given, the other we make.
Bloom where you are planted.

You are an important part of God's plan.
May He watch over you
And keep you safe.

LIFE IS A GIFT, WITH GOD'S HELP, YOU CAN LIVE IT WELL

LaVergne, TN USA
13 November 2010
204701LV00001B/4/P